Build the Ultimate Gaming PC

Build the Ultimate Gaming PC

K. R. Bourgoine and Matthew J. Malm

Wiley Publishing, Inc.

Build the Ultimate Gaming PC

Published by
Wiley Publishing, Inc.
10475 Crosspoint Boulevard
Indianapolis, IN 46256
www.wiley.com

ISBN-13: 978-0-471-75547-0
ISBN-10: 0-471-75547-8

Manufactured in the United States of America

10 9 8 7 6 5 4 3 2 1

1B/QV/RQ/QV/IN

For general information on our other products and services or to obtain technical support, please contact our Customer Care Department within the U.S. at (800) 762-2974, outside the U.S. at (317) 572-3993 or fax (317) 572-4002.

Wiley also publishes its books in a variety of electronic formats. Some content that appears in print may not be available in electronic books.

Library of Congress Cataloging-in-Publication Data

Library of Congress Cataloging-in-Publication Data
Bourgoine, K. R., 1973-
 Build the ultimate gaming PC / K.R. Bourgoine and Matthew J. Malm.
  p. cm.
 Includes index.
 ISBN-13: 978-0-471-75547-0 (paper/website)
 ISBN-10: 0-471-75547-8 (paper/website)
 1. Microcomputers--Upgrading. 2. Computer games--Equipment and supplies. 3. Computer input-output equipment. 4. High performance computing. I. Malm, Matthew J., 1978- II. Title.
 TK7887.B67 2006
 794.8'1416--dc22
                              2005020238

About the Authors

K. R. Bourgoine is a hard-core gamer of role-playing, online, and console games. He's an active beta-tester, having tested Magic Online, Asheron's Call I and II, World of Warcraft, and Diablo II. In his professional life, Kerry is an IT consultant, Network engineer, and Special Project Manager for a renown law-firm located in New York City with offices across the globe. He has been building computers for personal and professional use since the 1980s and is certified in 3D StudioMax, PhotoShop, Dreamweaver, and Director. Kerry is also the author of *The Acquisitioners* (www.acquisitioners.com).

Writing since 2001, his first published work came in the form of a short story, "The Adepth's Vault: The Bone Sword of Kelifex," which appeared in Gary Gygax's *Lejends* (co-Creator of Dungeons and Dragons) magazine in July 2002. That work expanded into a regular column in which he introduced new artifacts into the Lejendary Adventure world, through the tales of Meselin, The Master of Lore and Arcana for the Society of Lost Knowledge.

The Acquisitioners series was created in 2001 as an expansion of his Mordelack/Shadowcircle Series, a verbal trilogy that follows the rise, reign, and fall of Modelack the Vile. Interestingly, *The Acquisitioners* series was written before Mordelack ever was put to paper. In December 2003, www.Acquisitioners.com was launched.

In his spare time, he enjoys creating board games and building scenes for the world of the Acquisitioners. He currently resides in New York and shares a humble abode with two cats, Zoe and Gertie and his wife Kate.

Matthew J. Malm is a Microsoft Access Database Developer and VBA Programmer for a large insurance firm in New York, as well as a computer consultant, specializing in building and repairing PCs. Matthew has been programming and gaming since the days of the Apple IIc.

Credits

Executive Editor
Chris Webb

Development Editor
Kenyon Brown

Technical Editor
Loyd Case

Production Editor
Pamela Hanley

Copy Editor
Susan Hobbs

Editorial Manager
Mary Beth Wakefield

Production Manager
Tim Tate

Vice President and Executive Group Publisher
Richard Swadley

Vice President and Executive Publisher
Joe Wikert

Project Coordinator
Ryan Steffen

Graphic and Layout Technicians
Denny Hager
Joyce Haughey
Stephanie D. Jumper

Quality Control Technician
Laura Albert
Jessica Kramer
Joe Niesen
Carl William Pierce

Book Designer
Kathie S. Schnorr

Proofreading and Indexing
Christine Sabooni
TECHBOOKS Production Services

To Kathryn who will forever be my Valera

—*K. R. Bourgoine*

To my Mom and Dad

—*Matthew J. Malm*

Preface

Welcome to *Build the Ultimate Gaming PC!* If you love to play computer games and have always yearned to have a top end killer machine, this is the book for you.

Who This Book Is For

If you're a first timer, who has never really built a computer from scratch before, this is exactly the book for you. We'll teach you how to buy parts, build, and enhance a system from nothing into a super computer pushing the limits of its and your gaming capabilities.

If you have a little more experience, perhaps you tinkered with your machine before, upgrading memory — you will also benefit from this book. You'll find easily accessible information about the inner workings of the hardware you'll be installing; that kind of information can save you hours or even days of troubleshooting that you might spend on a computer that you aren't familiar with.

No matter what your skill level, think of this book not only as a step-by-step guide to building a computer but also as a foundation from which, with its knowledge, you can grow and build any type of computer you want. If you're apprehensive about spending all that money on computer parts and fear that you may ruin them in the process, have no fear — we'll walk you through each step.

If you're a hardware specialist, or someone who has built so many machines that they have forgotten half of them, this probably isn't the book for you. While there might be a few things here you would learn you could probably do everything in here on your own without our help.

What You'll Find in This Book

This book covers everything you need to know to build an ultimate gaming PC. We will show you how to make a plan for you computer so that you can figure out what you can get on your particular budget. We will also show you how to select, shop, and buy parts form the vast ocean of them on the market. We give examples on how to save money and cut corners while keeping in mind all the important factors that are key when buying a particular piece for you computer. We also tell you where to shop without getting ripped off — something that can happen quite often in the internet store age.

In each of the parts chapters, whether is be hard drives, video cards, CPUs, or sound cards, we list all the key factors of that device then based of those theories we talked about, at the end of the chapter, pick what is currently the best product on that market to show the methodology of the chapter in action. We walk you through the process step by step all the way from the initial planning of your computer through purchasing while trying to get the best price. After that we give very detailed instructions, with tons of pictures to help guide you, on how to assemble all the individual parts you have collected. Then once you are finally able to hit the power switch and see your ultimate Gaming PC come to life for the first time, we help you install the Windows operating system. Finally, you'll learn how to optimize and tweak your Windows operating system and which general computer settings make for a much better, sleeker, faster and powerful gaming rig.

After all that we delve a little bit into Multi-player gaming and how you can best set up your computer to play cooperatively or competitively with your friends with the most amount of game play and least amount of annoying networking quirks and glitches.

In this book we assemble one particular computer but don't worry if that particular system is not for you. Why? Because with the information we give you in these pages you will be able to adapt or change the system specifications with confidence. You will have the basic skills needed to determine what is best for you and what parts you will need. We not only suggest but we urge you to try out your new skills, put the information to use! You don't have to walk exactly in our footsteps because all the other paths will be just as rewarding the first time you get to turn on the very first computer that you built.

Don't Look For...

We cover a lot of topics in this book, all of which will help you build a great computer now and probably many more in the future, but there are a few things that we are not going to cover.

We are not going to cover overclocking. Overclocking is a way to tweak and manipulate your computer's hardware to work faster than it was designed to do. Our goal is to help you build a machine with enough power that you shouldn't need to overclock. But aside from that, over-clocking takes a bit more skill and knowledge to achieve, more than we could adequately provide within these pages. Overclocking is also risky--you can burn out parts and ruin them, throwing all the money you spent out the window. That is a pretty big risk to take if you're just starting out. We opt for the safer route and keep your parts intact.

We are also not covering modding in this book. Modding is changing or re-configuring any factory parts in some way. For example, you can cut out the side panel of your computer case, replace it with clear Plexiglas and insert light on the interior of your computer to give a nice cool blue glow. Or you can built a complete computer and stuff it inside an old Millennium Falcon toy. Modding is fun and we encourage you to try it out if it sounds like it suits your fancy. But again that goes beyond the scope of what we want to teach here. Our goal is to give you the knowledge to build the best machine that you can, what you do after that, well, we will let you decide.

Note

If you do want to try modding, take a look at *Going Mod*, another great ExtremeTech title also published by Wiley. It covers everything you need to know to delve into case modding, and includes really cool examples.

If you're looking to build a laptop or any type of portable computer, you won't find information here. There are computers available that are slim lined and smaller in size for easy transport just like laptops. These tend to be single unit computers, meaning that many of the pieces are already built in (for example, the video card, which gives you your display, is built onto the motherboard). These type of machines can't easily be upgraded or changed, so their gaming capability is limited to current technology.

How This Book Is Structured

As we mentioned, we're going to walk you through everything you need to know to be able to build the ultimate Gaming PC.

This book is organized into four main parts.

Part I: Spec-ing out Your Ultimate Gaming PC

In Part I we teach you everything you need to know to get started on building your new computer. We explain why it's favorable to build your own computer and where it is best to shop for your computer parts.

Chapter 1, "Let's Make Some Decisions" covers what is available as far as gaming systems go, and why you'd want to build your own from scratch. You'll also set your budget in this chapter and understand what you'll get for your money. We end this chapter with the basics on shopping for parts—OEM as opposed to Retail, the most popular stores, internet versus brick-and-mortar—and the decision process we'll be using in each chapter.

Part II: Let's Go Shopping for Parts

Part II, "Let's Go Shopping for Parts," is designed to get you hunting and on the right track to the best computer parts you can buy. It's a step-by-step process that takes you through how to find the highest quality pieces you will need to build your ultimate gaming machine.

Chapter 2, "How to Select the Ultimate Gaming Processor" walks you through the first part you'll need to purchase. The processor will determine which motherboard you'll need to buy, so we need to select one very carefully. You'll learn what a processor does, the key factors to look for when you make your purchase. And, we'll introduce you to the top players in this market, discuss their pros and cons, and finally make a decision on which processor we'll purchase for our ultimate gaming PC.

In Chapter 3, "How to Select the Ultimate Gaming Motherboard," you'll learn how to select the motherboard for your PC. We'll keep in mind our processor choice, but also learn about how to select a motherboard that will accommodate future technology developments. We'll introduce you to the key players in this market, and then select the motherboard for your PC.

The next purchase you'll make is the memory. Chapter 4, "Choosing Your Ultimate Memory" covers everything you need to know to buy the best memory for your machine. We talk about what memory is, and why you need it, how much is enough, and what happens when you don't have enough. We'll meet the major distributors of memory, learn where to buy it, and then select the one that's best for the PC.

What's a gaming PC without a video card? Not much! Chapter 5, "Choosing the Ultimate Video Card," covers everything you need to know to make this purchase. You'll learn how to figure out what type of memory you need (based on what motherboard you picked). We'll talk about the chipsets available, who the major distributors are, and finally select the best video for our PC.

Hard drives? DVD drives? Virtual Drives? We'll cover exactly what you need for storage in Chapter 6, "Choosing Your Ultimate Storage Device." There are a lot of things to consider when choosing storage, among them size and speed for both your operating system and the games you'll be playing, as well as more practical issues such as built in drives or removable (and thus semi-portable) drives. We'll survey the manufacturers out there, and then pick the one that will be the best for our Ultimate Gaming PC.

If you've played any game at all, you know how important sound is. Admit it, you can still hear the distinct sound from Pac-Man in your head if you think hard enough. Crucial to the gaming experience is the sound, and Chapter 7, "Choosing the Ultimate Sound Card and Speakers" covers not only the sound card you'll need but also what speakers will give you the best experience. We'll talk about the top sound card brands and models, the different types of speakers, and—you guessed it—pick the best sound card and speakers for our Ultimate PC.

In Chapter 8, "Choosing a Case for Your Ultimate Gaming PC," you'll learn what to look for when selecting the case for your computer. There are different sizes and materials available, and different port options that you'll need to consider. We'll talk very, very briefly about modding and what you'd need to think about when making this purchase if you intend to mod in the future.

In Chapter 9, "Selecting the Ultimate Power Supply," we cover exactly what a power supply does and how it converts household electricity to something that can be used by the various components of your PC. We also point out some of the identifying characteristics of a quality power supply before we select one for our PC.

In Chapter 10, "Choosing Your Ultimate Monitor," we move on to external purchases. This chapter covers the types of monitors available and helps you select the top of the line monitor for your gaming needs. We'll cover sizes, colors, resolution, and the different manufacturers out there. Wait until you see what we pick for our ultimate gaming PC—it's impressive!

And finally, what's a gaming PC without accessories? Chapter 11, "Selecting the Ultimate Gaming Accessories" looks at things like joysticks, keyboards, mice, and flight sticks—everything you'd want for the best gaming experience ever.

Part III: Bringing Your Ultimate Gaming PC to Life

Now that we have collected all our pieces, in Part III of the book we begin putting it all together. With a very easy to understand and a reference guide we show you how to put all the pieces of your computer together, complete with dozens and dozens of photos.

Now that you have all the parts, let's put this machine together! Chapter 12, "Assembling Your Ultimate PC" is a monster—but don't let the page count fool you. It is packed with detailed steps and photographs that will walk you through exactly what you need to do to put the machine together.

Once the machine is up and running, we'll install the OS in Chapter 13, "Installing Your Software/OS." We'll install Windows XP, test, tweak, and optimize for your best gaming experience.

Part IV: Advanced Gaming

In Part IV, "Advanced Gaming," we show you how to connect your computer with others for more intense and irresistible gaming.

And finally, we'll turn the machine on and start gaming! Chapter 14, "Multiplayer Gaming," is your introduction to the world of gaming over a network—whether it's a simple setup in your home or apartment, or over the internet. You'll learn about LANs and wireless networks, the best way to set up the home network for ultimate gaming experiences, and what you need to consider when you connect with your friends. Don't skip this chapter—we talk about protecting your computer here as well with software and hardware firewalls, essential when multiplayer gaming. And finally, we give you tips on how to host a LAN party, so that you can show off your new PC.

What You Need to Use This Book

The good news is that you don't need much to use this book. The most important thing that you do need is a desire to build the most powerful ultimate gaming PC ever. That aside, you will also need a bit of free time to help you on your journey. It takes a little time to shop and order parts as well as the time it takes for them to arrive. You will also need a clean area to work and store your boxes of parts as they arrive, and it is also worth mentioning that you should have something to ground yourself on (static electricity is a minor annoyance to you, but it can seriously damage your parts.) If you don't have thing its not the end of the world, you can work without one, but if you happen upon one, they are worth grabbing. Probably the biggest hurdle of the things you need will probably be money. Fortunately in this book we explain how to shave off a few dollars here and there, but money is one of things you will need for this project so that you can order all the parts that you pick.

Oh, and make sure you have a screwdriver! In terms of tools that is pretty much all you need — a simple Phillips head screwdriver. If you can get one that is not magnetic that is preferable.

Enjoy!

Acknowledgments

K. R. Bourgoine would like to thank:

First off I would like to thank my wife Kathryn. Her understanding and suggestions made this whole process much easier than it would have been. Kathryn, I thank you for your support, ideas, caring, and knowledge.

There are several other people I would like to acknowledge because without their impressive knowledge my share of work on this book might have never been done. I would like to thank Jonathan Rivera for his speedy responses, no matter how many times I emailed, and for his seemingly endless collection of informative links and fast typing.

I am very grateful to Jonathan Bourgoine and Owen Murray for their technical expertise, vast knowledge and for their patience. The scope of their collective knowledge is utterly mind-boggling, and unfair to those of us who don't have it!

I would like to thank Dustin Bourgoine II for being a sounding board and helping me work through everything that should be covered in certain areas of the book. I greatly thank you for helping me streamline and point out a few of the things that I might have missed.

Chintan Pandya also deserves thanks for his help in gathering some of the supplies, needed for this project as well as his in-depth application knowledge.

Similarly I also want to mention Paul Gallo for his thoughts and encouragement about making the most from the intricacies of the Windows OS to make it a screaming gaming machine.

Chris Webb, and family, I also thank for kicking off this project in the first place. Go Sith Go!

I thank Kenyon Brown, as well, our Developmental Editor for his help in kicking this book into shape and making the writing process as calm as possible.

Lastly, (many bad things might happen to me if I don't mention them), I would like to show my appreciation to the Sin-Forums Outposters. They are a community of stand up, just, righteous and pure people. They more than willingly offered ideas and brainstorms about how to tackle certain things helping to make this the most inclusive book that it could be.

Thank you to everybody once again. I really couldn't have done this without you. See you in game!

Matthew J. Malm would like to thank:

I would like to thank my sister Kathryn, who helped me lay my foundations for this book.

I would also like to thank my sister Elizabeth and my brother-in-law Michael, who have provided me with great advice over the years.

I would like to thank my friends James Greenan and Joe Berthiaume, who let me bounce ideas off of them.

Finally, I would like to thank my parents for their love and support.

Contents at a Glance

Contents

Part I: Spec-ing Out Your Ultimate Gaming PC

Part II: Let's Go Shopping for Parts

Chapter 2: Selecting the Ultimate Gaming Processor 23

Chapter 3: Selecting the Ultimate Gaming Motherboard 37

Part IV: Advanced Gaming

Chapter 14: Multiplayer Gaming 295

Introduction

Welcome to *Build the Ultimate Gaming PC!* If you are picking up this book, chances are you are very much like us — you love games and you love computers. The goal behind this book is to make sure you get the maximum entertainment from building a computer that can not only handle all the games on the market, but blow the doors off them as well.

Computers are everywhere – very little in the worlds of business or entertainment runs without some form of computer aid. They are the gateway to entertainment. With your computer, you can watch sports broadcasts from around the world, listen to music, write a story, watch a movie, keep in contact with friends, and, most importantly for us, play games!

Computers change as fast as the gaming market. It is theorized that that the greater push for faster and more powerful computers is driven almost solely by computer gamers. Gamers want more and more realistic games with better graphics, better sounds, more options, more details, all of which require processing power and continual hardware upgrade.

This book is about that hardware that you'll need to build the ultimate gaming PC. Within these pages, you'll learn exactly what each piece of hardware does, why it's important, where to buy it at the best price, and what can be done to make it run better, smoother and with less hiccups. With a little first hand experience in how to build a computer with the equivalent power of a nuclear reactor from the ground up, you'll soon be able to play any game you can find.

The purpose of this book is to help and introduce a computer gamer, who has had limited access to playing with computer parts. There is a joy and sense of accomplishment felt when you build your own computer. Not to mention the benefit gained by knowing everything about the inner workings of that computer.

Spec-ing Out Your Ultimate Gaming PC

part

Let's Make Some Decisions

Congratulations on taking the first step to building the ultimate gaming PC! After reading this book and following the steps, your PC will be able to run the latest games at peak performance, letting you completely experience the world as the game creators intended.

You may be asking yourself, "Why would I build this PC myself when I can just head to the store and buy one?" That is an excellent question. Let's take a look at why building your own PC is a much better way to go.

Buying the Ultimate Gaming PC: Why Your Wallet Will Never Forgive You

You can take the easy route and skip this whole "build your own PC" idea. Just whip out that credit card and buy the best PC that you can find. There are many places you can do this. You can get on the Internet, go to one of those configure-it-yourself computer Websites, and try to piece one together. You can also check out some of those specialty gaming computer Websites to see what they have to offer. You can also skip this whole Internet thing, drive over to a local computer store, pick one up, and carry it home.

It's Not Called the Generic Gaming PC, You Know

Take a look at what happens if you try to go to one of those general computer Websites and configure one for yourself. Of course, you have to try and find the best desktop model for gaming out of the 10 or 15 generic variations that they offer. All of these choices look a little different — some have big CRT monitors; others have sleek, thin flat panels. Some have big and tall cases; others are much smaller. And each and every one is labeled for some specific purpose, such as "Great for Home Entertainment," or "Cutting Edge Technology." In the best case scenario, one of these PC's is labeled "Ultimate Gaming PC" or such. More than likely, you'll be left trying to figure out whether "Cutting Edge Technology" or "Home Entertainment" is better for gaming.

Assuming that you managed to pick a base desktop model to build on, I'm sure that you'll be pleasantly surprised to find a price tag that is several hundred dollars less that you were expecting to spend, probably around $1,300 or less. This is great! You'll be able to grab your ultimate gaming PC for next to nothing! But first, check the configuration to see what parts are included.

Parts That Are Less Than Ultimate, Too

The first thing that you might notice is that the fastest possible processor is not included in this PC. Because this computer supposed to be the "ultimate," you need to add in what a processor will cost. Time to scroll down the page and find out how much memory is included. That won't likely be enough, either, so you have to add more memory. The hard drive may not be big enough for your needs, so add in the cost of a larger hard drive. By the time you look though the entire configuration and add all of the things you need, that $1,300 price tag is long gone. In all likelihood, the price is now probably hovering around $2,000.

Because you expected this thing to cost a pretty penny, you're not too concerned about the price. After all, you're getting some quality parts, right? The processor is a brand that you recognize, so that's good. And the memory...wait a minute. Exactly what brand of memory are you putting in this computer? And what brand of hard drive? A quick review of the entire list reveals that very few of the key components of the PC actually have a brand name listed. Are these the parts that you really want inside your ultimate gaming PC?

Warranties: We're Right Behind You...Way Behind You

Well, for the moment, try and put this whole "brand of parts" issue in the back of your mind. After all, computer parts are all the same, right? If something breaks, you can just send it back under warranty, right? Just in case, you might want to check that warranty policy.

Somewhere on that computer configuration page, there is likely a description of the warranty that comes with the computer. It's possible that you didn't notice it the first time; it's something that is often overlooked. After you do find it, you may be dismayed to see how long that warranty actually lasts. Most warranties only last for one year, with some basic warranties as short at 90 days. There are probably some extended warranty options available to you, but each one has a price tag associated with it. In the end, a four-year extended warranty can cost you an additional $200.

Freebies: Do You Really Want This Stuff?

Even though some of the pitfalls are getting harder to ignore, you're going to get this computer anyway. After all, this is much easier than building it yourself, right? Besides, the next part of this virtual shopping trip is the most fun: free stuff. No matter when you decide to buy this PC, something will be free. There may be a component upgrade, such as upgrade your 32x CD drive to a 42x drive, or some sort of free peripheral, such as a printer or scanner. Even though you're buying the site's "Gaming PC," the freebie is almost never a free gaming peripheral, like a joystick or gamepad.

The most important freebie is one that you never know if you're going to get: free shipping. If you manage to be on the Website the day free shipping isn't offered, be prepared to add another $100 to the price of this computer. When this PC is shipped to you, you might find even more freebies — free software. In fact, the hard drive and desktop are often littered with it: two or three different types of music software, maybe some extra "Internet protection" software, and some software for a free Internet connection. Of course, because you bought the PC online, you probably don't need a free Internet connection, but the software is free and included.

A Fine-Tuned Machine?

Now that you have your ultimate gaming PC, you can try to play some games. Unfortunately, all of that "free" software could be stealing valuable system power from your games because they have been set up to run in the background every time you turn on your PC. On top of that, there are a lot of other settings on your PC that can boost the performance of your games; however, the machine didn't arrive with those configurations, so you have to find and change these settings yourself. But once you do, you'll finally have your $2,500 ultimately generic gaming PC — with free printer!

In the end, this Website is probably a great place to get a solid, multipurpose PC. However, if you really want the ultimate gaming PC, you have to look elsewhere.

The Ultimately Expensive Gaming PC

The generic PC Website wasn't really the place to get the PC you wanted. The generic PC site offered something for everybody, but it didn't seem to understand what components go into an ultimate gaming PC. One of those specialized gaming PC Websites should be a better place to look.

High Tech, High Price

After the Web page loads, you can immediately tell that you came to the right place. First of all, you don't have to find your PC among hundreds of different home, business, and server models. Instead, you can narrow your focus to a great gaming PC rather quickly.

After you've chosen your model, you can head over to the configuration page. The difference on this site is immediately noticeable when compared to the generic PC site. There are many different choices for each part, and the brand of each component is clearly noted. This is great! You can run through all of these parts, pick the best ones available, and you'll have your ultimate gaming PC. Unfortunately, this is where the shortfalls of this method begin to show.

After adding all of the best components to your PC, you notice the price tag. $5,500! Wow! You could have had two of those generic gaming PCs for that price. And you haven't even chosen a monitor yet! Okay, you figure you'll worry about the price later. Better to check into how the computer will be configured when it arrives.

Luckily, all of this expensive technology can be properly tweaked for gaming before it even arrives at the door. This is a significant advantage to the generic PC site. Of course, that costs another $25 to $50. Checking the warranty on the parts and components reveals that they are just as short as that generic PC site. To protect your purchase a year or two longer will cost another $300. Forget the warranty; you may need an insurance policy for this $6,000 ultimately expensive gaming PC.

This seemed like a good idea at the time, but you don't think this Internet shopping experience is working out. Now it's time to pile into the car and drive to your local electronics store.

The One-Size Fits All Gaming PC

Now that you're at the local electronics superstore, you feel much better. First of all, there are many PCs lined up for you to look at. You can see all of them in action, check the images on the monitor, and compare them side by side.

Because you've been worried about the warranty policies online, you are comforted by the fact that the superstore has their own warranty policy. If you're not satisfied in a few days, you can bring it back for a full refund. Of course, if that happens, you'll be back at square one, looking for the ultimate gaming PC. And you will most likely have to pay a restocking fee for returning the machine. But you can worry about that later. Let's see what kind of computer you can get.

After you begin to look closely at these PCs, you notice that they are all similar. Some are a little better than others, but not by much. Very few, if any, are offering the latest technology that you saw on that gaming PC Website. And these PCs all come with peripherals that you already have, such as printers, and items you don't really want, such as digital cameras. You can't customize these machines, either; what's in the box is what you get. In the end, these one-size-fits-all gaming PCs don't really fit your needs any better than the ones you saw on the Internet.

Building the Ultimate Gaming PC

Just because you couldn't find the ultimate gaming PC available for purchase, or available at a reasonable price, doesn't mean that building it yourself is a much better choice. After all, these other companies put computers together all day long. How could you possibly do a better job than they do? Believe it or not, you can do a much better job. The following sections show the reasons why you want to build your own PC instead of buying it already assembled.

Fully Customizable

When you build your own PC, it can be completely customized to reflect your needs. You can pick any brand of processor, not just the brand that is affiliated with a particular Website or computer manufacturer. If a particular feature, such as high-quality sound, is important to you, the very best sound card can find its way into your PC. You are not limited to the sound card offered by a particular PC manufacturer. This theory applies to every computer component that you want to use; you are in complete control.

Pay for What You Want

When you build your own PC, you pay only for what you want. You don't have to buy that new printer just because it's part of the package. Your computer does not come with preinstalled software that you do not want or need. Just like dictating what parts you do use, you have the power to leave out the components, peripherals, and software you don't need.

Save Money

When you build your own ultimate gaming PC, you can save significant amounts of money compared to a fully assembled PC. You can buy each part from the store or Website that offers the lowest price. In addition, you don't have to pay for the labor that is required to assemble and package your PC for shipment.

Also, when you buy your fully assembled PC, you are often charged sales tax at the time of sale. If you buy individual parts from Websites whose warehouses are not located in your state, you may not be charged sales tax at the time of sale.

A Better Protected Investment

When you buy individual parts for your PC, you will be pleasantly surprised by the warranties that are offered for each product. It's nearly impossible to find a retail product that has a warranty less than one year in duration. In fact, most companies cover their products for at least three years, with many now offering lifetime warranties! Compare this to the 90-day and one-year warranties offered by most Web-based computer sellers. To have your pre-built PC covered for as long as the one that you assemble yourself, you could be forced to pay an additional $200 or more!

Gain Knowledge

The greatest thing you gain when you build your own PC is not something that can be bought in a store. Building your own PC gives you a tremendous amount of knowledge about how a PC works. You learn about all of the parts that comprise your PC and how they work together. You learn about your operating system and drivers, and how they affect your system performance. And you use what you learn to keep your system in peak operating condition. This knowledge comes in handy long after your PC has been assembled.

This knowledge also allows you to upgrade to the latest technology as it is released. When that next great video card comes out, you know exactly what it takes to uninstall the card that you currently have and pop the new one in without a problem. Knowing your PC inside and out lets you get the most out of it.

Your Budget: What You Get for Your Money

Hopefully, all of the benefits that we noted have convinced you to assemble your own PC. If so, it is important to understand how much money you will need to complete this project. Knowing what kind of computer you are going to get based on what you spend is also vital. Here are some general guidelines for understanding your budget.

$1,000 — Basic PC

A budget of $1,000 is not going to build a very good gaming PC. If you shop very carefully, you may be able to find a few quality parts; however, you will wind up cutting too many corners to build a solid gaming PC that remains up-to-date for any extended period of time. You'll probably run out of storage before long, your mid-range video card will probably need to be upgraded before long, and there may not be enough money left over to buy the latest games or computer accessories. At best, the computer you build with this budget will be decent; at worst, it will be a disappointment.

If you only have $1000 to spend on your PC, you may be better off buying a PC from a generic PC Website. Because these companies build and sell a great number of these budget PCs, they can buy low- and mid-level components in bulk, saving more money than you are able to by purchasing them yourself.

$2,000 — Solid Gaming PC

A budget of $2,000 ensures that you can run every one of today's top games as well as those that are released in the near future. Not every game will run at its maximum settings, but the average gamer should be happy with this PC.

Because the quantity of high-level PCs that are sold by major manufacturers is significantly less than basic PCs, they do not realize as much of a savings on these components. In addition, the prices of these premium components are higher, which adds to the PC manufacturer's overall cost. At this price level, you get more value for your money by buying parts yourself and building your own PC.

$3,000 and Up — The Ultimate Gaming PC

A budget of $3,000 lets you buy all of the components you need for the ultimate gaming PC. You can have both the latest processor and graphics card, along with more than enough memory and storage to get the job done. You also can get a great monitor for viewing all of the latest graphics that your games throw at you. A full set of gaming accessories round out the total package, truly making this the ultimate gaming PC.

How to Set Your Budget

The general guidelines mentioned in the previous sections shouldn't be the only things that dictate how much money to spend on your new PC. Here are a few points to keep in mind as you set your budget.

Honestly Evaluate Your Cash on Hand

If you replaced all of the wallpaper in your home with sheets of dollar bills, you can skip this section and move on to the next chapter. For the rest of us, it is important to understand how much we *should* spend on this PC. First of all, the point of building the ultimate gaming PC is to play the greatest games. If there's no money left after assembling your PC to buy those games, you've done something wrong. Leave some cash on hand to have some fun after you've purchased all of your parts.

Assess How Long Your Computer Will Be "Ultimate"

If you're trying to build the ultimate gaming PC, you will wind up spending a lot of money to do it. However, if you break the bank today, it is important to understand that your computer won't be the best forever. Every year, new technology is allowing manufacturers to improve processors, video cards, and every other computer component that you can think of. Because of this, today's best computer will be bumped into second place in one to two years. You'll still be able to run every game out there, but you might find that you have to lower a setting or two to get the best overall performance. In two or three years, your top-of-the-line computer will become more mainstream, just slightly above the average PC. As time goes on, you'll begin to realize that your computer is becoming obsolete.

Because you're building your own PC, you have the unique opportunity to upgrade individual parts as better ones come out. And because you installed the original components, it shouldn't be much of a problem to repeat the task as technology improves. If you spend every last dime you own to build it in the first place, however, or if by this time next year you can't pay off that credit card you used to purchase the components, you won't be able to afford the newest technology as it comes out. Keep this in mind as you set your budget.

How to Save Money on Your Ultimate Gaming PC

Now that you set your budget, are you falling just short of being able to afford the parts you want? Luckily, there are many ways to save a few bucks along the way. The following are some ideas.

Harvest Parts from Old PCs

As much as processor and video card technology has come a long way in recent years, certain computer parts haven't evolved since the last decade began. Floppy drives are useful to diagnose broken PCs and assist during OS installations, but they still work in the same way as they did 10 years ago. The difference between a 32x CD-ROM drive and a 48x CD-ROM drive is negligible at best. Keyboards have had the same layout and keys since the 1970s.

Because these parts have undergone such little change, they are great items to salvage from older PCs. By grabbing these and throwing them into your new PC, you could save yourself $50, $100, or more. While that may not sound like much, every dollar helps when you're reaching for the next best processor or that top of the line video card that you've had your eye on.

Decide What's Most Important to You

Another way to save money, although slightly less desirable to some, is to determine what computer features are important to you and what areas you can cut. For example, if you can settle for a small symphony coming out of your PC instead of a full orchestra, you might be able to buy a mid-line sound card, or a slightly less-powerful speaker system. Focusing on the areas that are most important to you ensures that you will get the most satisfaction out of your new PC, rather than thinking about how much better your computer could have been.

Read Each Chapter for Part-Specific Savings

In each of the part selection chapters of this book, there is a section labeled "How to Save Money." Read through these sections carefully to prevent yourself from throwing money away. These sections also point out ways to save a few dollars with part selection and not compromise the overall quality of your PC.

Understanding Computer Parts

Purchasing all of the parts that are necessary to build a working PC can be a daunting task. Luckily, there are chapters in this book to help you search for each part. Before delving into the specifics, let's discuss the general quality of computer components.

Bargain Parts and Brands

The lowest level of computer parts is an unbranded component. Very often these are the lowest priced components available in a selection. If you are shopping in a brick-and-mortar store, these parts may even be labeled with the store's name, or with a particular logo or color that belongs to that store.

It is important to understand that the quality of these parts can vary widely. The performance of a single store brand component puts the reputation of all similarly branded items on the line. As such, a little more care may go into the manufacturing of these components when compared to other generic parts. Even so, the primary purpose of all generic parts is to be one of the lowest priced items on the shelf; you don't know if anything was sacrificed to achieve a particular low price point.

These parts are not recommended as primary components in an ultimate gaming PC. When we select parts, we choose them for reliability as well as performance. In general, these parts are good for emergency replacements of malfunctioning network cards or for meeting a sudden need for a dial-up modem. For important pieces of your PC, always use parts with solid reputations of quality.

Retail Parts

On the other end of the spectrum, you have retail parts. These components come complete in a box from the manufacturer. They contain not only the purchased item, but any accessories that may be required to install them, including screws, bolts, clips, cables, and similar pieces of hardware. These products also come with CDs that contain any drivers or other pieces of software that are necessary for them to run properly. Complete documentation and instructions are also found in the box.

Some retail parts include bonus items to make your purchase even more enjoyable. Sound and video cards may contain demo CDs, or even complete games that best demonstrate the part's unique capabilities. There may even be bonus pieces of hardware that compliment the original, adding value to the purchase.

Finally, the greatest item you get with a retail part isn't found in the box. Retail parts come with a complete warranty from the manufacturer. As mentioned earlier in this chapter, the majority of these warranties last for at least three years, if not for the lifetime of the product. Considering that you plan to spend significant amounts of money on these parts, you don't want to have to spend it a second time if the part fails within a year or two.

OEM Parts

Somewhere between bargain parts and retail parts lies the world of OEM (original equipment manufacture) parts. These components are the same brand name items that you find inside of a retail box; however, they do not come with the colorful packaging of retail parts. They most likely do not come with the necessary mounting screws and cables. Often, they do not come with any drivers; instead, you are directed to download any necessary software from the company's Website. Documentation is probably omitted, as well, and there are no bonus items.

Note The term *original equipment manufacture* is a misleading term for a company that has a special relationship with computer producers. OEMs buy computers in bulk and customize them for a particular application. They then sell the customized computer under their own name. The term is really a misnomer because OEMs are not the *original* manufacturers—they are the customizers.

The warranties that come with OEM parts can vary. It may match the warranty of the retail version exactly, or it may exist in a limited fashion or for a shorter duration. In some rare cases, there may not be any extended warranty at all.

These OEM parts represent a great opportunity for computer builders to save money, but they require some caution. OEM parts may simply be retail parts without documentation, or they could be "factory reconditioned" items. This means that the part previously failed inspection by the manufacturer, was repaired, tested, and passed a second inspection. The reliability of these products should match their retail counterparts, but it is ultimately up to you to decide if you are comfortable with them.

If you are considering OEM parts for your PC, read the entire product description very carefully. Check to see if the manufacturer's warranty still applies to the product. If the maker of the part is willing to stand behind it, you can feel comfortable in using it in your PC. Also, be sure that you have any necessary screws and cables to install it properly; otherwise, you could end up spending the money you saved to purchase the accessories that would have been included in the retail box.

Where to Buy Computer Parts

Now that you know a bit about part quality, you need to know where to look for the components. Similar to buying an entire PC, you can look on Internet sites specifically for computer parts, or you can look to one of your local retailers. Let's take a closer look at the places where you can shop for your parts.

Internet Shopping

There are hundreds of Websites selling computer parts. Some may specialize in a particular area, but most tend to be the Internet equivalent of a computer part superstore. Here are some things to be aware of as you shop these Websites.

Good Selection

Websites such as these often offer a superior selection when compared to their brick and mortar counterparts. Because they do not have to worry about stacking parts on shelves or advertising a particular brand over another, you should be able to find almost any part that you have read about or seen advertised.

Unfortunately, this wide selection can be both a benefit and a curse. If you shop at these sites without a particular product in mind, the selection can seem overwhelming. Something as simple as a network card can have 10 to 15 brands available for purchase. Avoid any confusion: research parts first before shopping at an Internet superstore.

Superior Prices

Product prices on the Internet are often less than your local store. Because these Websites do not need to advertise or maintain a storefront, they can usually offer the consumer a lower price than a physical store. Just don't use this as an excuse not to shop around. Prices can vary from site to site, and you could miss out on substantial savings by simply making a purchase from the first site you come across.

Virtual Selection

Unfortunately, products on a Website can't be physically examined. You are forced to rely on the product descriptions listed on each site. Some of the better sites offer several photos of each product, giving you some idea of what will be arriving at your doorstep in a few days.

Generally speaking, not being able to physically scrutinize an object should not be a problem for most components; however, if you are shopping for mice, keyboards, cases, or similar items, you may want to find them in a local store first and then shop and compare prices online. The comfort level of human interface devices such as these varies from person to person; just because your best friend likes the way a particular mouse fits in his or her hand doesn't mean it will be comfortable for you! Get a hands-on impression before buying.

Delayed Gratification

Another issue to be aware of when shopping online is the amount of time it takes to receive your product. There is usually one or two days of processing time before your order is shipped, and the shipment itself can take another three to five business days to arrive. Faster shipping methods are often available, but they can be costly. Be prepared to wait at least a week before you can play with your new toys.

Warning Some Websites offer "faster processing" or "priority processing" for your order in exchange for an additional fee. The amount of time you save with this option is usually negligible. Save your money for other purposes.

Quality Merchants

Unfortunately, for every quality Website that exists, there are two or three sites that have a questionable reputation. Beware of Websites where prices are significantly below all other Websites because there may be hidden fees or high shipping costs that are not readily apparent.

The best method for finding a reliable Website is to ask a friend, or check message boards for recommendations. The two Websites that we visit most often — www.newegg.com and www.zipzoomfly.com — are great places with solid reputations.

Overall, Internet shopping is wonderful, especially when you're planning to build a new PC. The amount of money you can save and the tremendous selection available will have you scouring the Internet again and again.

Internet Shopping Portals

With so many Websites selling computer parts, wouldn't it be great to search them all at the same time? With the help of Internet shopping portals, such as www.pricewatch.com, you can. Sites like this don't actually sell anything. Instead, they scour hundreds of merchants at once, returning any that are selling the product you identified. Here are a few points to keep in mind, if you plan to enlist the help of these search sites in your quest for quality merchants.

Component Price Range

The greatest advantage to using Internet shopping portals is that they can quickly identify the price range that you should expect to pay for a particular component. Simply take the highest and lowest prices found by your search, and average out how much you should expect to pay no matter where you look.

Estimated Availability

Another advantage to these shopping portals is in determining the average availability of a particular product. If your search reveals 10 Websites and they are all out of stock, the demand for your product may be particularly high. If you find it in stock somewhere, you may not want to wait very long before purchasing it, no matter the price.

Similarly, if only one or two merchants are returned by your search, it may be a sign that your part has been discontinued or replaced by a better model. You might benefit from a little more research before making this purchase.

Inexact Matches

It is important to read your search results very carefully. Some shopping portals may return items that are similar to the one you are searching for, but may not be an exact match. For example, if you are searching for Expansion Card 13ab, your results may include Expansion Card 13, Expansion Card 13a, and Expansion Card 13b along with your desired item. Be sure to read the product descriptions carefully before completing your purchase.

Variable Merchant Quality

Unfortunately, there isn't a single search engine that can scan every possible Website. Thus, your search results may include a few merchants that you don't recognize. Before purchasing a component from one of the merchants from your search results, compare prices with some of your favorite Websites. It may be worth an extra $10 or $15 to get your component from a reliable source.

In general, shopping portals are great one-click tools for gathering information from many online merchants; however, be cautious and read your results carefully. You may be better off using the information that you gather to shop at a more reputable merchant than you would be in giving your credit card information to an online retailer you have never heard of before.

Brick and Mortar Stores

Sometimes, the oldest methods are the best methods. Visiting your local computer store can have some advantages over browsing the Web. The following are some points to ponder if you decide to take a shopping trip.

Great for Getting Your Feet Wet

If you are buying computer parts for the first time, heading to you local store may be a great way to get your feet wet. The limited selection that these stores offer may be less overwhelming than what you find at some Internet superstores. You can also pick up retail boxes and read the detailed descriptions about the component. These experiences can help you visualize products that you find when shopping on the Web.

Advertisements

Brick and mortar stores generally advertise on a weekly basis. These circulars can usually be found in your local paper or at the store itself. The benefit of these flyers is that they deliver price information right to your door. Read over a flyer for an item of interest and make a note of its price. You can then compare that price to your favorite Internet retailer without ever leaving your home.

Rebates

Brick and mortar stores often have extensive rebates on a large array of products. These rebates can save you significant amounts of money in return for a little homework on your part. At the time of purchase, you usually receive a rebate form to send to the manufacturer. Fill out the form and send it, along with any required materials (usually your dated sales receipt and a proof-of-purchase symbol from the product box) to the address on the form. In six to eight weeks, the company will send you a check for the amount of the rebate.

Many people purchase a product and never complete the rebate applications. Fill out the application immediately after you are certain that the product fits your needs and is in good working order. This ensures that the rebate doesn't expire before you get around to filling out the application.

Note Some rebates are also available for Internet purchases. Check the retailer's Website or the manufacturer's Website for special offers.

Warning Don't clip out proof of purchase symbols from the product packaging before you have verified that the component works. Many merchants do not accept returns if you cut up the original box.

Easy Returns

After waiting two weeks for something to arrive from an Internet retailer, it can be a tremendous disappointment to find that it doesn't work. Luckily, when buying parts from your local store, you can try the part and return it almost immediately. And no shipping is required. Just hope that the return line isn't very long....

Note Always check your local store's return policy. Often, it is different for computer components and software than it is for general merchandise.

Reward Programs

Some stores are creating frequent shoppers' programs to reward repeat customers. For a small fee you can enroll in a program that rewards you with gift certificates after spending a certain amount of money. If you can get the majority of your parts in a particular store, this may be a significant benefit to you. Do the math; compare the fees with your expected reward to see if it is worthwhile.

Price Match Policy

Often, stores have some form of a price match policy for their products. If you bring in a circular from a competing store offering a lower price, the store may match the price and offer the product to you with an additional discount. If you have many competing stores in your area, you may be able to use a price match policy to your advantage by shopping around and comparing store circulars.

Instant Gratification

The best part about shopping in your local store is the fact that you don't have to wait for the part to be delivered. Some people find it more fun to run through a store on a shopping spree than clicking "Add to Cart" 20 times on a Website. No matter how you feel about this, there is one practical purpose to shopping a local store — emergency parts. If you need a part quickly to get your computer up and running, just head to your local store. You can waste much more time and money trying to find the best price for a product on the Internet and paying to ship it overnight than you would by grabbing it at your local store.

The Decision Making Process: How to Pick the Best Parts

Even though this chapter has discussed general part quality, you need more knowledge than this to select one brand or model over another. Part II of this book has specific information related to the computer components you need to get your ultimate gaming PC up and running. However, this book could be around a lot longer than the parts mentioned in those chapters. If that happens, the following section outlines some steps that help you perform your own research and select different components.

It's very tempting to just ask a friend or go to a Website and use a pre-published list of parts to build your ultimate gaming PC. Unfortunately, if you use that list three or six months from now, at least one of the components on it will have been replaced by newer technology. Rather than blindly using a random list of parts, it would be better to pick the best parts yourself.

The following section outlines a method for you to use to research your own part selection. We used these strategies, along with a few other resources and our own experiences, to select the components used in these books. The part selection chapters do not simply hail the praises of a particular component or brand. Instead, they identify the qualities that were important to us when we chose each part. You can use those qualities, along with the strategies outlined in the following sections, to choose new parts in the future.

Places to Look for Information

The Internet may be the greatest research tool ever created. With literally a whole world of information one Google search away, you should be able to research just about anything. Unfortunately, with the thousands of search results that can be returned by every search engine, finding the most relevant information can be difficult. Instead of wading through thousands of search results, try looking in some of the following places.

Review Sites

The Internet is a great source of computer hardware review sites. On these sites you find reviews of a wide range of components; hopefully they have some for the parts in which you are interested. They also have articles that compare several components side by side, a process that may provide more information than simply reading about the special features of a single component.

In general, good research sites also list some of the latest computer news, which keeps you abreast of any changes coming to the industry. If the newest technology is right around the corner, you can learn about it here and keep it in mind as you plan your new system. This could prevent you from buying a component that will be obsolete next month.

Good general review sites also contain a number of guides that may be useful to you. These guides may focus on hardware installation, which helps someone new to building their own computer avoid common troubles. They may also cover software and operating system installation, which assist you with installing programs that have a history of being difficult to install. Check these sites often to see what articles are available; they are a great way of learning more about your PC.

Tip   Most sites offer a search function that enables you to quickly find a review or an article. For best results, type the model number of the component that you are interested in (i.e. P4B-533e). If the search does not return a useful article, try another one using the band name and a part description (i.e., Creative sound card).

If you want to get started with your research right away, here are some of our favorite sites:

- AnandTech: www.anandtech.com

- Tom's Hardware Guide: www.tomshardware.com

- ExtremeTech: www.extremetech.com

- CNet: www.cnet.com

Message Boards

Message boards are great places to look for information about computer technology. A message board is a site where a visitor can post a question or information for other visitors to read. If someone wants to comment on your post or add additional information, their response is attached to yours. As more responses are posted, this online "conversation" (called a thread) incorporates the knowledge and views of many different people. By posting a question about a computer part on one of these message boards, you can get the views of many different people, instead of the opinion of a single reviewer who has written an article.

Some message boards operate independently, but many review sites have their own message board capabilities. You can often find links at the bottom of articles that take you to a thread on an associated message board that is currently discussing what the reviewer wrote. This is a great way to get answers to any questions you have on a particular article. You can also see if other readers agree with the opinions stated in the article.

Basic Concepts for Reading Reviews

Most review articles follow the same basic format. Now that you know where to find these reviews, expect to see the following sections in them:

- Introduction: A paragraph that usually introduces the part or parts being reviewed, and possibly the manufacturer as well. The introduction may also make note of other models that are essentially the same as the one being reviewed. Most of the information in one of these articles can be applied to the model mentioned.

- Body: The body of the article discusses features of the product, along with general impressions. Sometimes, the body features simple descriptions of the part. Often, it includes measurements and specifications that may or may not be useful to you.

- Test Results: Most reviewers run a component through several lab tests to measure its performance. This is the easiest way to compare the capabilities of one part to another in the same category. There are usually graphs and charts that display these comparisons in a visual format.

- Summary: At the end of the article, the reviewer quickly summarizes all of the key points made in the article, usually in one or two paragraphs.

- Score: Many reviews offer scores for each part, either on a 10-point scale (i.e., 8.2 out of 10) or as a percentage (i.e., Our Score: 96%).

Because these articles can often be several pages long, it can be difficult to gather the information that you need. Here are some hints on how to get the most out of your research.

Check the Date

The most important (and often overlooked) item to check is the date the article was published. If an article is over six months old, components with more advanced technology may have already been released. If this is the case, the product under review may match up favorably with similar parts mentioned in the article, but not with ones that have recently been released.

Start at the End—Read the Summary First

The best way to get a quick understanding of a particular review article is to jump right to the summary. This section of the article offers quick recaps on the positive and negative aspects of the component without detailed test results and performance measurements.

Don't Worry About the Score

Many Websites list a part's review score on a sidebar or in the header of an article in large font, making it the first thing visitors see. Unfortunately, readers often use this score as the first and last judgment of a product. A better way to use the score is as a general statement of quality and performance. For example, a part that receives a 3 out of 10 likely has several shortcomings, and you should avoid it, especially when compared to a component that received a 9 out of 10. If you are trying to compare a component with a score of 95% to one that received 97%, however, you need to look at the articles closely. That 2% point difference may be a result of a specific reviewer's experience and may not be a reflection of the product itself. You may arrive at a different conclusion after reading the article.

Read the Body and Ignore the Technical Jargon

The body of the article can contain a tremendous amount of information, some of which is not important to a reader who is just looking for a basic understanding of the product. Read through the body, but don't get hung up on anything too technical. Focus on statements that back up the points made in the summary; you should be able to find enough information to support the writer's opinion. Don't get discouraged if you don't understand every word.

Also, keep an eye out for phrases that are important to novice computer builders. For example, look for sentences that state the component is "easy to install and configure," or that the product has "good documentation." These qualities are often minimized by a seasoned reviewer, but they can be very significant to you.

Rinse and Repeat—Go to Other Sites!

After you have found all of the information you are looking for from a particular site, go to another. If possible, read two or three reviews on each part that you are considering for your PC. It is most important to see if each reviewer has the same general opinion on a product. A good computer component generates good reviews on all sites that review the product, not just one.

Advanced Concepts for Reading Reviews

After you are comfortable with getting useful information from review articles, you can expand your research to gain greater knowledge. The following tips may be more time consuming than you'd like, but you learn more about computer technology in the long run.

Expand Your Search — Read Other Articles

A great way to learn more about a particular type of component is to read review articles for other products in the same category. Almost all reviews make note of the leading manufacturer in a particular category when evaluating the reviewed product. See how your product stacks up against the top-ranked component in that category; when the results are in, you may want to switch brands.

Reviews of other products by the same manufacturer as your chosen part give you insight as to the quality and reliability of the company as a whole. If the majority of their products are rated poorly or have bad track records, you may want to purchase from a manufacturer with a better history of quality.

Reading reviews for competing products may point out additional features that are not part of your chosen product. Versatile products that have the latest features exist for a longer period of time before becoming obsolete.

Research the Technical Jargon

When reading the body of the article, we previously recommended skipping over complicated sections with extensive amounts of technical information. As an alternative, you can do additional research on the technical information to fully understand the discussion. Look on the manufacturer's Website for more information about a particular product. Use an Internet search engine such as Google to look up definitions of technical words that appear several times in the same article. If a particular piece of software was used to test the product, go to the Website for that software to learn about the tests and why they truly measure a product's performance. All of these steps provide the background for you to fully understand product reviews.

Basic Concepts for Using Message Boards

Message boards can be hit or miss when it comes to finding information about a product. Messages are not always entirely accurate, and important details on a product can be left out in favor of promoting another aspect of it. The best message board posters include hyperlinks to technical information, quotes from product literature, or other such back-up to support the things they post.

Message boards are extremely useful in registering many opinions in regards to product reliability and overall usefulness. Threads that have several responses indicate a particular topic is generating a significant discussion. If a product has poor reliability, you see many posters complaining about product returns, or insufficient warranties. If a product is difficult to set up, you see many questions about settings, product installation, and error messages. In the end, learning about actual user experiences via the message board can be as useful as any single review.

If you cannot find any threads on a particular product, feel free to create your own. If you are asking technical questions, be sure to include system information in your post (i.e., motherboard model, processor speed, OS, etc.). This ensures that people looking at your post are able to understand your situation and offer appropriate advice and feedback.

What's Next?

Now that you've decided to build your own PC, its time to start looking at the specific components that you'll be putting into your ultimate gaming PC. It's time to go shopping for your parts!

Let's Go Shopping for Parts

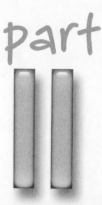

part

Selecting the Ultimate Gaming Processor

The Brains Behind the Operation

The processor is one of the most important components of any PC, let alone an ultimate gaming PC. It is quite literally the "brains behind the operation." Unfortunately, when it's time to choose the processor for your Ultimate Gaming PC, you will probably feel like a mad scientist. With two different brands, each with their own models and part numbers, it may seem like choosing from a bunch of brains on the shelf, all in unlabelled jars. Which one is the best for your monster?

When you finish reading this chapter, that question will hopefully be answered. We provide you with the information you need to pick the best processor for your ultimate gaming PC. We show you how we used this information to narrow down the choice of "brains" available to us and pick a specific brand and model.

The Basics: What Is a Processor?

The "brain" analogy used in the introduction to this chapter is quite appropriate to this discussion. The processor is the brain inside of your computer. Its primary job is to take information provided by your computer programs and "process" it, returning a result or instruction to be sent back to your program. It then acts on the instructions, which enables it to send more information to the processor, repeating the cycle. These cycles are how the processor "thinks."

Key Terms

Before you delve too far into the discussion and examination of processors, you should learn the "technical" jargon.

- Processor: Abbreviation for microprocessor.

- CPU: Abbreviation for central processing unit, which is a synonym for processor.

- Front Side Bus (FSB): The connection through which the processor and the memory on the motherboard communicate.

- Clock Speed: Measurement of the internal "clock." Every PC processor has one or more of these internal "clocks." The ticks from these clocks, which occur millions or billions of times per second, keep the data flow and calculations inside the CPU synchronized.

- Frequency: A measurement of the number of cycles something can complete in a period of time, usually 1 second; also known as clock rate." Frequency can be used in connection with different components of a PC; it is not limited to a processor. The following are typical units of frequency that you may encounter:

  - MHz: Abbreviation for megahertz, which is how many millions of cycles are completed in 1 second.

  - GHz: Abbreviation for gigahertz, which is how many billions of cycles are completed in 1 second. When comparing frequencies, GHz is much faster than MHz.

- Cache: Memory that is built into the processor, as opposed to the general memory located in chips on the motherboard. Cache is subdivided into different levels, with Level 1 (L1 Cache) and Level 2 (L2 Cache) being common on current processors. CPU cache memory is considerably faster than the main memory inside your PC.

- Hyperthreading: Intel-specific term used to describe the way their latest CPUs handle processing tasks. Also known as simultaneous multithreading, older processors can only handle one task at a time, albeit very rapidly, thus giving the illusion that many things are happening at once. Hyperthreading actually allows the CPU to assign idle parts of the processor to a second task, which improves response time and CPU efficiency.

- Dual Core: Terminology currently being used to describe the next generation of processors. Dual core CPUs actually embed two complete processors inside a single CPU package.

- 32-Bit Processor: A processor that can handle 32 bits (a measurement of size) of data in one cycle. A pure 32-bit processor can address a maximum of 4GB.

- 64-Bit Processor: A processor that can handle 64 bits of data in one cycle. Note that various 64-bit CPUs can address differing amounts of physical memory, due to the way they handle memory accesses internally.

However, having the fastest brain is useless if there is nothing to think about. Although a fast processor can "think" quickly about information, it needs to be supplied with information about what to think. Thus, it is important to look not only at the speed at which a processor does its job, but at how fast the processor can be supplied with information by other computer components. If all of the related components cannot keep up with each other, system performance suffers.

While the actual details of how a processor executes instructions from start to finish can be an interesting subject, that discussion is not going to help you in building the ultimate gaming PC. Instead, you need to stay focused only on the specific features of available processors that affect the gaming performance of your PC. In addition, you should examine how the processor works with other parts of your PC, affecting performance. Understanding all of these concepts enables you to pick the best processor for the job.

The Tech: Which Parts of a Processor Affect Gaming?

Because processor performance is vital to many uses of your PC besides gaming, it can be difficult to look at product specifications to find the ultimate gaming processor. Understanding the following categories and how they affect gaming allows you to focus your search and find what you need.

CPU Core: Think, Man, Think!

When most people try to determine the most powerful processor from a varied line-up, they tend to focus on one factor: clock speed. Whether the specs that you find call it "operating frequency" or "clock speed," a 3.8 Ghz processor sounds impressive. This is especially true if you've been gaming since the days of the original Pentium, when a 100 Mhz processor was cutting edge. In the world of today's games, however, clock speed is not necessarily the ultimate factor.

Clock speed is a determination of how fast a processor can complete a set of instructions in a period of time. This is probably the easiest concept for people to grasp when considering a processor. Just like a race car, faster is better, right? A faster race car reaches the finish line sooner than a slower car. If your CPU is given a set of instructions by a program or an OS, and it completes those instructions really quickly, those programs should show the results faster.

Unfortunately, this analogy is a little too simplistic to give you the real answer. Your race car may be fast, but doesn't the race track also have an effect on the race? If the CPU speed is like a race car, a computer game is the race track. What you are really interested in is how the two interact.

Computer games that involve explorable, 3D environments are great examples of how the processor does and does not affect actual gameplay. Games such as this usually contain numerous objects with which the player can interact. As the player walks across the landscape, the game typically asks the CPU to calculate several things. The CPU is in charge of physics calculations, which affects how your character walks, falls, jumps, and maybe even flies. The CPU is processing character-triggered events that occur when a player walks into a particular area or onto different terrain. The CPU is also used to handle the reactions of other objects to the player's actions. This can be as simple as opening a door, or as complex as determining how a computer-controlled character is going to react to the player's actions. Having a CPU that can process these events quickly can be a great advantage to many games.

There are also many actions in the game where the speed of response is not a factor of the CPU. Just because your processor can quickly calculate how fast you are flying though the sky doesn't mean your graphics card can draw those clouds and birds that are whizzing by at a sufficient rate to keep up with the player.

Another factor is processor *efficiency*. Think of efficiency as how much work the CPU can do per clock cycle. The Pentium 4, for example, has a high clock rate, but divides up any task into many small parts. So the amount of work done per clock cycle is relatively small. On the other hand, AMD's Athlon 64 doesn't split up the task into as many parts and thus can do more work per clock cycle. That's why a 2.4 GHz Athlon 64 can often keep up with, or even exceed the performance of, a 3.4 Ghz Pentium 4.

A high clock speed is a great asset to gaming, especially games that involve complex physics and use many interactive features. Just be aware that it is not the sole factor in choosing a great gaming processor.

Cache: How a Processor Avoids Going to the (Memory) Bank

As mentioned in the introduction to this section, a "quick thinking" processor becomes less important when there is nothing to think about. In a radical example, what is the difference between someone who can finish a math problem in 1 minute versus someone who takes 1 hour if a teacher only comes to get the answer and offer a new problem every 60 minutes? For a processor to make a difference, it has to be supplied with information as quickly as possible. To properly address this issue, it is important to understand where the information that a processor thinks about comes from.

There used to be only two places from where information could be gathered and given to the processor. The hard drive stored large amounts of information, for extended periods of time, but took the longest amount of time to be accessed and sent to the processor. The onboard memory bank of RAM was significantly faster but couldn't hold as much information at once. That information disappeared if power to the RAM was interrupted.

As processor calculation speed increased, the gathering of this information became tremendously slower than the processing of it. This accessing of information became the primary roadblock to improving system performance. The creation and utilization of processor cache (pronounced the same as the word "cash") became one way to get around this roadblock. Cache is memory located on the processor itself, a place where information used frequently by the processor can be stored. This memory can operate almost as fast as the processor can, rapidly providing information for the processor to "think about."

Cache is divided into "levels," which are simply terms used to define exactly how this memory is physically connected to processor. Level 1 (L1) cache is the most basic form of cache. Every processor since the 386 was developed in 1988 has had a small amount of L1 cache. Its presence is not an important aspect in your processor search, nor is it advertised as a key processor feature. Level 2 (L2) cache, however, is a factor in the performance of current processors. A larger L2 cache allows more frequently used information to be stored on the processor and accessed at speeds significantly greater than the other storage options in the system.

Current processors are available with 512KB, 1MB, or 2MB of L2 cache. If your programs or your OS are designed to properly utilize much of this L2 cache, you see a significant boost in performance. Because this is not always the case, however, the size of your L2 cache is one of several factors in your CPU decision, but not the most important.

Note Some processors even have Level 3 (L3) cache. At this time, it has not produced a significant effect on gaming performance. This may change if future games are specifically designed to take advantage of this additional on-chip storage.

Intel Versus AMD: Apples and Oranges

As you may or may not know, there are two primary manufacturers of processors for your desktop: Intel and AMD. No matter which brand you buy, each processor performs the same tasks. Their designs, on the other hand, are completely different from each other. Each brand has unique features that the other does not. Even features that sound the same, such as clock speed, are based on different concepts. This can make comparing these two brands a real chore.

The following section discusses the unique features of each brand, how common features such as clock speed are different between the two, and how to go about comparing CPUs from different manufacturers.

Intel: Apples (No, Not Those I-Pod People)

Today's processors boast some special features that are designed to set their chips apart from their rivals. Gamers are specifically targeted by many of these. It is important to understand what these terms mean, and whether or not they actually accomplish their intended goal.

Hyperthreading

Hyperthreading is a feature that causes a processor to be seen by an operating system as two separate processors, even though it's really a single CPU. The OS divides its workload into groups (called threads) and sends them to these two processors. In theory, this should allow twice the work to be done at the same time because the "virtual" processor and the real processor are sending results back to the OS.

In actuality, this isn't quite as helpful as it sounds. It is very difficult for a program to split up the workload for two processors. You can visualize this single processor as a car wash. One day, you build a second car wash next to the first. If a car pulls up, you can evenly distribute the workload (thus maximize the benefit of two car washes) by cutting the car in half. This way, each car wash would only have to wash half the car (which is half the work) and they would finish at the same time.

Obviously, you can't cut the car in half. It would be much more practical to divide the workload—have only one car wash and hire an extra worker to clean the inside of the car while the car wash cleans the outside. These tasks would not be an equal distribution of the workload, and the man cleaning the inside probably couldn't get out until the car wash was finished with the exterior of the car. But it would result in a small speed improvement.

For hyperthreading to really increase performance, the software using it has to be specifically programmed for this optimization. Most of today's games are not multithreaded. At this time, hyperthreading does not offer noticeable benefit for gaming. In the future, though, game developers are taking a serious look at how to split their games into multiple threads. The next generation of dual-core CPUs and the next generation game consoles will work best with multithreaded games.

Extreme Edition

The headline "Extreme Edition" (EE) is Intel's way of flagging certain processors to catch the attention of gamers. In general, Extreme Edition processors are simply derivations of "regular" P4 processors, except for three points:

- "Extreme" cache: The first Extreme Edition CPUs had a 2MB L3 cache, more than any other Intel desktop CPU at the time.

- "Extreme" overclocking: Intel EE processors have "unlocked" their frequency multipliers, which is a fancy way of saying they are easier to overclock. In fact, some systems builders are actually selling Intel Pentium Extreme Edition 840 dual-core systems running as high as 4GHz, even though the rated clock speed is 3.2GHz.

- "Extreme" price: Intel EE processors are significantly more expensive than regular P4 processors.

As mentioned earlier in this chapter, the addition of cache to the processor can be a great advantage; however, according to many Internet testing sites, the additional amount of cache on the Intel EE chip does not translate into any noticeable gaming improvement. Because this book is about building an ultimate gaming PC and not about how best to overclock a PC, the unlocked multiplier is not significant to you. Paying more for this chip is definitely not a "feature" that appeals to us, either. All in all, an Extreme Edition label is not a great incentive to buy an Intel EE chip.

Note The latest Intel P4 EE chips may not be the best gaming processor, but they have proven to be a great addition in another area—media encoding. If you are doing any sort of processor-intensive video or sound editing, the performance of these CPUs beats any other, hands down.

AMD: The Oranges

AMD (Advanced Micro Devices) processors were originally slightly modified copies of Intel processors. As this brand of processors evolved, they broke away from the Intel design. AMD processors now use different motherboards, communicate with the RAM differently, and are even capable of "thinking" differently. The following sections discuss the features that set the current AMD chips apart.

64-Bit Capabilities

AMD makes sure to point us to the capability of their latest generation of processors to handle 64-bit instruction sets. Unfortunately, many people mistakenly believe that this capability offers some sort of significant advantage over Intel processors and previous AMD models in regards to current computing needs. This is incorrect. On top of that, the latest generation of Intel CPUs are now 64-bit capable.

The 64-bit processing refers to the size of information that can be processed by the CPU in one processing cycle. Previous generations of processors could only process 32-bit instructions. This implies that a 64-bit processor could handle twice the amount of information in one cycle, which sounds like a great improvement. Just because the processor is capable of handling 64-bit instructions, however, doesn't mean it is actually going to receive any.

Also, a 64-bit CPU can talk to much greater quantities of memory than a 32-bit processor. In some respects, this is actually more important than doing 64-bit math. Modern applications are becoming more memory-hungry, and the ability to address larger quantities of memory is highly desirable.

The sizes of the instructions that are received by the processor are actually dependant on the operating system that is in use. Most gamers run some version Microsoft Windows—as old as Windows 95 to the most recent version of Windows XP. These two versions, and all of the variations in between, are 32-bit operating systems. This means that the instructions they send to the processor are 32-bit, not 64-bit. Without a 64-bit OS, the 64-bit capabilities of the AMD processor are not relevant to computing today.

Microsoft has released a version of Windows XP that's 64-bit ready, called Windows XP Professional x64. But even if you have a 64-bit processor, you don't necessarily want to rush out and get this OS. For one thing, critical device drivers — the piece of software that allows Windows to talk to hardware—may not be ready. And although most 32-bit applications run well on Windows x64, not all do.

Microsoft's next generation operating system, code-named "Longhorn," ships in both 32-bit and 64-bit versions.

Integrated Memory Controller

Normally, the communications between the processor and RAM is controlled through a chip on the motherboard known as the memory controller. The latest processors from AMD have taken this memory controller and integrated it directly on the CPU. This creates a more direct path between the processor and the system RAM, allowing faster and more efficient communication between CPU and RAM. The result is a significant improvement in system performance. In particular, games seem to benefit substantially from the Athlon 64 integrated memory controller.

Intel Versus AMD: Just Because It Sounds the Same, Doesn't Mean It Is

Believe it or not, discussing the differences of each brand of processor is an easier task than discussing the things they have in common. These features are clearly pointed out by each manufacturer and can be evaluated on their own merits. It is when discussing features that the brands have in common, such as core frequency, that the conversation can become confusing. This section focuses on two similar-sounding features that the brands share — how they are completely different from each other, and how they affect your purchase.

Core Frequency

Both Intel and AMD have a core frequency listed for their processors. In fact, some people immediately point to this as the "speed" of the processor. If you fall into that camp, I have no doubt that you own an Intel processor. Why? Because when you match up an Intel CPU with its competing AMD version, the Intel frequency always appears higher. Be careful: this does not imply that the Intel CPU is better.

To truly understand how to interpret the core frequency of each brand, you have to understand its meaning. The core frequency is a way of measuring how much a processor gets done in a given period of time. A good analogy is two children who are given one page of math problems to complete. If the first child is finished in 1 minute and the second child is finished in 2 minutes, you would probably conclude that the first child was faster. This is only true, however, if the two children were given the same page of math problems. What happens if the first child's page has only 5 problems and the second has 100 questions?

This uneven page analogy describes exactly what is happening with Intel and AMD. The AMD processor completes less "math pages" in a given cycle than Intel (thus resulting in a lower clock speed), but it gets more work done in those same cycles than Intel.

This leaves you with a very large problem — if the core frequencies for each brand are not measuring the same amount of work, how do you compare the two? This question is answered later in the chapter. For now, it is simply important to know that you cannot directly compare the core frequencies of an AMD processor with that of an Intel processor.

Front Side Bus

The Front Side Bus (FSB) is a term used to describe the communications between the processor, the on-board system memory (RAM) and the expansion cards in your computer. The faster these communications run, the better your system performance. Because the graphics card for your computer usually communicates with the processor via the FSB, having a very fast FSB is beneficial to game performance.

If the front side bus is so important to gaming performance, why wasn't it listed in the section that described the parts of the processor that affect gaming? Well, you can credit AMD for that.

AMD has made significant changes to the way the processor communicates with the rest of the parts of the computer. One way that has already been discussed is the integration of the memory controller with the processor. With this connection taken care of, that's one less task for the FSB to handle.

The remaining tasks are handled using Hypertransport technology, which has changed the way the FSB communicates. Hypertransport technology allows the FSB to send *and* receive information from its connected components simultaneously. A good analogy is the human heart. With each pump, it takes in blood from other parts of the body while sending blood back out at the same time.

The end result of these two technologies has completely reconfigured the FSB when compared to Intel. Just like the core frequency, this means that FSB frequencies cannot be directly compared to each other as a way of finding the best processor.

Note that Intel CPUs still use a more traditional approach, with the CPU communicating with the memory controller via the front side bus. So with Intel systems, a faster FSB often means somewhat improved performance.

How to Compare Intel with AMD: Benchmarking

The goal of this chapter is to help you choose the best gaming processor. It appears that all we've actually done is say that the two brands, AMD and Intel, cannot be compared by simply looking at the label. Then how, exactly, are you supposed to decide between the two? The answer? Benchmarking.

Benchmarking

Benchmarking is a testing process designed to measure the performance of a particular computer component or a PC as a whole. The test results have a specific unit of measurement, allowing them to be compared to the results of a different brand or model in the same category. For example, you can use the results to compare an Intel processor to an AMD Processor, or you can match two different Intel models against each other

Having a measurable standard is the key concept behind benchmarking. You could not run Doom III on two computers and simply say one is "faster" or "smoother" than the other. These perceptions could be different depending on the person playing. Instead, you need an actual measurement to compare the two. Comparing the number of frames per second displayed onscreen is usually the determining factor is this sort of test.

Even though we discuss benchmarking in depth throughout Chapter 13, it is important to introduce it here. Benchmarking is the only way to directly compare the effects of an Intel and AMD processor on gaming performance. Fortunately, you do not have to buy several different processors to benchmark because this subject has been covered extensively on numerous Websites and in magazine articles. Gathering information from all of these sources made one fact perfectly clear: AMD processors consistently match the performance of or outperform an equivalent Intel processor in the gaming environment.

The latest processors from Intel excel in many other benchmarks, especially ones that involve multitasking or video encoding.

Finally, you have some concrete information on which to base your decision. However, we want to ensure that you have all the facts before you make your final decision. Take a moment to examine some less measurable factors that are part of your decision-making process.

The Future of Processors

If you were trying to build an ultimate gaming PC during the last 10 years, you would have found it to be a task that was never finished. Video cards were constantly improving. PC sound evolved from beeps and buzzing noises to 7.1 surround sound. Processors alone were constantly increasing speed, forcing consumers who wanted the fastest system to upgrade often. Manufacturers were constantly inventing ways to make processor components smaller, fitting more on a chip and increasing speed; there didn't seem to be an end to how fast they could become.

Unfortunately, that end has unexpectedly appeared. As the number of processor components on a CPU has increased, so has the amount of heat they produce. This could fry the processor or the other components of your PC. The technology used to shrink processor components is also reaching the limits of current technology, preventing continued speed increases that result from simply cramming the processor full of more transistors.

As a result, the processor industry is moving in a different direction, that of multicore technology. This concept is to place two or more CPU cores on one physical processor, creating a direct connection between the two. This gives your computer two "brains" on one chip! Tasks that take up a lot of processing power, such as burning a CD, could be given to one core, leaving another free to handle other tasks. In the gaming world, a game could split up tasks, giving physics calculations to one core and running game events with the other.

Why is this important to discuss now? Both Intel and AMD are now shipping dual-core processors suitable for desktop PCs. If you want to run out, grab one, and pop it into your computer the moment they arrive, you should be aware that AMD has stated that their first dual-core processor has the exact same connections as their latest processors. With a simple BIOS upgrade, you can pop out your Athlon 64 processor and pop in your new dual-core CPU. Intel dual-core CPUs do require motherboards built around that company's 945 or 955X chipsets. If you don't already have one of those, you're stuck with investing in a new motherboard. You may even have to replace your memory.

Top Brands and Models: Which Processors Are We Considering?

While we were discussing the future of processors, your Web browser was gathering information on the "now" of processors. Because you're building the ultimate gaming PC, we grabbed the specs on the top processor from Intel and from AMD. Their specs are listed in Table 2-1.

Table 2-1   Intel Versus AMD: A Competitive Comparison

	Intel	AMD
Name	Pentium 4, Extreme Edition	Athlon 64 FX-55
Core Frequency	3.73 GHz	2.6 GHz
Front Side Bus Speed	1066 MHz	1000 MHz
L2 Cache	2 MB	1 MB
Hyper-Threading Technology	Yes	No
64-Bit Processing	Yes	Yes
Integrated Memory Controller	No	Yes
Typical Internet retailer Price	$1,067.99	$839.99

Our Results: What We Chose and Why

In the end, we chose the Athlon 64 FX-55 over the Intel P4 Extreme Edition 3.73 GHz. After scouring the Internet for benchmarks and considering all of the results, the Athlon 64 FX-55 was clearly the top gaming processor. We mentioned in the previous sections that for every AMD chip there is a comparable performing Intel CPU, and the performance benchmarks of the P4 Extreme Edition definitely made things close. However, some other AMD features made this decision easier.

In part, our choice was based on the established 64-bit processing history of the AMD line, readying this processor for the Windows OS of tomorrow. We also chose this processor because it allows us to use future AMD technologies without having to buy a new mother-board for our PC. Finally, the $200 price difference was a great plus. In the end, the AMD processor was exactly what we wanted, both now and in the near future. Take a look at our selection in Figure 2-1.

FIGURE 2-1: Our pick—the AMD Athlon 64 FX-55.

How to Save Money in the Processor Category

If you don't have $1,000 to throw around on a processor, that's OK. Luckily, there are many processors from which to choose, providing you with numerous options. Here are some ways to save a few bucks.

Buy the Next Best Processor

The two processors we looked at were definitely the best each company had to offer; however, you can save quite a bit of money by taking one step down the ladder. For example, the previous version of the processor we chose, the Athlon 64 FX-53, is selling for $50 to $100 less.

This is still a quality processor and is a great example of how to grab a discount on a processor that just got knocked out of the top spot. If you need to save more, simply take another step down the ladder. Eventually, you will find a good combination of performance and price.

Don't Go to the "Extremes:" Leave the FX and Extreme Editions Behind

The AMD FX series and the Intel Extreme Edition series are designed specifically for gamers. As a result, they come at a premium. Both companies, however, have general performance processors that are quality purchases. Finding the best one takes a little bit of research on your part. Use the discussion throughout this chapter to check the specs on the processor of your choice. Hopefully, we have told you what to look for, and you can find the best bang for your buck.

Some of the older (and cheaper) processors only fit in some outdated motherboards. Be sure to check out our discussion on processor sockets in this chapter to ensure that you don't purchase an outdated processor. This could limit your performance today and your upgrade potential in the future.

What's Next?

Now that you have chosen your ultimate processor, you need to have a place to plug it in. Of course, it's not as simple as it sounds. It's time to move on to Chapter 3, "Selecting the Ultimate Gaming Motherboard" and see what you've gotten yourself into!

Selecting the Ultimate Gaming Motherboard

N ow that the processor has been selected, you need to find somewhere to plug it in. In fact, you need a place to put all of the ultimate gaming components that you are going to buy. Looks like it's time to talk about a motherboard.

The Basics: What Is a Motherboard and What Does It Do?

The motherboard: a flat printed circuit board that has strange looking, long, drab-colored plastic pieces, tiny electrical things, and blinking lights soldered onto it. If you paid attention in physics class, you might even recognize some of those tiny things as capacitors and resistors. If you've explored inside a computer before, you might know that those long plastic pieces are slots for components like video cards and memory. If you're really skilled, you might even see those small metal twigs sticking up from the motherboard, standing really close together, and recognize them as jumpers. Unfortunately, if you're like many people out there, you just see this rectangular-shaped mess and hope that you never have to do anything with it. With any luck, after reading this section, you will be able to make sense out of the electrical mess that is your motherboard.

Before you can even begin to identify the essential parts of your motherboard, it is important to understand what it does. The motherboard acts as a home for all of your computer parts, with slots and sockets specially constructed for each component. Your processor has a socket on the motherboard uniquely shaped to fit it. The memory slots on your board are fashioned in a manner that prevents you from installing a memory chip backward. Every component of your PC has a specific home on your motherboard.

Key Terms

Before you take a close look at how a motherboard works, here are some key terms that might help you understand the discussion:

- Mainboard: Synonym for motherboard.

- Slots: Long, plastic pieces on your motherboard where each PC part is connected. These slots are usually color coded to indicate what component can be inserted. Also referred to as *expansion slots*.

- PCI slot: General slot that holds many different expansion cards. Examples include sound cards, USB cards, FireWire cards, modems, network cards, older video cards.

- AGP slot: Slot for AGP video card.

- PCIe video slot: Slot for a PCI Express video card. Often referred to as the PCIe x16 slot, because it uses 16 PCI Express "lanes."

- PCIe expansion slot: New type of slot for general expansion cards that communicate faster than PCIe. Defined by the number of PCIe "lanes": x1, x4, x16, etc.

- PCI Express lanes: A direct connect serial interface. A single PCIe lane can deliver up to 2.5GB per second in either direction. Lanes can be combined to work in concert. For example, PCIe graphics cards are typically plugged into a slot with 16 lanes, called a PCIe x16 slot.

- Ports: Sockets on the board where external devices can be connected.

- USB ports: Sockets for a wide variety of peripherals ranging from mouse devices and keyboards to gaming aids to even external hard drives or optical drives. All current generation USB ports support up to 480 megabits per second (Mbps).

- FireWire ports: Ports used primarily for digital video I/O, MP3 players, and external storage.

- Chipset: Consists of one or more semiconductor chips that handle all the "traffic cop" duties. The chipset shuttles data from the processor to PCI or PCI Express slots, interfaces with USB, and so on. In some systems, the chipset also handles communications between the processor and main memory. Commonly known as "core logic." The five most common manufacturers of chipsets are

  - Intel
  - NVidia
  - ATI
  - VIA
  - SiS

- Bus: Term describing a shared connection between multiple points or peripherals, such as the PCI bus or USB bus.

- Point-to-point connection: Alternative to the bus, point-to-point connections are dedicated connections between two devices. For example, PCI Express is a point-to-point connection, as is the HyperTransport links used in many PC motherboards.

- Front Side Bus (FSB): The connection that your processor uses to communicate with the chipset. The speed of this communication is described by a particular frequency (i.e., 800 Mhz FSB). You may see the terms "actual" and "effective" clock rates. For example, a Pentium 4 with an 800 MHz effective FSB really runs at 200 MHz, but transmits four data items per clock cycle.

- Form factor: The size and shape of your motherboard.

- ATX form factor: Most common size motherboard, 12 in. x 9.6 in. Also popular are microATX (9.6 x 9.6) inches.

- BTX form factor: More recent form factor, currently used mostly in off-the-shelf systems built around Intel processors. The main advantage of BTX is a component layout that maximizes cooling of hot components.

The motherboard also acts as a telephone switching system for each installed component. When your memory needs to work with your processor, they "talk" to each other through the motherboard. When your hard drive wants to store some data, the motherboard lets it join the conversation between your processor and your memory, enabling them to work together to accomplish the task.

The Tech: How Does the Motherboard Do What It Does?

When browsing motherboards, most people check the specifications of each product being considered. However, this can often be like reading a restaurant menu written in a foreign language — very confusing and very frustrating. We've already taken the first step in preventing that by listing the key terms, but just because you can now translate what is on the menu doesn't mean you can tell if you will like it. That is what this next section is all about. It will add context to the vocabulary you just learned. For example, now that you know what the different types of slots on a board are, you need to decide which ones are important for your ultimate gaming PC. (Knowing why they're important won't hurt, either.)

Let's begin by taking a close look at a motherboard's chipset.

Basic Communications: Chipsets

As mentioned earlier in this chapter, one of the primary roles of the motherboard is to allow every component to communicate with each other and work together. This task is handled by the motherboard chipset, also known as core logic. The term "chipset" is used to describe one or more semiconductor chips that act as "traffic cops" for all the data flying around your system. It is the motherboard chipset that actually handles the communications between components. Chipset circuitry is not usually developed by the motherboard manufacturer. The manufacturer simply incorporates existing chipset designs into their motherboards.

For many years, Intel has been designing and constructing chipsets suited for their own processors. Their most recent chipset design utilizes a two-chip configuration to handle component communication. This two-chip design is also referred to as a north bridge/south bridge configuration. In boards that are a few years old, and even in some of today's boards, the north bridge was designed to handle communication between the processor, the onboard memory, the video card (AGP), plus the PCI bus. In fact, the terms "north" and "south" referred to "north of PCI" and "south of PCI" because the two chips were connected by the PCI bus in the early days. The south bridge handles all of the input and output needs of your PC, like USB ports and internal connections to storage devices (hard drives, CD drives, and so on).

Intel's more recent chipsets also use this setup, but the roles of each chip have changed. The major change is that PCI communication has been moved from the north bridge (called MCH in this setup, which stands for Memory Controller Hub) to the south bridge (called the ICH, with stands for the I/O Controller Hub). This reconfiguration was done to optimize the communications performance of each chip by grouping slower devices on the ICH and faster ones on the MCH. (Chipsets with integrated graphics, such as Intel's 945G core logic, add a "G" to the term, as in "GMCH.")

This basic design has been the model on which other companies have built their own chipsets, giving motherboard many manufacturers from which to choose. Three of these companies, NVidia, SiS, and Via, join Intel as the names that you are most likely to see when looking at the specs of a motherboard.

Note that Athlon 64 processors no longer have a traditional north bridge because the memory controller is actually built into the CPU itself. A dedicated, point-to-point connection between the CPU and memory now exists in Athlon 64 systems. You may see this connection incorrectly referred to as the "FSB," but it's really just the memory clock rate, not a true front side bus.

Advanced Communications: Unified Chipset Design and Processor-Based Memory Controllers

Although all of this information may be interesting to some (and utterly boring to others), it is an important basis for discussing two features that play an important role when choosing your monster motherboard.

The north bridge/south bridge chipset setup introduces a new factor in component communications. Instead of just dealing with the speed of communications between components, the speed of communications between the north bridge and the south bridge can become a factor in system performance. The optimized design of the latest Intel chipsets dealt with this issue by isolating the most important components in terms of performance on the MCH (processor, memory and graphics), but NVidia has taken this concept to the next level.

Recent NVidia chipsets have used a unified construction to simplify communications. Instead of having two chips sharing the communications load with each other, the latest NVidia Nforce3 and Nforce4 chipsets has one chip that handles all communication between motherboard components, eliminating the issue of chip-to-chip communications within a chipset from impacting system performance. Because the memory controller is actually embedded in the CPU, the core logic mainly handles PCI Express and other, slower input/output devices.

Because AMD has given their processors an integrated memory controller, the motherboard architecture can be simplified a bit. The chipset no longer has to provide a memory controller, simplifying chipset design. Also, the processor can communicate with memory directly, which is a much faster method than having these communications run through the chipset. This gives motherboards with AMD-compatible chipsets a significant performance advantage in applications that rely heavily on the processor, memory, and graphics cards. What applications might those be? Well, games, of course!

Plug in! Slots and Sockets on the Motherboard

Now that you've learned how a motherboard handles component communication, you can move on to its other key role: motherboards need to have a place for all of your components to plug in. Thus, you have to ensure that your board has the correct type of connections for everything you want to add. Also, you have to ensure that you have enough of each type of connection to meet your needs.

For example, video cards can connect to your motherboard in three different ways — PCI, AGP, or PCIe. If you want the latest and greatest video card that connects via PCIe, you better make sure that your motherboard has a corresponding PCIe video card slot for your fancy card; otherwise, it's time to take that card back to the store.

Cross-Reference Don't worry about the details of the connections right now. We cover them in Chapter 5, Choosing the Ultimate Video Card.

Also consider someone who buys a video card that fits in a PCI slot. The PCI slot-type is shared by many other components. Your sound card will likely be a PCI card, as will a FireWire expansion card or a 4-Port USB 2.0 expansion card. If you motherboard only has two PCI slots, you have to decide which one you're giving up to install that new video card.

The following is a list of slots and connections to look at when choosing a motherboard.

Processor Socket

Your processor is the brains of your computer and is one of the most vital pieces of your PC; however, your processor can't process anything unless it has a place to go on your motherboard. Unfortunately, not every motherboard matches up with every processor, and the purchase of one may control the purchase of the other.

The processor slot on the motherboard connects to your CPU using a series of pins that can either be on the motherboard or on the processor itself. The number, size, and arrangement of these pins vary, depending on the brand and the computing power of the processor. Each pin pattern has a name given to it by the CPU manufacturer, enabling you to match it up with motherboard that has a similarly named CPU socket.

It is important to remember that the processor socket on your motherboard is designed to handle only one possible combination of pin size and arrangement. If you purchase the motherboard as the first component of your system, the processor socket on the board dictates the brand and design of the processor you purchase. Certain boards work only with AMD branded processors, and others are designed to work with Intel brand processors. If you purchase your processor first, the same theory applies as the pin count on the CPU controls where it fits. For example, if you selected an AMD processor for your PC, you will be unable to use an Intel brand board at all because they are competing manufacturers. Your selection from the remaining motherboard manufacturers is limited to the portion of their product designed for your product.

Table 3-1 matches the most recent processor slot descriptions from motherboard specifications with the brand of processor that can be used and its maximum speed.

Table 3-1   Processor Slot Names

Processor Slot Name	Processor Brand	Maximum Processor Speed
Socket 939	AMD	2.8 Ghz
Socket 754	AMD	2.4 Ghz
Socket LGA 775	Intel	3.8 Ghz
Socket 478	Intel	3.4 Ghz

Cross-Reference   In Chapter 2, we selected the AMD Athlon 64 FX-55 as the CPU for our Ultimate Gaming PC. This 2.6 GHz chip fits in a Socket 939 connection.

When we pick the motherboard for our PC later in this chapter, we need to ensure that it has this type of socket. A picture of this type of processor slot is shown in Figure 3-1.

Note   The next AMD FX chip, the FX-57, will run at 2.8 GHz. Although it was not available at the time this book went to press, it should soon be available at your favorite retailer.

FIGURE 3-1: An example of a Socket 939 connection.

Memory Slots

In a manner similar to processors, computer memory comes in different brands, types, and sizes.

Cross-Reference

All of these issues are covered in detail in Chapter 4, Choosing Your Ultimate Memory.

There are two points to keep in mind regarding memory and your ultimate motherboard. The type of motherboard that you buy determines the type of memory that you are able to use. Also, the number of slots that are available on your motherboard determines how many memory modules you can purchase for your machine. When buying your motherboard, having three or four slots for your memory offers you greater flexibility than one or two slots offer.

To identify and count the memory slots on your motherboard, look for slots similar to the ones seen in Figure 3-2.

FIGURE 3-2: An example of a motherboard's memory slots.

Video Card Slots

Your video card is one of the most important pieces in your ultimate gaming PC. To play the most demanding games, you may want to purchase the latest and greatest card on the market. Unfortunately, as mentioned in the introduction to this section, the available video card slots on your motherboard have the final say in whether or not that card can be used.

Currently, there are three possible ways of connecting your video card to your motherboard — PCI Express (PCI*e*, for short), AGP, or PCI.

Cross-Reference   For specific information on each of these video card standards, you can jump to Chapter 5, Choosing the Ultimate Video Card.

For now, however, you need to be aware of a few important details. AGP is currently the most common video card connection today, with PCI*e* being the newest (and the fastest). Regular PCI video cards can still be found, but they are the slowest connection type and not recommended for ultimate gaming.

In terms of choosing your motherboard, one fact is vital: the best video cards currently in development are using the PCI Express interface. Therefore, be sure to pick one that has a PCIe video card slot to ensure that you can keep up with current and future video technology. This video card slot information is summarized in Table 3-2.

Table 3-2   Summary of Video Card Slot Information

Slot Type	Used for	No. Needed	Notes
PCIe	Video Card	1*	Highly Recommended
		— or —	
AGP	Video Card	1	Not Recommended
		— or —	
PCI	Video Card	1	Not Recommended
	Total:	1	

Note Some PCI Express motherboards have two PCIe x16 slots. Two graphics cards can be used in these systems and run in concert for better performance in some games.

If you need to determine if your motherboard has a PCIe video card slot, look for a slot that is similar to Figure 3-3.

FIGURE 3-3: An example of a PCIe video card slot.

PCI Slots

PCI slots are slots on your motherboard that accommodate general expansion cards. When you need some additional USB ports, you can grab a PCI card that contains four additional ports. Did your motherboard come without a FireWire port for that cool MP3 player or DV camcorder you just bought? Grab a FireWire PCI card. Do you need some wireless networking capability to be added to your PC? You can grab a PCI wireless network card and simply plug it in. PCI slots are extremely useful for adding functionality to your motherboard that was not available at the time of purchase.

The primary PCI expansion card that many gamers purchase is a PCI sound card. If a key part of your gaming experience is feeling the room shake when something explodes onscreen and hearing the dying wails of that mutated creature you just filled with holes, you want to purchase a 5.1, 6.1, or 7.1 surround-sound PCI card for your machine.

Cross-Reference

For more details on sound cards, check out Chapter 7, Selecting the Ultimate Sound Card and Speakers.

The versatility of PCI slots could make it sound as if the more slots you have, the better. In years past, this might not have been a bad strategy; however, today's motherboards come with a significant number of capabilities built onto the board that would have required a PCI card purchase in days past. Network adapters are built right into the motherboard now, when many older boards needed a PCI card. Although you can get a PCI card for those extra USB ports, most boards come with four or six built in. The same idea applies to FireWire connections.

Keeping all of this in mind, don't panic if your motherboard only has two or three PCI slots. The days of computers having six expansion cards are long gone; three PCI slots are more than sufficient. The recommended number of PCI slots and their possible uses is summarized in Table 3-3.

Table 3-3   Summary of PCI Slot Usage

Slot Type	Used for	No. Needed	Notes
PCI	Sound Card	1	—
PCI	Modem	1	Optional
PCI	Wireless Network Card	1	Optional
PCI	USB or FireWire Expansion Card	1	Optional
	Total:	4	

You can identify and count your PCI slots by finding slots that look like Figure 3-4.

FIGURE 3-4: An example of PCI slots.

USB Ports

USB ports are the probably the most useful connections available on today's motherboards. The peripherals that can plug into these ports range from the most basic of items to some very useful gaming toys. Thus, your ultimate motherboard needs several of these ports to keep up with your gaming requirements.

The most basic items that will be plugged in via USB are your keyboard and your mouse. These days, you are more likely to find a comfortable mouse and an ergonomic keyboard with a USB connection than with the older format, PS/2. Also, useful features like shortcut buttons on your keyboard and Internet browser buttons on your mouse may need a USB connection to work properly.

Additional gaming devices such as gamepads, flight sticks, and other advanced game controllers also use your USB ports. While many games are designed with a viable keyboard and mouse control scheme, don't be surprised to see more gamepad compatibility in the future as PC games manufacturers try to lure new customers from the console gaming market (Playstation, Xbox, Nintendo, and so on).

For gamers who like to take their games on the road, many CD drives, DVD drives, Flash Memory readers and even hard drives are available with a USB 2.0 connection. If you need to back up a series of saved games and take them to a friend's house, you can use an external USB drive to get the job done.

While I wouldn't classify them as necessary for gaming, connecting printers and scanners to your ultimate gaming PC also requires some available USB ports. When you need to print out that online guide to your favorite game, be sure that there is an available USB port for your printer.

Knowing how many different devices can be plugged into your USB ports, it is not unrealistic to look for a motherboard with six or eight USB ports built in. Don't panic if your dream motherboard doesn't have enough to meet your needs; you can always grab a PCI card for the extra ports or add an external USB hub. The recommended number of USB ports and their likely uses are listed in Table 3-4.

Table 3-4   Summary of USB Port Usage

Slot Type	Used for	No. Needed	Notes
USB	Mouse	1	—
USB	Keyboard	1	—
USB	Gamepad	1	Optional
USB	Gaming Aid	1	Optional
USB	Printer	1	Optional
USB	External Storage	1	Optional
	Total:	6	

Are you trying to figure out how many USB ports are on your motherboard? Just count the ports that look like Figure 3-5. Beware! Not all USB ports are grouped together on your motherboard. Look at the entire back panel to find them all.

FIGURE 3-5: An example of USB ports.

FireWire Ports

Unlike USB, FireWire ports (also know as IEEE1394) aren't as versatile. Primarily, they are used to connect external drives and some MP3 players to your PC. If there are no built in FireWire ports on your motherboard, don't fret. You probably won't need one anyway. (If you do, you can always grab a PCI card.)

Built-In Components: Helpful or Not?

Like it or not, you may wind up with two sound cards in your new PC. There may also be more than one video card, too. Why? Many motherboard manufacturers are adding some common features that used to be handled by separate expansion cards right onto their motherboards. In fact, you will probably find that your ultimate motherboard has more than a few of these added "features." The questions is, how useful are these additions?

The most useful addition is probably the built-in communication devices, specifically network cards and modems. With the Internet becoming integrated into our daily lives, having the ability to connect via dial-up or through a high-speed connection right out of the box is extremely useful. It also saves the cost of purchasing and installing separate expansion cards to handle these tasks, and it frees up the expansion card slots for other purposes.

An add-on that may or may not be useful is onboard sound. Many motherboard manufacturers have integrated audio directly on the board, with some of them even offering 5.1 surround sound or better. The primary advantage to this setup is that your games have music and sound right out of the box, without a need to install and configure a separate sound card. This saves both time and money; however, the quality of these devices can be hit or miss. They may make your game sound wonderful, or they may cause you to wonder why your game sounds muddled, as if the action takes place underwater. Also, most motherboard integrated audio is *host-based*, which means that all the audio processing is handled by the CPU. A good PCI sound card, by contrast, can offload audio processing from the CPU.

As an alternative, a PCI sound card gives you the ability to select the best sound for your games, no matter what motherboard you choose. It also lets you control how many speaker inputs are available on your card. It may also come with some handy features such as headphone jacks, audio outputs and inputs, and volume control knobs.

 Cross-Reference Be sure to weigh the pros and cons of this built-in option carefully, and consult Chapter 7, Selecting the Ultimate Sound Card and Speakers, for assistance in your decision.

The least useful integrated feature is onboard video. Usually, you only find this in low-end motherboards, and it might be called something like "integrated video." If you see this, run far, far away from this motherboard! (Or just don't buy it; your call.) Onboard video is substandard when it comes to meeting the needs of today's top games. Often, the video card does not even have dedicated onboard memory like a PCIe or AGP video card; it "shares" the same memory that the rest of the system uses, reducing system performance. Onboard video is not a viable substitute for even a midline video card.

In the end, built-in motherboard features are hit or miss. They may be extremely useful, or just another item to add onto the manufacturer feature list. Keep an eye out for them when browsing motherboard selections, but don't get too concerned over them. If an onboard feature is not up to par, you can usually replace it with a PCI expansion card.

Selecting Our Ultimate Motherboard

It is finally time for us to pick a motherboard to go with our AMD processor. To do this, we checked out many different sites and gathered information on the most popular brands that would fit our needs. Here's what we found out.

Top Brands and Models

Our motherboard is going to come from one of the top motherboard manufacturers. Currently, ASUS, and Gigabyte are two of the leaders in the market for AMD motherboards. Table 3-5 is a quick rundown of the top model for each brand.

Table 3-5   Comparison Between ASUS and Gigabyte Features

	ASUS	Gigabyte
Name	Asus A8N-E	GA-K8N Ultra-9
Chipset	NVidia Nforce 4 Ultra	NVidia Nforce 4 Ultra
FSB	1000 MHz Hypertransport	1000 MHz Hypertransport
Max Amount of Memory	4 GB	4 GB
No. of PCI Express Video Slots	1	1
No. of PCI Express Expansion Slots	2	2
ATA Controllers	2 (4 devices total)	2 (4 devices total)
SATA Controllers	1 (2 devices total, SATA 150)	2 (4 devices total, SATA II 300)
RAID Capability	Yes	Yes
Integrated Video	No	No
Integrated Sound	Yes	Yes
USB 2.0 Jacks	4	6

At first glance, it may appear that these two boards are exactly the same. In fact, for most of the important factors, they are. They both support the AMD processor that we selected in the previous chapter. They both have PCI Express slots to support the latest graphics cards. They both support up to 4GB of memory, which would be more than enough for our needs. Each of these boards would be a fine addition to our ultimate gaming PC.

Both of these boards do not include integrated video, but they do have onboard sound capability. This offers the option to skip the purchase of a separate PCI sound card, saving a few dollars.

Because we need to make a choice between the two boards, we look a little closer and find the subtle differences between the two. One of the most noticeable items is that the Gigabyte board comes with an additional SATA controller. This allows us to have an additional two SATA hard drives, offering more storage options. The additional SATA ports are made available by an additional SATA controller chip on the motherboard. Finally, the Gigabyte board's controllers are SATA II, which support the greater transfer rates of the latest SATA II hard drives. All of these storage options start to swing our support toward the GA-K8N Ultra-9.

The Gigabyte board also offers an additional two USB 2.0 jacks. This is a nice addition for those gamers who like to use many USB gaming devices in addition to a USB keyboard and mouse.

Taking all of this information into account, we chose the Gigabyte GA-K8N Ultra-9 as the motherboard for our ultimate gaming PC, as seen in Figure 3-6. However, the reputation of both brands for quality construction would make either board a worthy choice for your ultimate gaming PC.

FIGURE 3-6: Our choice–the Gigabyte GA-K8N Ultra-9.

How to Save Money on Motherboards

Because your motherboard is the central component of your monster gaming PC, it can be difficult to save money in this category. Features and options that you omit because they appear unimportant may be vital for future upgrades. Here are some better suggestions on how to save money in this category.

Lesser-Known Manufacturers

Brand names such as ASUS, Gigabyte, MSI, and Intel dominate the motherboard market, but there are a few hidden gems available that can save you a few bucks. Some lesser-known brands, such as DFI or Abit, have been known to come out with some quality products in the past year. In fact, these boards may come with some features that the big manufacturers have not yet implemented. Because these companies are not the most well known, their boards could be significantly cheaper than a comparable board from the big boys.

If you want to try and find some of these hidden gems, scour the Internet for some general reviews. Many sites offer a "motherboard roundup" every few months that compares several boards considered to be in the same class. Pick one of the lesser-known boards and find two or three other reviews elsewhere on the Internet. This gives you a broad range of opinions on which to base your buying decision.

Also, check out reviews for different motherboards from the same manufacturer. Have 98% of all boards from that manufacturer received bad reviews? If so, that may be a sign of some problems down the road if you buy their newest board. If recent products have also received favorable reviews, you may have found a board worthy of your ultimate gaming PC.

Ripple Effect

Although it may be hard to find a cheap board with all of the features that you need, be aware of the ripple effect your motherboard will have on your other parts selection if you settle for a lesser model. For example, if you are willing to use onboard sound, you will not have to spend money on a video card. This can be a money-saving compromise.

A bad compromise to make would be to buy a board with an AGP video card slot instead of a PCIe slot. Although you may be able to buy an acceptable (and cheaper) AGP video card instead of the latest and greatest (and most expensive) PCIe card now, it may limit the number and quality of graphics cards that are available to you in the future.

Keep reading through this book to get a better idea of how this motherboard ripple effect can save you money on your part selection. Future chapters give you an idea of features that are too important to leave off you motherboard.

What's Next?

Now that you have a motherboard for your processor, you also have a place to put all of your other components. Move on to Chapter 4 and see what kind of memory you can slide into those new memory slots.

Choosing Your Ultimate Memory

Now that you've chosen a motherboard and processor, it's time to pick your ultimate memory. In general, memory is any form of electronic storage. Many gadgets and products around your home contain memory, such as your VCR or your car radio. You are also likely to have heard of storage devices such as Flash Memory and memory sticks. Even the cache of your Web browser is a form of memory. For the purposes of this chapter and your ultimate gaming PC, memory refers to a temporary data storage device, also referred to as physical memory. For your ultimate gaming machine, what you need is RAM.

The following section defines all of the key terms you need to know to evaluate memory and how to choose the memory that's right for your ultimate gaming PC.

in this chapter

☑ Memory defined

☑ Memory choices

☑ Shopping for memory

Key Terms

Before you take a close look at how memory works, here are some key terms that can help you understand memory and be better able to choose the memory that is right for your needs.

- RAM: Stands for *Random Access Memory,* also referred to as read/write memory. It is used by the computer to run programs. You may also hear RAM referred to in conversation as "main memory" or "physical memory."

- Module: A small printed circuit board that holds the RAM chips and plugs into a socket on the motherboard.

- Bus: A shared connection between components attached to your motherboard (for example, the PCI bus).

- Front Side Bus (FSB): The specific connection between the CPU and the memory controller. Note that the Athlon 64 actually replaces this with a more sophisticated crossbar switch built onto the CPU itself. The faster the front side bus can transfer information from the memory to the memory controller, the faster your applications appear to run. The speed of this communication is described in units of frequency (for example, 800 MHz FSB).

- Bandwidth: The rate or frequency at which the information is transferred from one point to another. Here, we're referring to memory bandwidth, which is the rate that data is transferred between the CPU and main memory. Bandwidth is measured in Megahertz (MHz) that defines how fast the memory can "talk." The speed at which it can talk or its bandwidth is represented as a number, for instance PC3200. The 3200 indicates that the module has a bandwidth of 3.2GB/sec. The data cannot be transferred faster than the FSB clock rate allows, even if the memory is rated at higher speeds.

- SDRAM: Stands for Synchronous Dynamic Random Access Memory. A slightly older type of memory.

- DDR: Stands for Double Data Rate (DDR) SDRAM. It is the most common type of RAM currently found in computers. Double Data Rate transfers two data items per clock cycle. DDR modules have 184 pins.

- DDR2: The second generation of DDR. The purpose of DDR2 was to increase memory bandwidths. DDR2 continues to increase the data rate from where DDR capped out. One of the big improvements in DDR2 is that it greatly reduces the amount of power needed to read and write from the memory. Currently DDR2 cannot be used on motherboards designed for AMD processors and is compatible only with motherboards using Intel chipsets or Nvidia chipsets for Intel processors.

- ECC technology: Error checking and correction technology that is built into more expensive memory. Memory that has ECC technology looks for errors in data traveling through the memory and corrects them. ECC is not ideal for gamers because performance is slightly degraded by the additional error checking, but rather is used for mission-critical servers.

- **Non-ECC:** Memory with non-error checking and correction technology is much cheaper than ECC, and is ideal for gamers.

- **Memory Controller:** Controls the data flow between the CPU and the main memory.

The Tech: How Does It Do What It Does?

Random Access Memory, or RAM, is a temporary storage area used by the processor to perform any of the calculations it needs to do to make your game run or render graphics, such as the explosion you get when you finally destroy the base on Malik 5 with a thermal detonator to win the game. So even though the game is stored on the hard drive, the processor needs a space where it can process the calculations that make the game play. This is also the space where the processor figures out what the game should do when you press the Jump button on the controller.

The RAM module is covered with millions of cells. Each cell can hold 1 byte of information. For example, 512MB of RAM means that the chip of memory has 512,000,000 million cells that the computer can use to run any program that you launch. One byte of information is roughly equivalent to a single letter or number.

Every cell has an individual address that the processor can call upon when the desired information is required. The faster the processor can access to the information stored in RAM, the faster the game reacts and plays. As mentioned in Chapter 2, the processor communicates with memory through the Front Side Bus (FSB) or, in the case of the Athlon 64, the CPU communicates directly with main memory because the memory controller is now part of the processor

Note   RAM is considered random access because the processor can read or write information or values to any of its millions of cells upon request as long as the processor knows the address of each cell.

The amount of memory you have also affects the speed at which the game reacts. You need to have enough RAM for the processor to process requests. After the RAM is full, any overflow or remaining data is written or *paged* to the hard drive. The speed at which the hard drive can page the information and gather it back up for the processor is vastly slower than the speed at which the processor can send and receive information from RAM. The more RAM the computer can use for its calculations, the faster your computer can do what it does best — compute. Increasing the amount of memory in your gaming PC is the most reliable and least expensive way to increase the entire performance of your system. Information sent to the RAM is sent along the busses (circuitry connecting the processor to main memory), which connects all the devices on the computer to the memory and the CPU. You may recall this is one of the things discussed in Chapter 2. The following section goes into a little more detail about how the bus directly affects your RAM choices.

How the Intel Chipset Does It

Computers with the Intel chipset have a bus that is broken into two distinct parts. These two parts run along parallel wires, but perform very different tasks. The first part is the data bus that transfers actual information. The second part is the address bus that directs the data bus to where to bring the information it is sending.

Each bus line to each part of the computer is separate and designed differently. The bus on an Intel motherboard is the Frontside Bus and runs from the main memory to the CPU. Communication between the FSB and the main memory to the CPU is controlled by the Memory Controller, which also sits along the FSB. FSB is defined by its width in bits and it speed in MHz, which in total is its bandwidth. Data is sent form the processor to the memory controller and then routed to the memory as needed.

How the AMD Chipset Does It

When AMD created the Athlon 64, they reinvented the wheel. They moved the memory controller from the motherboard directly onto the processor chip, changing the way the archetypical bus works. No longer did information have to leave the processor and travel all the way to the memory controller and then to the memory. Because the memory controller is part of the chip, the information doesn't have to waste time traveling since the controller is right there. This results in a significant boost in performance because the CPU can talk directly to the memory controller at the full speed of the processor, which lowers the access latency to memory, and is not slowed down by a bus.

Because the manufacturer changed the way things work, AMD uses different terminology for front side bus; it is no longer really doing the same thing. With their new architecture, the data pathway is called the *DDR Memory Controller*.

What does this all mean to you? By understanding how the memory talks, all you have to know when shopping for memory is what that maximum speed of dialogue can be, or the maximum frequency or bandwidth it runs. You want to buy the fastest memory your motherboard's FSB or DDR Memory Controller can handle.

What Are Frequencies?

You should be familiar with the differences between bandwidth and frequency. In actuality they are similar and it's easy to get confused. The following is a basic overview of how memory works, but it is enough to show you what you need to know when dealing with memory. Bandwidth can be thought of as the size of the pipe along the bus that sends information between the CPU and memory. Frequency is how fast the memory can send that information through the pipe. Think of it this way — you installed a long metal pipe running underneath your lawn to help keep the farthest area watered on those hot summer days. Now say that the pipe is 4 inches wide. Consider that as its bandwidth. because that maximum amount of water any point of it can hold is 4 inches. The frequency is how fast you can push that water through the pipe. At any point the pipe can hold 4 inches worth, but the speed that your tap can force the water into the pipe is your frequency. In computer terms, that's how fast the memory can talk.

Slower memory or a slower tap might on fill the lower 3 inches of the pipe, leaving unused bandwidth. But regardless of how fast the tap tried to push the water through, it capped at the 4-inch diameter.

With that in mind, *frequency* is how often information can be written to or read from the pathways or bus between the CPU and RAM. With DDR and DDR2 memory, frequency is noted in the following format: PCxxxx where xxxx is a number that stands for the actual bandwidth rating of that memory. For example, PC3200 is rated to move data at a rate of up to 3200MB/sec, or 3.2GB/sec.

Memory can also be rated by frequency. For example, the PC3200 memory mentioned earlier is also known as *DDR400,* which implies that the frequency of the memory is 400 MHz. In actual fact, DDR400 runs at 200 MHz, but moves two data items per clock rate. So 400 MHz is usually referred to as 400 MHz *equivalent.* The higher the frequency, the faster the information travels between the memory chips and the processor. Make sure you don't buy memory with too high a frequency than your BUS can handle, or that is too small for your computer. You always want to make the frequency of your memory match up with the BUS's bandwidth as determined by your motherboard.

For example if you have a Gigabyte GA-K8N Ultra-9 motherboard, like what we have chosen for our ultimate gaming PC, you know by checking the manual (or online) that the compatible DDR SDRAM frequencies are PC2100, PC2700, and PC3200. Now if we bought PC3700 modules that run at 66 MHz faster than the PC3200, which is the fastest memory our motherboard can handle, we would lose that extra 66 MHz of speed because the motherboard can't talk that fast even if the memory can. It's just too much water to fit through the pipe at once. We would have spent more money for faster memory, but it would have been wasted money because there is a cap in the architecture of the motherboard.

In actuality, you can run the memory speed higher through a technique known as *overclocking.* This allows you to boost the processor speed or memory controller speed to actually support the faster speed. Overclocking, however, has the potential to cause data loss or even damage memory modules or CPUs, so it's a topic for advanced users who understand the risks. Most gamers tend to prefer stability over pushing the system a little harder. After all, what's the use in playing a game on an overclocked system if it's unstable?

Caution Pay attention to the motherboard's bus speed when you begin shopping for memory. You should buy the fastest RAM possible for your monster gaming machine without overspending on something that you can't use. Spending money on RAM that has a faster frequency than the specifications of your CPU or motherboard would be a waste because it would cap out at its lowest frequency and any extra speed will be lost.

What Are the Frequencies?

The numbers that come after the letters "PC" refer to the maximum speed of the memory chip. Table 4-1 shows the breakdown of what those numbers mean so that when you are looking through your manual or online you know what they correlate to.

The bus may run at the frequencies listed in the table, but the actual DDR memory chip and memory module run at a double data rate. That is the meaning of DDR (Double Data Rate). It can send the information twice as fast as other memory. Because of the available frequencies, standards have been set by the computer industry for the DDR memory speed.

Overclocking

For a long time overclocking was done by manipulating the bus speed. All you had to do was increase the bus multiplier (how fast the bus runs). This simple switch on the motherboard forced the information to move faster between the CPU and the RAM, increasing the total computer speed. The side effect of this, like most overclocking, was an increase in heat on the motherboard. The solution was to add cooling such as extra fans and cooling gels to the motherboard.

Over time, processor manufacturers tried to stop this; they wanted the hardware hacker to pay for a faster chip, not modify their own for free. They began to hardcode the CPUs to only work at precise designated speeds.

Table 4-1   DDR Memory Bus Speeds

Speed of Motherboard Bus	Frequency of DDR Memory Chip
100 MHz	PC1600 modules or DDR200
133 MHz	PC2100 modules or DDR266
166 MHz	PC2700 modules or DDR333
200 MHz	PC3200 modules or DDR400
233 MHz	PC3700 modules or DDR466
266 MHz	PC4200 modules or DDR533
333 MHz	PC5400 modules or DDR667

As already mentioned, we are not going into detail on how to overclock in this book. Be assured it is still possible; it just requires a little more work on your behalf than before.

What Are the Different Types of RAM?

You would think that the increase in speed and power that came along with CPUs would be reflected in RAM, but that's not the case. RAM hasn't changed nearly as much as CPUs have. In the last decade RAM's performance increased perhaps 20 times; CPUs have increased about 10 times over memory. This is because memory manufacturers have focused more on increasing memory capacity rather than speed. One good thing to come from the evolution of RAM is the introduction of DDR.

DDR/DDR2

The evolution of memory has produced DDR-SDRAM, currently the most common type of memory, and DDR2-SDRAM is currently on the rise to replace plain old DDR. DDR SDRAM (Double Data Rate Synchronous Dynamic Random-Access Memory) is often referred to as just plain DDR, although DDR2 has achieved parity in pricing. DDR has taken the speed of older SDRAM and doubled the rate at which the memory can send data. When you take a motherboard and processor designed to handle DDR memory, there is a dramatic increase in speed over that of SDRAM.

Note

If you are choosing AMD over Intel CPUs, DDR is your choice in memory. The AMD chipset is not currently designed to work with DDR2 technology, leaving you with no other options. That is not as big of an issue as it may sound. The current benchmarking differences between DDR and DDR2 are almost unnoticeable in their current states.

As processor speed increases, the memory needs to be able to pass information at faster rates to keep up at some level. But no matter how fast you get your memory to go, it is still never fast enough in the ultimate gaming world. DDR2, the second generation of DDR, was introduced in late 2003 and is still on its speedy rise to center stage, outshining its aging kin DDR. Table 4-2 compares DDR2 with its predecessor. But while DDR 2 offers larger memory frequencies and some improvements over DDR, it doesn't offer any groundbreaking increases in performance just yet.

Many users see great results with DDR2 in overclocking. As mentioned, this book doesn't cover overclocking; however, if overclocking is one of your goals for your ultimate gaming PC, this might be a selling point for you. You may also consider DDR2 for future expandability. Technology that can make full use of everything that DD2 has to offer, such as its boost in speed and much needed increase in bandwidth, probably won't be available too long from now.

Note

Don't forget when shopping for memory that currently DDR2 is also only compatible with chipsets that support Intel processors, and not AMD-based core logic.

Table 4-2   Comparisons DDR and DDR2

	DDR	DDR2
Data Rates	200/266/333/400 Mbps	400/533/667 Mbps
Bus Frequencies	100/133/166/200 MHz	200/266/333 MHz
DRAM Frequencies	100/133/166/200 MHz	100/133/166 MHz
Module Sizes	256MB, 512MB, 1GB	256MB, 512MB, 1GB

RDRAM/SDRAM

There are two other types of memory that you may come across, depending on which motherboard you choose: RDRAM and SDRAM. These types of memory are not common anymore, but there is a small chance you might come across them when shopping for motherboards.

RDRAM or Rambus DRAM (Rambus Dynamic Random Access Memory) was created in a new and revolutionary DRAM architecture that has a much larger memory frequency than the standard DRAM; however, RDRAM pays for its increase in speed with a high latency and a larger cost to you as a consumer. An interesting fact in regards to gaming is that RDRAM was the memory Nintendo used in its Nintendo 64 gaming console. So chances are if you are an avid gamer, you have already used RDRAM for many hours of digital entertainment.

SDRAM (Synchronous Dynamic Random Access Memory) is even older than RDRAM. The approach of SDRAM is that it actually synchronizes itself with the CPU's bus, which saves time in transmitting data and thereby increasing the overall performance of the system. By synchronizing, it can obtain higher clock speeds than the memory before it of 100 MHz. Even so, it is much slower than RDRAM, which could reach 800 MHz.

Note   Just keep in mind that the biggest bang for the buck is with DDR RAM. Although you may find that SD-RAM is faster, it's really only economical for servers.

ECC Versus Non-ECC Memory

ECC (Error Checking and Correction) is an algorithm for checking the integrity of data stored in DRAM memory. If it detect or sees an error passing through the memory, it will do its best to fix it on the fly. For this to happen, special circuitry and an additional memory chip is put onto the memory module. This allows the algorithm to run so that it can test the accuracy of data as it passes through the memory.

Memory that has ECC technology looks for errors in data traveling through the memory. For gaming this is really not necessary because today's memory is pretty reliable, and few errors are generated in normal use. ECC is designed more for mission-critical business servers or architectural modeling where extreme reliability counts.

Non-ECC doesn't note or correct any errors. It is the same memory but without the error checking and correction technology. The reason they make both is because the majority of the computers running don't need to be that exact or precise. In word processing, for example, any small error in memory has no real effect.

ECC memory is also more expensive than non-ECC memory. There is no need to spend extra money on buying ECC memory because you gain no real results in the PC game world. It is a common opinion that when building your own machine that you buy non-ECC memory because otherwise you are just wasting money.

At the end of the day it is your decision which type of memory you want to buy, but we recommend you choose DDR RAM if you use an AMD processor, or DDR2 is you are going the Intel way. If you do choose to go the SDRAM direction, you have a much smaller selection of motherboards from which to choose. Most motherboards manufacturers have come to support DDR RAM because that is what most people are buying.

Warning Different types of memory are not compatible and cannot be used together. You cannot use DDR and DDR/2 together at once. There are a handful of motherboards for Intel CPUs that support both types of memory, but not at the same time. So keep in mind the type of memory you want to use as you shop for a motherboard. Remember—there can be no mixing and matching of RAM types.

How Much Memory Do I Need in My Ultimate Gaming PC?

Because this is a gaming PC, can there really be a limit on how much memory you have? The fun answer is no. The financial answer is yes. But regardless, it is an ultimate gaming machine, and, therefore, it has to have monstrous quantities of its parts.

When deciding how much memory you want to put in, there are a couple of factors to think about. The big one, of course, is cost. The bare minimum you would ever want is 512MB of RAM. That will get you off the ground and run most of your applications fairly well. But keep in mind that Windows XP itself takes 256MB of memory to run, leaving you only with 256MB left for your games. You could technically go even lower than 512MB (which would not be the ultimate thing to do), but keep in mind that the recommended requirement of high-end games, like Half Life 2, is now reaching 512MB. So if your goal is extreme gaming, don't drop down to 256MB or you will be sorely disappointed with the amount of games you can run, let alone using high textures and having a good frame rate.

Tip If cost is a big factor, go with 512MB of RAM. Although Windows XP uses up half of that, the remaining memory allows you to run most games. You can always upgrade later when prices come down.

If cost is a problem it's fine to stop at 512MB for now. In about six months or so, you can upgrade. When the new string of games are pouring out, grab another 512MB for a bit cheaper because prices will likely have gone down over time. This is one place where you could trim the total cost of your machine if there is a great budget concern. It will have an effect on total performance, no doubt, but nothing that is a complete showstopper.

When it comes to an ultimate gaming PC, we recommend no less than 1024MB of onboard RAM, perhaps even going up to 2GB if your budget allows. A normal computer user who uses word processing, e-mail, chat, and so on, would very likely never see the difference between a computer with 512MB of RAM and one with 1024MB because not all applications are designed to take advantage of all available memory past 512MB. Some programs do, such as Adobe

Photoshop, but those programs are more uncommon. And if you are also a programmer besides a gamer and do a lot of compiling, relational database sorting, or video editing, having 1024MB shortens the length of time it takes to perform these tasks.

You are not an ordinary user, though, wanting ordinary uses from your computer. You want an insane monster machine that can handle whatever the gaming market has to throw at it. And that requires a bit more punch of at least 1GB of memory.

> **Tip**
> If you want smoother all-around operating, at least 1024MB of RAM is the way to go—even higher if you can afford it. That guarantees that the caching your hard drive has to do is kept to a minimum. Honestly, 1GB is just too cheap currently to pass up.Remember—whatever is not processed in the physical memory, the computer has to write to a hard drive. This is a much slower exchange than how fast RAM can handle the same information. With 1GB of RAM, you can save the hard drive from doing a lot of unnecessary and sluggish work.

What Happens If I Don't Have Enough Memory?

If you don't have enough memory in your computer to run your game, hard drive paging begins. Paging is what we just mentioned where whatever the CPU can temporarily hold in the computers memory it writes to the hard drive. This occurs at a much slower rate than the speed at which the CPU can retrieve information from the main memory. So how would this affect your gaming? Well, that depends on how far under the recommended requirements your game is. Here are some examples of what you may see if you don't have enough memory and the CPU has to page information:

- A slower frame rate, as well as stuttering frames.
- Game response becomes slightly or extremely sluggish.
- Temporary computer lockups.
- Solid computer lockups that can only be fixed by a reboot.
- Textures disappear off 3D models and are replaced by blank white polygons.
- The game may not even start up; sometimes you see a warning dialog box or an insufficient memory error.
- A great increase in hard drive activity as the computer tries to page all extra information that couldn't be handled by the RAM.

There are other problems you might experience, but those are the most common and all of them can really ruin the feel or excitement of a game. Nothing is more annoying, frustrating, and anger inspiring than working your way through some grand and final sequence of a game, then after an extremely hard fought battle as you are about to get your reward the computer locks up and everything you did was lost. The first thing most gamers do to juice up their system is to add more memory, and they do so for good cause.

Can I Have Too Much Memory?

As is often said, especially as a gamer, the answer is no, you can never have too much memory. But in reality the question is: *Is there a point where there is more memory than the programs can actually utilize?*

We said previously that an average user would never need above 512MB with the current software available. But games require a much stronger backbone. Games have to be designed to take advantage of available memory, and most quality games are. But even so, it is doubtful there are any designed to fully utilize 3GBs of RAM because so few people in the general gaming community have that much memory in their computer. Most of today's desktop motherboards max out at either 4 or 8GB of memory.

It's reasonable to say that 1GB of RAM is enough for the current market of games. Two gigabytes is also becoming worth splurging for as the next generation of gaming engines come on the market. So really the current point of excess memory begins at about 2GB+.

 Tip   If you can afford it, have the 1GB onboard. When the new engines come out, you can add as much additional memory as you think you need.

Most importantly, there is a maximum amount of RAM supported by your motherboard. You should check your motherboard's product specifications and manual for details to confirm the maximum physical memory you can possibly add.

Database servers can and do use up to 16GB of physical RAM. On your motherboard you are unlikely to find that much, but having 2 to 4GB of RAM, which is possible, is one way to guarantee that you won't need to add RAM until you replace the box.

Is There a Cheap Way to Save on Memory?

If you need to save money, memory is not the area you should skimp on, if at all possible. Memory is so integral to every other part of your computer. If the systems memory is not running well, chances are not much else will, either. Memory prices fluctuate, making it difficult to develop a sure-fire strategy to buy memory as cheap as possible. When shopping for memory, here are a few ideas that might help you save a little cash.

OEM

If you can buy OEM memory, this is likely to be the best way to save on memory without risk of reducing the quality of your machine. You get the same memory, just without the pretty box. Most online retailers sell OEM products and send you the RAM in simple plastic holders.

The one problem with OEM is that is normally only comes with a 30-day warranty instead of several year to unlimited you would get if you bought a retail version.

The good news may be that in our experience, and it may be different for you, with electronics, if it is doomed to fail it almost always happens early in its lifetime. There are exceptions, of course, but usually if an electronic part is bad it becomes apparent very quickly. So if the OEM memory is going to go bad, it will probably happen within a month, making the 30-day warranty adequate. It's a risk and a decision you have to make for yourself.

Proper Frequency

Another way to save is making sure you buy the right frequency of memory and no more. As we mentioned earlier in this chapter, anything beyond what the BUS can handle is not utilized, and there is no reason to pay for anything you cannot use.

No-Name Brands

Some might think buying no-name brands is a good way to save money. While it could save you money, you still pay in performance. Buying an unknown brand is a risk because it's hard to know exactly what its past track record has been.

We do not recommend no-name brands as a way to save money on your ultimate computer — or any other computer, for that matter. When you add in potential stability issues that can cause the system to crash, its ability to work with other types of RAM, its weak warranty, and its usually high latency, no-name brands become not worth the trouble.

Buying Direct

This is the best tip we can give you. When possible, buy directly from the manufacturer of the RAM instead of through any middleman who increases the price. This is a good way to save money without reducing or risking the quality of your memory.

Dell memory is made by Crucial. You can buy memory from Dell, but you can also buy the same exact memory directly from Crucial, which comes out a bit cheaper. Don't buy the Kingston memory from Best Buy when you can buy it cheaper from the Kingston Website. Use the Internet — it's your friend.

Tip Crucial supplies memory to Dell; Kingston supplies memory to Best Buy. If you do some research, you're sure to find a better price for the exact same product.

DDR Versus DR2

If money is a concern and you are buying an Intel motherboard you can save money buying a motherboard that uses regular DDR instead of DDR2. The difference between their current performances is negligible, and the only reason to buy a motherboard and DDR2 memory is so that when a breakthrough in the technology happens, you are ready to take advantage of it.

If you are using an AMD motherboard, this point is moot because DDR2 is not yet supported by their chipset.

What Are the Things to Look for When Buying Memory?

Memory can be one of the most confusing parts of your computer to buy. Why? Well, because there are so many different specifications that you have to worry about, such as type, frequency, and pin count. When you begin browsing the Internet for your memory purchases, it's good to know why one brand may be better than all the others that you find. Here's what to look for.

- **Reliability:** You want memory that is reliable and has a good track record. There are numerous review sites on the Internet that can help you gauge what is currently the best and what isn't. Here are a few examples:

    - http://www.cooltechzone.com

    - http://www.tomshardware.com

    - http://www.hardocp.com

    - http://www.anandtech.com

- **Brand Compatibility:** Try to ensure that all your memory is of the same brand. Mixing and matching does not always yield the best results. Sometimes they won't even boot up together, or they cause continual system crashes. Memory is very specific; the slightest difference in the memory chips can cause you problems. Although this is not always the case, it is not recommended. The potential hassles aren't worth it.

- **Speed:** Try to keep all the memory the same frequency. Don't buy one chip of PC2700 and then another of PC3200. If you do this, the PC3200 with be sending and receiving information at a much faster rate than the PC2700. The problem with this is the CPU can store data wherever it wants on either chip, and might have divided some of the information it now needs among the two. So it can get what it needs from the PC3200 but will wait — or in the worst case scenario, crash — for the PC2700 data. Mostly, though, the faster memory runs at the speed of the slower memory.

- **Motherboard Compatibility:** Buy only what the motherboard manufacturer recommends. Don't buy faster or slower memory than is suggested. Know your motherboard. Your user manual or online support can help you answer the following questions before you shop for memory:

    - Who is the manufacturer of your motherboard?

    - What is the model number of your motherboard?

    - What is the specific type of memory that my motherboard uses?

    - How much memory can your motherboard hold?

While all of this can be found in your product manual, it's sometimes hard to understand. The book may tell you that you can use DDR SDRAM but not tell you exactly which frequencies you can use, such as PC2100, PC2700, or PC3200.

- Fortunately the good news is that there are Websites out now designed to make sure you don't make a wrong purchase. Crucial, who is the only American memory manufacturer, has such a Website. So does Kingston.

Tip   If you plan to use these sites, and we recommend that you do, all you need to know is the model number of your motherboard.

Crucial guarantees that the results of a search will be compatible with your motherboard. They give you a list of all your system specs and also a list of all their memory products that match your results for a quick shopping experience, or just as a good way to gauge price.

After you know exactly the type of memory that you need to buy as well as a general price, you can either shop around or buy it directly from their site. It is important to note that the quality of Crucial's products is impressive and very fairly — and by that we mean low — priced.

You can search through their memory checker by the kind of memory your computer takes, by the name and/or model number of your motherboard, or, if you happen to have a brand name computer like Dell, by the model number of the computer that you have.

- **Price**: Keep the price reasonable to what you can afford. It's good to plan out your whole computer on paper so that you know the total cost of everything and can see if it fits into your bank account. If it doesn't, buy the next frequency down in memory that is still supported by your motherboard. This way, you can save a few dollars.

Finally — and this is very important — make sure you buy the exact type of memory you need the first time. If you don't, you might be stuck paying RMA fees and return cost for shipping, or you might even be stuck with the wrong memory you bought because not every seller accepts returns. We can't stress enough — make sure you buy the right memory the first time. Double-check and triple-check what you are about to purchase.

Before You Buy Memory

- Make sure it is the correct type of memory for your motherboard, DDR, SDRAM, RIMM, etc.
- Make sure the memory you are buying has the correct pin count.
- Make sure the speed or frequency you choose matches your memory BUS speed.
- Make sure you're not buying more memory than your motherboard can handle.
- Make sure you're shopping at a reliable source.
- Make sure you're not buying ECC memory.
- Make sure you shop around for the best price.

What Are the Top Three Manufacturers of Memory?

It's hard to pick the top three manufacturers of memory because there are a good many contenders, such as Mushkin and Viking. The criteria we used when we decided who the top three are included reliability, a good track record, stability, warranty, and price. With that in mind, we compare our final three in Table 4-3.

Table 4-3   Memory Comparison

	Kingston	Crucial	Corsair
Name	Hyper X KRX3200AK2	CT12864Z40B	TwinX 2048-3200C2
RAM Type	DDR	DDR	DDR
Module Sizes	2 x 1GB modules	2 x 1GB modules	2 x 1GB modules
Frequencies	PC3200	PC3200	PC3200
Pin Count	184 pin	184 pin	184 pin
ECC or Non-ECC	ECC	Non-ECC	Non-ECC
Compatible with AMD Motherboard	Yes	Yes	Yes
Good for Overclocking	Yes	No	Yes
Designed for Gaming	Yes	No	Yes
OEM/Retail Box	OEM	OEM	Retail box
Warranty	Lifetime warranty	Lifetime warranty	Lifetime warranty

Our Pick for the Best Memory

When we were deciding on the best memory, our factors were based on speed, cost, motherboard compatibility (which is why there were no DDR2 choices), and price. All three top choices offer a lifetime warranty, so that was not something that concerned us.

We liked the Kingston Hyper X, and if it wasn't so much money we might have chosen it. Being nearly double the cost of other memory, even if it is uber gaming memory, it just wasn't worth it for the results, especially since we don't plan to overclock. It is also ECC, which is part of its huge price. That is money we really don't need to spend.

Crucial DDR memory was nothing flashy, but it's still powerful memory that wants nothing more than to do its job. But because this is a gaming machine, we wanted memory that was designed for this purpose and this purpose only.

In the end we went with the Corsair memory we mentioned. It is highly praised and our only desire is pure power, which the TwinX memory offers in spades. This memory was also made for gaming. It's non-ECC, and its retail box is still cheaper than the others that are OEM. We also know that just because we won't overclock doesn't mean some of you won't, so this covers that base as well.

Our memory speed is PC3200 or DDR 400. This is the maximum bandwidth for memory that our motherboard allows. So already you can see how your motherboard can help dictate what other parts you buy, and how knowing what kind of memory you want to use when you start shopping can also help determine which motherboard you want.

Many of the pieces in your PC are deeply intertwined. Knowing your end goal is the easiest way to help you collect the best parts to serve your needs. But keep in mind that some of your choices will ultimately limit your choices for other parts.

Our chosen Gigabyte motherboard, the GA-K8N Ultra-9, can hold a maximum 4096MB of DDR-SDRAM: a nice, even, and impressive 4GB. We have chosen for now to go with 2GB and not fill up the board just yet. Although we would like to, it is not cost effective. The 2GB is more than adequate for the current stock of games. In six months to a year from now, when games are driving hardware forward again, we can pick up the last 2GB to update our machine. With that in mind, we are getting two 1GB chips for now.

We are not going to design a system with the idea to eventually overclock it. We want a system that by itself, unmolested, can handle whatever the game developers throw at us. So in making our decision, we didn't weigh the benefits of overclocking, where you might want to.

What's Next?

Now that picking your ultimate memory is behind you, it's time for you to take the next step. You have your processor, motherboard, and memory. Now you need a way to see all that technology in use. In Chapter 5, "Choosing the Ultimate Video Card," you can see all those games come to life. Flip the page and enjoy!

Choosing the Ultimate Video Card

I f you're a casual observer of PC hardware, you're probably under the impression that the video card is the most important part of gaming. After all, every four to six months, there's news of a new model that's supposedly far superior than the last. Video card manufacturers are constantly putting out new drivers, indicating they provide better performance and support than the last version. Message boards constantly feature posts about the best settings for a particular game, based on the card someone is running. Video cards are always on gamers' minds.

Just because gamers think about their video card doesn't mean they actually know how they work. Sure, it's easy to throw around related words like "anti-aliasing" or "pixel shaders." But in the end, most believe that the latest technology is the best technology and they leave it at that. Well, that's not good enough for your ultimate gaming PC.

In this chapter, we're going to take a look at how a video card improves your game performance. Specifically, we're going to focus on the parts of a card that usually see an upgrade when a new model is developed. Before we're done, we are going to test that idea that the latest technology is the best. What do you get in return for buying the most expensive card available?

The Basics: What Does a Video Card Do?

The video card is one of the easiest and yet at the same time hardest computer component to understand. It's easy because the job of the video card is very clear: connect your monitor to it, and you get pictures. That's what it has done since its original incarnation, and that's what it still does today. Exactly how it generates the images you see on the monitor, though, is where things get much more complex. We'll discuss that shortly.

Of course, the role of the video card has expanded with the advent of 3D gaming. Instead of just displaying images for a 3D game, the video card now handles the calculations that determine the shape, size, color, and effects that you see onscreen. The capabilities of your graphics card determine exactly how many of these calculations can be completed and how fast their results are displayed.

Key Terms

- Graphics pipeline: The process by which a video card draws a 3D image on your 2D screen.

- Anti-aliasing: The process by which a video card smoothes the appearance of jagged lines.

- GPU (Graphics Processing Unit): A programmable processor on your video card that performs all the necessary calculations to draw 3D images.

Of course, there is a small selection of video cards that have branched out to do even more. These cards come with a built-in TV tuner, turning your monitor into an extra television. All that is required is to plug your cable box, satellite receiver, or rooftop antenna into the connection on the back of the card. Many of these TV-capable video cards can also record TV programs and store them on your hard drive, letting you watch them at a more convenient time.

Other than these two primary functions, that's really all a video card does. Because you're building the ultimate gaming PC, there's no need to concern yourself with watching TV on your PC. Instead, focus on how a video card produces 3D images on your PC, making the world of games more realistic than ever before. Before getting into this chapter, review some key terms that are a significant part of this discussion.

The Tech: How a Video Card Generates 3D Images

Generating realistic 3D images on a 2D surface (your monitor) is a very complex task. It is so complex that your PC needs the help of another computer to do it. That other computer is your video card. Each video card is, in fact, a miniature computer. It has its own processor, its own memory, and its own input and output ports. Unlike its larger counterpart, this mini-PC that is your video card has only one task to complete: generating graphics.

The Graphics Processing Unit (GPU)

The Graphics Processing Unit (GPU) is the driving force behind your video card. Generating 3D graphics requires intensive calculations, and the GPU is the calculator that gets it done. Because an object is not simply generated by the video card, it is built from the ground up. Its position onscreen has to be determined. Its color has to be determined, not based simply on the object itself, but also by the environment that is being drawn. For example, if the lighting in the scene being drawn is very dim, the object color needs to appear darker than normal. The texture of the object affects the way it is drawn — smooth objects differ visually from objects with a rough surface. Transparency and object distortion can come into play. Is the object being viewed through a window? Is it being reflected in a fun house mirror? All of these things cannot be done without the help of the GPU.

GPUs were originally limited in their capabilities. If the GPU is a calculator, these early processing units were calculators with only three or four buttons. They were only capable of handling a certain number of mostly pre-defined tasks. As GPUs have evolved, they have become more flexible. Now, they can be programmed, giving game programmers greater control over their 3D images.

Video Ram (VRAM)

The video card has its own memory built right into the card, which is called VRAM. Its primary role is to store information regarding the objects being drawn and provide this information to the GPU for processing. Because this memory is integrated into the card, it can communicate very quickly with the GPU. However, there has to be a balance between the speed of the GPU and the speed of VRAM for the card to work effectively. The VRAM cannot provide more information than the GPU can process, as this would simply create a "traffic jam" of instructions for the GPU to process. Conversely, the GPU shouldn't outpace the speed at which information is supplied, as the full power of the GPU would be wasted when information could not be provided.

The amount of information that your video card can accept is determined by the amount of VRAM on the card. Different models of cards contain different amount of VRAM. A smaller amount of VRAM can slow the rendering process because there has to be more frequent communication between the PC and the video card. These communications are slower than those between the VRAM and the GPU. If your video card has larger amounts of VRAM, it can accept more data, thus reducing communications with the PC and increasing the rate of the rendering process.

Random Access Memory Digital-to-Analog Converter (RAMDAC)

The RAMDAC is the link between your video card and your monitor. After all the calculations are complete for 3D graphics, you are left with just a bunch of numbers. It is the job of the RAMDAC to convert this digital information into analog signals that can be processed by your monitor. However, if you're connecting to a DVI-equipped display using the DVI connector on most of today's video cards, the entire signal path is digital and the RAMDAC isn't involved.

Graphics Pipelines: The 3D Image Assembly Line

Just because you can now identify the individual pieces of a graphic card, it doesn't mean you truly understand how they work. As we said earlier, 3D graphics are essentially "built" by the video card, one pixel at a time. The real question is, exactly how does this piece of hardware build a pixel? By using a pixel assembly line, of course! A graphics pipeline is the method by which a video card generates the pixels that form 3D images. This is achieved by following the same series of steps for each pixel to determine a pixel's location and appearance onscreen. The exact order of processes in this assembly line can be different depending on the video card, but they all have to complete the following tasks to generate a pixel.

The first step in this pixel assembly line is to receive information from the computer program that is running. Before the video card ever gets involved, the application must determine exactly what needs to be drawn and how to draw it. This starts by determining perspective. In the example of a 3D game, each game screen is viewed from a particular perspective by the player, be it from the eyes of game character (a first person perspective) or from a different vantage point to the side or above the character. The application must determine what objects can be seen from this viewpoint and decide what their visual characteristics should be, based on environmental conditions such as lighting and fog.

The perspective set by the application not only determines what can be seen by the player, but also what cannot be viewed. While the player can see the front of certain objects, he or she has to circle around it to see what's on the opposite side. As a result, only the portion of an object that is facing the character needs to be drawn. At an early stage of the pixel pipeline, calculations are completed to determine what parts of objects do not need to be drawn, and information related to those parts are discarded.

For example, consider a cube-shaped object in a 3D game. If your game character approaches one of the faces of the cube directly, the video card only needs to draw the face of the cube that your character is going to see. If your character approaches at an angle, you may be able to see more than one face at a particular moment, and the video card has to draw the appropriate faces of the cube at the correct angles. Either way, there are still some faces of the cube that are not going to be visible to the player. Because there is no need to draw these faces of the cube, no calculations are performed to determine their color, location, or texture. Essentially, this focuses the resources of the card only on the parts of the scene you see.

At this point, the video card can begin its calculations to convert the information from the application into actual pixels. Because the video card cannot simply create an entire object at once, it has to construct it in a manner similar to Lego building blocks. Instead of blocks, the card uses small polygons to generate 3D shapes. The video card determines the location on your monitor where pixels need to be placed in order to draw the polygons, and thus the resulting object, as they would be seen from the perspective set by the application. If this viewpoint causes an object to appear stretched or distorted from its original shape, such as when viewing something underwater, these calculations take that into account.

Finally, the video card takes into account the environmental effects of the scene to determine the appearance of the pixels that compose an object. For example, the appearance of a rough object is different than the appearance of a smooth object. A smooth object may reflect light or other objects, depending on the environment. Fog may cause an object to appear hazy or washed out. These effects, along with others, determine the appearance of each pixel.

After all of these steps, the assembly line spits out one perfectly colored pixel along with information on where it belongs onscreen. While you were following your pixel through all of these steps, there was always another pixel right behind it. The pipeline continues with this process until it completes all of the pixels required. At that point, they can all be sent to the monitor to create a 3D image.

Cleaning up the Mess: Anisotropic Filtering and Anti-Aliasing

Unfortunately, this 3D image created by your video card is not a perfect masterpiece. Lines drawn on the screen horizontally and vertically may not have any problems, but lines drawn at an angle may appear jagged. This is due to the fact that the resolution of today's monitors isn't sufficient to display all of the data in a particular scene. This means that the actual location of a diagonal line may fall between two pixels on your monitor. To accurately draw this line, your monitor needs to light up only a part of two different pixels. However, your monitor can only draw a full pixel; it can't draw half a pixel or three-quarters of a pixel. Thus, your monitor has no choice but to fill in all the pixels that your line touches. This effect, called aliasing, can be seen in Figure 5.1.

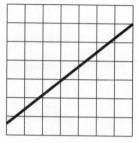

This is the diagonal line that needs to be displayed on a monitor.

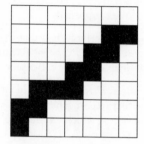

Your computer can only activate the entire pixel, resulting in the jagged line above.

FIGURE 5-1: Drawing a diagonal line on the screen causes aliasing.

To solve this problem, your video card can apply an effect called anti-aliasing. Instead of generating all of these pixels and creating a jagged line, the graphics card will fill in the surround pixels with different shades of the line color. When this revised line is viewed at a distance by the human eye, it creates the optical illusion that the line is smooth.

Unfortunately, a similar drawing issue can happen to the textures, or the "skin," of onscreen objects that are far away from your game character, or objects that have been rotated at a sharp angle. The textures of these objects should appear slightly different due to the viewing angle and distance rather than if you were looking at them close up and with no rotation. If the textures on these far away objects are not distorted slightly, they may "look wrong," disrupting the illusion of a realistic 3D world.

Several techniques are available to mitigate this. MIP-mapping uses several textures of differing resolutions that get swapped in as you move closer to, or farther away from, the object in the virtual world. Trilinear filtering—blending colors between the MIP maps—minimizes "popping" of the different textures. Finally, anisotropic filtering smoothes out the lines that may lie in differing directions, including "into" the monitor.

Unfortunately, these filtering techniques require complex calculations and chew up lots of memory bandwidth by the GPU. This can require additional resources, in excess of what the GPU has available. This can cause onscreen movements to appear slow and "jerky." To prevent this, these features can be enabled or disabled by the drivers of the video card, or through the settings within games. Depending on the capabilities of your card, it may be up to you to balance the need for quick and smooth gaming with the image-enhancing effects produced by these filters.

Bottlenecks: What Limits Graphics

When the newest PC games are demonstrated at developer conferences or trade shows, they can look astounding. Between the varying colors and the levels of detail displayed, gamers won't be able to wait until the game is released and they can play it on their own PC. Unfortunately, when they finally get their own copy, the results can be disappointing. Gameplay can be slow, and the graphics underwhelming. What happened?

As you can see in the complex "assembly line" that was discussed earlier, gaming performance relies on many different parts of your PC being able to work together. If one of these interlocked components is too slow, it drags down the entire process. This component is the bottleneck.

If you follow the entire process closely, you can identify many places where there can be a potential bottleneck. The first step in generating 3D graphics was for the video card to get information from an application, which, in this case, is the game. This information is generated by your processor and your system RAM. A slow processor or insufficient amount of RAM can cause a bottleneck before your video card ever gets involved.

The transmission of this information is handled by your motherboard. The information is transmitted through the video card slot (either AGP or PCI Express, depending on your motherboard) to the video card itself. This transmission line can only send a specific amount of information at a time. This is similar to a road that passes through a tunnel. A wide tunnel can accommodate more lanes of traffic, and thus more cars, than a narrow tunnel. Even though a PCI Express slot can transmit more information than an AGP slot, it is important that the game is not trying to cram too much traffic through these tunnels, creating its own bottleneck.

After the instructions from the game reach the video card, the GPU and the VRAM must work together to fill the graphic pipelines and generate pixels. As mentioned earlier, the VRAM and the GPU must communicate at compatible speeds to keep one from waiting for the other to finish a task. The VRAM must also be of a reasonable size and speed to keep feeding information to the GPU without running out and having to get more from the PC. If the size of the VRAM is too small, or the speed of the VRAM and GPU are insufficient, you can have a bottleneck.

Preventing Bottlenecks

How do you prevent these bottlenecks? To prevent the processor and the system RAM from being a bottleneck, make sure you have a processor and RAM that is fast enough for gaming. (Check the appropriate chapters of this book for more information.) As mentioned in

Chapter 2, an AMD system has its memory controller integrated into the processor, speeding up the transfer of information between the CPU and RAM, reducing the likelihood that these parts ever become a bottleneck.

A bottleneck in the video card slot is mostly the responsibility of the game designer. He or she knows the bandwidth of the VGA and PCI Express slots and should program their games to not exceed this limitation; otherwise, they're creating their own traffic jam. You can help them by using a PCI Express video card and PCIe motherboard, ensuring you have the widest "tunnel" available for use.

You can minimize the graphics bottleneck by buying the best possible graphics card you can afford. The most obvious thing to do is to buy a video card that is capable of running your games. (We'll discuss this in detail a little later.) If your card can't handle its current load, turn off anisotropic filtering and anti-aliasing. If that doesn't help, reduce your game's graphic settings until you find the right balance between beauty and performance.

New Card = Better Performance?

One of the common assumptions about video cards is that buying a better one instantly increases the performance of current games. This is true to a certain extent, but the relative performance increase can be disappointing. This is related to how games are programmed.

To generate 3D images and create an immersive game world, designers do not assemble images pixel by pixel. Instead, they use an Application Program Interface (API), which is essentially a set of programming tools. Essentially, an API is like a set of wooden building blocks, and the game designer uses them to build what's in his imagination.

Currently, two primary API's are used to create 3D images: DirectX and OpenGL. Using these tools, programmers can send commands to the video card that, in turn, generates 3D images. Games that are several years old used older versions of these APIs that gave programmers less control over their work. As new versions of the APIs are released, programmers can tap into the greater power offered by newer video cards. This gives birth to new lighting effects, new shading effects, and other such improvements now seen in today's games.

Games that use these early API versions limit what the program asks your video card to do. For example, if the hardware built into your new video card offers great improvements in generating realistic textures on in-game objects and in creating realistic lighting effects, you see the most benefit in games that rely heavily on these things. If older games do not make extensive use of such effects, you see a moderate increase in game performance, but not a tremendous amount. In these cases, the actual cause of your performance problems may have been unrelated to your old video card; take a look at the section on bottlenecks to see if other components of your PC are in need of an upgrade.

Although new card technology may not be a savior for your favorite older games, it becomes a driving force to improve your gaming experience. Newer technology can lead to improved APIs that can take advantage of the hardware. This gives greater control to game programmers, who in turn develop newer and better methods for rendering objects. These methods push video cards to their limits, once again spurring research toward improving card hardware.

Evaluating Game Performance

So, you just purchased a brand new video card that's supposed to be one of the best available. After installing it, how can you tell how much of an improvement you've gained? You might be able to generalize, saying a game is running better or worse than before, but how do you measure these changes? The answer is to measure frames per second.

Frames per second (FPS) is a term that describes how many scenes are drawn onscreen during a single second of gameplay. The best way to understand it is to think of a movie. Movie film captures a single scene per cell on the reel. In the next cell, there is a slight change in the scene as the characters move about. When the movie projector runs these individual cells back rapidly, they form "moving pictures" on the screen.

This same process happens on your computer when you play a game. The game rapidly displays a sequence of static images. In each successive image, your game character moves a small amount. When these "frames" are played back rapidly, they create the illusion that your character is moving across the screen.

Each of these frames takes a fraction of a second for your video card to draw. If your video card struggles to draw these frames, the game appears to stutter because it has to skip frames to keep up with the movement of the character. If your video card can render the scene very quickly, there is a complete frame for even the smallest change in your character's position, giving the impression of fluid and realistic movement.

How many frames per second does your video card have to render for the human eye to perceive the onscreen action as fluid? According to many different publications, 60 frames per second is the target value for realistic action. If your card can render this fast or faster, you shouldn't have a problem with graphic related game performance.

There are many factors that can affect the frame rate of your game. Higher game resolutions require more pixels to completely fill the screen. The advantage to this is that more pixels create a higher level of detail in each frame. However, this increases the amount of work required for each frame and lowers your frame rate. In addition, the extra GPU processing required for anisotropic filtering and anti-aliasing makes each frame take longer to complete. Finally, the complexity of the game programming affects your frame rate. Specifically, if the game calls for a large amount of shadows and textures, each frame requires more work by the video card, reducing the frame rate.

Benchmarks and FPS

Almost every article published evaluates the performance of a video card by performing benchmarks tests. Exactly what tasks these tests consist of can vary. Sometimes, the reviewer simply plays a graphically taxing part of one of the latest 3D games. Unlike normal gameplay, some form of frame counting is enabled, either through the game itself or by using a separate program. The game is played on different resolutions, and with different combinations of anisotropic filtering and anti-aliasing enabled and disabled. The frame rate of a particular card is then compared to another card under the same exact situations, allowing the tester to compare.

There are also specific programs designed for the purpose of benchmarking. The programs run different graphical tests, often stressing the card more than would occur while running a game. The advantage to these programs is that they ensure the same tests are performed every time the benchmark is run, ensuring that every card is tested on a level playing field.

Optimization

Video cards can get a helping hand on these tests from their creators. When a card manufacturer sees that many benchmarks and games are using a particular graphics engine, they can use their drivers to take advantage of the situation. A specific graphics engine usually has particular strengths and weaknesses when rendering a frame. It may handle shadows and lighting effect very well, but the way it draws specific textures could be taxing to the video card. A card manufacturer can program their driver to shift its power among these strengths and weaknesses in a manner that is different than normal. These optimizations improve gaming performance not just for the original game, but for all other games based on its graphics.

Drivers are not all about game optimization. They also give the user more control over how the video card functions. The can include the capability to adjust color setting for your monitor. They may include software that allows you to use two monitors with a single computer. They may also allow you to turn settings such as anti-aliasing on and off, giving you the ability to manually balance game performance with image-enhancing effects.

Split Personality: The Chipset and the Manufacturer

Unlike most other PC components, a video card is not always produced by a single company. In most cases, there are two companies that work together: the chipset manufacturer and the card manufacturer.

The GPU Manufacturer

The GPU manufacturer plays two key roles in the manufacturing process of the video card. They design and manufacture the graphics processing units for the card. They also set the specifications for building the rest of the card. The minimum requirements for components, such as type and speed of memory, capabilities of heat sink and cooling fan, are set by the chipset manufacturer and must be followed by their business partners.

The two primary GPU chip manufacturers at this time are ATI and Nvidia. Nvidia focuses only on producing the GPU itself. They use various business partners to manufacture the complete video card. ATI both produces GPUs and manufactures their own cards. Similar to Nvidia, they also partner with other firms to manufacture cards based on ATI graphics processors to ensure that a sufficient quantity reaches store shelves.

Card Manufacturers

The card manufacturer uses the GPUs and the specifications issued by a chip manufacturer to build a complete video card. They market these cards with under their own brand name while listing the chipset on the box. For example, ASUS manufactures a line of cards for Nvidia and sells them under the name ASUS V9999 Ultra Deluxe. The Nvidia logo is placed in a prominent place on the retail box.

A line of cards must meet ATI's or Nvidia's specifications and use their GPU, and the remaining components of the card are selected by the card manufacturer. This can lead to a few "tweaks" thrown in by each manufacturer to get ahead of the competition.

For example, a card manufacturer may slightly overclock the GPU on the card during the manufacturing process. If necessary, they can use a better heat sink or fan than specified by the chipset manufacturer to deal with excess heat that may be generated. This is usually not necessary because the components can handle this small increase. This overclocked card scores better in benchmark testing than another manufacturer who followed the specifications exactly. When the scores are posted in a review, the overclocked card catches the eyes of readers and probably increases sales.

Of course, card manufacturers may cut a few corners on some of their lower-end cards to gain a price advantage. For example, if they are able to use a slightly cheaper heat sink or cooling fan, they can save money and allow them to lower the price of the card. When a consumer on a budget compares two similar cards, the lower price tag probably catches his or her eye, increasing sales for the manufacturer.

Two Heads Are Better Than One? SLI and Crossfire

Just when you thought we couldn't possibly find anything else to discuss about video cards, we pop up with this question: Are two video cards better than one? Thanks to SLI from Nvidia and Crossfire from ATI, we may just get a chance to find out.

SLI

SLI (Scalable Link Interface) enables you to link two Nvidia graphics cards, allowing them to work together to render your graphics. They can divide the workload for a single frame by each rendering a portion of it, or they can alternate frames with one card rendering frame 1, the other rendering frame 2 and so on.

While this sounds like the best idea ever, it is not the easiest thing to build and configure. Here are the points you need to even attempt an SLI setup:

- An SLI compatible motherboard
- Two identical, SLI compatible Nvidia video cards
- Bridge chips to connect the two cards (comes with the motherboard)
- Power supply capable of supplying both cards with power via a PCI Express cable
- A game that is supported by Nvidia's drivers

The motherboard is not hard to come by; there are several manufacturers who currently have SLI boards available. However, two top-of-the-line SLI video cards can strain your budget, costing between $800 and $1,200. These two cards must be identical in every way: same manufacturer, same capabilities, and even the same BIOS revisions. A solid power supply isn't too hard to find, but this, too, can add to the total cost. The final requirement is a game supported by Nvidia's drivers. Nvidia has to predetermine the best method of load sharing for each game; then, their drivers have to be encoded with this setting for a game to be played with SLI.

At this time, an SLI system offers a significant performance boost over a single card system. This boost is the most noticeable when running the latest games at their maximum resolution with anisotropic filtering and anti-aliasing activated, resulting in an 80% to 90% increase in frame rate when compared to a single card setup. If you're not running games with high resolutions or with these settings enabled, the performance boost will be smaller.

Crossfire

ATI's response to Nvidia's SLI is crossfire, their own version of dual video card support. Crossfire has its own set of requirements:

- Crossfire compatible motherboard
- One ATI Crossfire video card, one compatible ATI video card
- Connector cable to connect the two cards
- Power supply capable of supplying both cards with power via a PCI Express cable

This list may seem similar to the requirements for SLI, but there are a couple of key differences. The video cards do not have to be the exact same make or model. The first must be a Crossfire-enabled card. The second can be selected from ATI's latest generation of video cards. This could offer a little wiggle room to lower the cost of a dual card system, depending on the price of the Crossfire card.

Another difference is that the games do not have to be pretested by ATI for Crossfire to work due to the different method that Crossfire uses to split the workload between two cards.

Shouldn't the Ultimate Gaming PC Use One of These Systems?

You may wonder if your ultimate gaming PC should be using SLI. We debated including it in this book, but eventually decided against it. Early on, some people experienced problems building SLI systems. These problems ranged from issues with particular brands of video cards to the BIOS of a motherboard. For inexperienced system builders reading this book, little bugs such as these would needlessly complicate the setup of their system. If we can't be sure that installing SLI would be a perfectly smooth experience, we aren't going to recommend it.

Of course, there is an even larger drawback to Crossfire. At the time this book went to press, ATI had not yet released Crossfire motherboards or video cards to the general public. It is nearly impossible to recommend the significant monetary investment that SLI requires without first comparing its performance to ATI's own dual card system.

By the time you read this, Crossfire may be available, and any difficulties in an SLI installation may have been ironed out. It's also possible that comparisons between both dual card systems have been published, making it easier to decide on your video card setup. If this additional information makes you want to build an SLI system, you can do it without changing most of the parts listed in this book. Simply replace the Gigabyte GA-K8N Ultra-9 motherboard we recommended with an SLI version from Gigabyte. After that, purchase two Nvidia video cards instead of one, and you're ready to go.

Unfortunately, because ATI hasn't released its products yet, we can't help you in selecting parts for a Crossfire system. Use some of the research methods noted in this book to do some homework on this system and see if it's something you want to pursue.

What to Look For When Shopping for a Video Card

After reading through this chapter, selecting a video card may seem like a difficult task. The following are some key things to look for in a card to make your shopping easier.

GPU Manufacturer

The first thing you need to decide is which chipset manufacturer to use. Depending on who has recently released their latest generation of cards, either ATI or Nvidia could be considered to have the "best" card available.

To assist you in this decision, we can offer a few suggestions. Don't directly compare card features between an ATI card and an Nvidia card. Because each chipset renders graphics with a different internal process, one card may be able to do more with a slower GPU and faster memory than the other could. The only reliable statistic that can be compared across chipset brands is game performance: frames per second.

Because most gamers are building the ultimate gaming PC to play the latest 3D games, consider two that are currently very popular: Doom 3 and Half Life 2. The graphics engines in these two games each place different stresses on a video card. At this time, ATI's chipset performs slightly better than Nvidia's in Half Life 2. For Doom 3, Nvidia's chipset handles the demands of the graphics engine slightly better.

If you want to build an SLI or a Crossfire system, your decision has already been made. An SLI motherboard needs two Nvidia cards; a Crossfire board uses ATI cards.

Right now, there is no conclusive evidence that says Nvidia is better than ATI, or vice versa. A card from either manufacturer would be a great asset to your gaming PC.

Chipset Version

After you settle on a chipset manufacturer, you need to select the version of chipset you want. At this time, Nvidia's latest chipset is the GeForce 6800. ATI's latest chipset is the Radeon X850. This version number simply indicates that the video card is using the latest architecture from the manufacturer. Within each of these versions, there are several specifications that can vary:

- GPU Speed
- Amount of VRAM
- Speed of VRAM
- Number of pixel pipelines and vertex phader pipelines

These qualities can vary, and simply knowing that you want a card based on Nvidia's GeForce 6800 is not enough. Check these specifications to ensure that you're getting the best card available.

Card Manufacturer

The manufacturer of a card has a great influence on the quality of the product you choose. It is important to buy your card from a manufacturer that stands by their work; check the length of the card's warranty to get a good picture of this.

Some companies that manufacture other components of your system, such as the motherboard and system memory, also make video cards. ASUS is a good example of one of these companies. If you purchased their brand of motherboard and believe that it is of good quality, feel free to purchase a video card from them as well. It's probably of equally high quality.

Finally, check to see what else the manufacturer has included with the card. Often, the manufacturer bundles full-version games that can display the 3D power of the video card. These freebies might be a benefit that will help you select one quality brand over another.

Interface

As mentioned in Chapter 3, there are two different types of slots on your motherboard in which you can install a video card: PCI Express and AGP. The majority of PCs already on the market use AGP slots for their graphics cards, but the newer PCI Express slot is definitely the choice for the future. The PCI Express slot offers more bandwidth for communications between your video card and the rest of your PC. At this time, there is little performance difference in between an AGP card and an identical PCI Express card; the full potential of the PCI Express slot has yet to be utilized by card hardware and PC game programmers. Using PCI Express cards now, however, ensures that you are ready to take advantage of new hardware and programming when it arrives.

Warning
Your motherboard determines what interface you use, not your video card. Be sure that you purchase a motherboard with a PCI Express video card slot. For further information, refer to Chapter 3.

Supported APIs

Powerful hardware is useless if PC game programmers cannot take advantage of it. Purchase a video card supports the latest versions of DirectX, currently 9.0c, and OpenGL, currently 2.0. This ensures that the power of your card is put to good use by your favorite games.

Power Requirements

The GPUs on new video cards use a tremendous amount of power, much more than ever before. Video card specifications list the requirements that your power supply must meet to run a particular card. If you are building a system from scratch, this shouldn't be a problem because you can select an appropriate power supply when shopping for your parts. If you are upgrading an existing system, or using a power supply that from an old PC in you new one, this could be more of a concern. Be sure that it meets the needs of your new video card.

Note For further information on selecting a power supply, refer to Chapter 9, Choosing the Ultimate Power Supply.

Selecting Your Ultimate Video Card

Now that we have covered some of video card features, it's time we selected the card for our ultimate gaming PC.

We need to settle on a chipset manufacturer. Knowing that both ATI and Nvidia are excellent choices, we had to fall back on our past PC experience. When we looked back on all of the systems we have built over the years, we found that the majority of them used different versions of Nvidia's chipsets. Due to our familiarity with them, we settled on a variation of Nvidia's GeForce 6800 chipset.

Now that we've selected a chipset, we can start to browse some of the different manufacturers who are producing Nvidia cards these days. When browsing through our favorite Internet shopping sites, the following cards caught our eye: e-GeForce 6800Ultra by e-VGA, GeForce 6800 Ultra OC by BFG, and the PX6800 Ultra TDA by Leadtek. Take a look at how their specifications match up in Table 5-1.

Table 5-1   Video Card Comparison

	e-Geforce 6800Ultra	GeForce 6800 Ultra OC	PX6800 Ultra TDA
Manufacturer	e-VGA	BFG	Leadtek
GPU Speed	400 MHz	425 MHz	400 MHz
Amount of VRAM	256MB	256MB	256MB

	e-Geforce 6800Ultra	GeForce 6800 Ultra OC	PX6800 Ultra TDA
Memory Clock	1100 MHz	1100 MHz	1100 MHz
No. of Pixel Pipelines	16	16	16
API Support	DirectX 9, OpenGL 2.0	DirectX 9, OpenGL 2.0	DirectX 9, OpenGL 2.0
Interface	PCI Express	PCI Express	PCI Express
Warranty	1 year + 1 year extra	Lifetime warranty	2 years

We picked these three cards as candidates for our ultimate gaming PC for several reasons. Leadtek has been in the video card business for some time now; when picking a card of that brand, we know we're getting one from an experienced, quality manufacturer. BFG also has a good reputation, especially for their customer service and support. Recently, cards from e-VGA have been seen not only on computer part Websites, but they've also found their way into our local electronics superstores.

If you stop to compare their specifications, you notice that, in terms of hardware, there is practically no difference. This is due to the GPU maker's specifications and the fact that they supply the actual graphics processors. Don't be fooled by the BFG's GPU speed. The extra 25 MHz comes from the manufacturer overclocking the GPU slightly, not from better hardware. (Thus the OC in the name of the product – OverClocked.) Because we don't plan on overclocking the video card ourselves, the extra 25 MHz does provide a free performance boost.

Other than the GPU speed, the rest of the hardware capabilities are exactly the same. The 256MB of VRAM is more than sufficient to run today's games extremely well, as well as any that are released in the near future. The 16-pixel pipelines ensure solid performance, and they all support the latest 3D APIs. This leaves us with only two points to help us choose between each brand: the extras that come with the card, and the manufacturer's warranty.

In terms of extras, the Leadtek bundle is the best of the bunch, coming with full versions of Prince of Persia: Warrior Within and Splinter Cell: Pandora Tomorrow. Not fantastic, but better than nothing. Some older bundles of the eVGA card comes with a full version of Far Cry, but most current bundles on the store shelves do not. The BFG card comes with some game demos, but not with any full versions. With none of these bundles really jumping out at us, we'd better take a look at the warranties.

There were significant differences in the warranty coverage for each of these cards. The eVGA only comes with a one-year warranty; you have to register your product to gain the second year. The warranty on the Leadtek card lasts for two years, no strings attached; however, the warranty on the BFG card blows them all away. It comes with a lifetime warranty and free tech support by phone and email. Don't underestimate the value of free phone support. While almost every manufacturer has a Website full of useful information, it's useless if you can't install your video card to turn the PC on.

With the small extra punch that the manufacturer's overclocking brings, and the excellent tech support, the BFG GeForce 6800 Ultra OC is the video card for our ultimate gaming PC. Check out a photo of it in Figure 5-2.

FIGURE 5-2: Our ultimate video card—the BFG GeForce 6800 Ultra OC.

How to Save Money in This Category

Chipset manufacturers have created many different versions of their cards to sell to all corners of the market. Whether you're a hardcore gamer for whom money is no object, or just someone who wants enough power to run a specific game, there's a card for you. Having many cards on the shelves can lead to a great deal of confusion, but it also offers many ways to save some money.

For example, we looked for video cards with the GeForce 6800 Ultra chipset. The GPUs that Nvidia puts in these cards runs at 400 MHz, and the cards have 256MB of VRAM. They also have a nice price tag hovering around $500. If you look at cards based on the GeForce 6800 GT chipset, you loose 50 MHz off the GPU, a handful of FPS in your games, and about $100 off the price tag. A GeForce 6800 card has a 325 MHz GPU, and a sub-$300 price tag, but you also lose four pixel pipelines, knocking the card down to 12 pipelines total.

The same sort of scale applies to cards based on the Radeon X850 chipset. The X850XTPE has a GPU operating at 540 MHz, memory with a clock of 1180 MHz, and 16-pixel pipelines. These cards retail for around $600. By switching to a X850XT, the GPU slips to 520 MHz and the memory clock is lowered to 1080 MHz; however, you also save about $100. An X850Pro has the same speed GPU and memory as the X850XT, but only 12-pixel pipelines. Selecting this card can save you between $75 and $100 more.

Any of these cards are a great purchase for your PC. If your budget has to come first, don't worry if you have to select a less powerful model. You can still run all of today's games.

What's Next?

Your PC is shaping up nicely; however, to play the latest games, you need a place to install them. Looks like it's time to check out the storage devices you're going to use in your ultimate gaming PC. On to Chapter 6, "Choosing Your Ultimate Storage Devices."

Choosing Your Ultimate Storage Devices

I n this chapter we discuss our choices for storage devices and how we came to those decisions for our ultimate gaming PC.

To begin with, it might be a good idea to define a storage device. A storage device is anything that acts like a permanent depository or container for data such as the OS, software, and personal files. Storage devices come in many forms, and each of them can have many different roles. For instance, there are hard drives, DVD drives, CD drives, flash cards, and floppy drives. They are kind of like a file cabinet that holds information or *data* until it is needed. At that point, data can be retrieved, modified, deleted, and placed back inside for continued storage when done.

The storage device covered in this chapter is the hard drive. Hard drives are the masters of data storage in computers, and the more space you have to hold data the better. As an example, just look in your closets. Chances are they are full and you still have a few things you would like to cram in there. Too much is never enough.

We are not looking just for space in our hard drives, but performance and speed as well. It's these three factors that are the core of hard drives. Performance and speed often get overlooked in the hunt for maximum capacity, but we are not going to let that happen here. We want all three for our ultimate machine: storage, speed, and performance.

Note When is a gigabyte not a gigabyte? Hard drive manufacturers use a different definition of megabyte and gigabyte than memory or CPU makers, which can lead to confusion. CPU and memory makers define a megabyte as 1,048,576 bytes, which is based on powers of two (1,048,576 bytes happens to be 2 to the 20th power). Hard drive makers define a megabyte as 1,000,000 bytes. Similarly, a gigabyte of memory is 1,073,741,824 bytes, while a gigabyte of hard drive space is 1,000,000,000 bytes. So that may lead to some confusion, making hard drives appear to be smaller than their rated size.

Key Terms

- **RPM:** Revolutions per minute rate. RPM is determined by how fast the pieces inside a hard drive spin to read and write data. Basically, the faster the pieces can rotate, the quicker they can find, retrieve, and store files onto the drive. Low-end speeds for desktop hard drives are 5400RPM; most performance drives run at 7200RPM, and drives that spin at 10,000RPM and even 15,000RPM are now available.

- **IDE (Integrated Drive Electronics):** The most common and standard interface used to connect a personal computer's hard drive and the system's motherboard by a single ribbon of bound wires.

- **SATA (Serial ATA):** The current successor to the IDE interface. It is a single serial cable similar to an IDE cable that connects the hard drive and the system's motherboard. The transfer rates of SATA are currently 150 Mbps with the future prospect of SATA II being 300 Mbps.

- **SCSI (Small Computer Systems Interface):** Another type of interface between the hard drive and the motherboard. It is a parallel interface that provides faster data transfer rates than standard IDE. SCSI hard drives cost more, mostly because they're designed for high-reliability, enterprise server environments.

- **Serial Attached SCSI:** A set of protocols that define the command set for hard drives. Using a serial attachment, similar electrically to Serial ATA, serial attached SCSI is replacing older, parallel SCSI in servers.

- **Gigabyte:** A measure of a hard drive's storage capacity in terms of data. A gigabyte is approximately one billion bytes of information. Common hard drives have gigabyte sizes from 20GB to 400GB.

- **Cache:** A small amount of random access memory on a hard drive where the most recently accessed data can be held for quick access. Cache sizes on hard drives range from 2MB to 16MB.

The Tech: How Does a Storage Device Do What It Does?

What are hard drives? A hard drive is a device that consists of a rotating, magnetic disk that can permanently store bits of information. As mentioned in the introduction to this chapter, the hard drive stores the operating system files, programs, and data. Some of the more popular hard drive makers are Maxtor, Seagate, and Western Digital. Hard drives have several main factors that determine the cost and usability of the drive. Let's go over these factors so that when you are searching for your drive you know what you are looking for. With all this in mind you should have basic understanding of what specificationsare used to define hard drives.

There are revolutions per minute (RPM). Hard disk rotation speed is the most basic determination of hard drive performance. The faster the drive can spin, the faster it can get to the data you need. A speed of 7200 RPM is the most common speed found in today's hard drives. Hard drives with lower rpm speeds, such as 5400 RPM, are slower in read and write times, but as a result of less rotations on the drive they put out less heat. This can be considered a good thing. Higher-end drives can reach 10,000 RPM but as a result put out more heat along with their great performance increase. Only recently have the 10,000 RPM drives come to the home PC. Before that, they were only built for servers; however, as the technology becomes cheaper and cheaper to make, the home user gets the benefit of what they can do.

Note that how fast a drive rotates doesn't always determine performance. Another key determining factor is *platter density*, which is how many bits can be stuffed onto a specific area of the drive. This may be defined as *tracks per inch, gigabits per square inch*, or *gigabytes per platter*. A 5400 RPM drive that has 100GB per platter may actually transfer data off the drive faster than a 7200 RPM drive that only has 60GB per platter.

Another factor of hard drives is seek speed. Hard drives consist of a series of magnetic heads, similar to the head on a tape recorder or VCR; however, a hard drive head flies just above the surface of the disk platter. How fast that head can move from one point to another on the drive is the seek time, and defines how fast the hard drive can find a particular item data. The average seek time for hard drives in personal computers ranges from 8 to 15 milliseconds. Remember — the lower the seek time, the faster the drive works and the better performance you get.

Next there is cache. Cache is one way a hard drive improves its speed and performance. Some hard drives have memory chips built into them that they can use to temporarily hold data for a short time instead of writing the data to the hard disk itself. Most hard drives that have cache now have it in 8MB chunks, but a few of the newer ones are heading up to 16MB. The low end of cache is a mere 2MB, which is the minimum you should get on any of your hard drives.

The size of the drive is the next factor you must understand. How big is the hard drive? How much data can it hold? The size of hard drives is currently measured in gigabytes; years ago it was measured only in megabytes. Fortunately, things have changed. The sizes of hard drives vary greatly, as do the prices for them. The lower end of hard drives in terms of space is about 40GB drives, which is probably more than an average user might ever need anyway. The high end is currently reaching past 400GB of storage.

Another factor to keep in mind is Sustained Transfer Rate (STR). STR reflects the hard drive's capability and performance to work with large-sized files. STR is a determination of how many megabytes of data a drive can transfer to at a continuous rate. For instance you have a super fast DVD-ROM drive and you want to copy the data off of it to your hard drive. The Sustained Transfer Rate is how fast the hard drive can receive that data. The more data the drive can continually transfer, the better. If you have a couple of hard drives, you can test the speed difference of a drive's STR by copying small files, but you won't see any major differences until you try writing data in at least 1GB chunks. You could then write the same data to the other hard drive, time it, and note the difference in speed.

The last thing to know about how hard drives work is what kind of connectivity or interface they have to connect them to the motherboard. There are several interfaces for moving information or data between a hard drive and the rest of the computer. Currently you are most likely to come across IDE and SCSI, and more recently SATA. We go over these in detail in the next section.

What Are the Different Types of Hard Drives?

For most PC users, hard drives can be classified as external or internal drives. Every PC or laptop has some form of internal hard drive built in. Internal hard drives are drives that reside somewhere within the chassis of the computer, normally in a slot called a bay. If there are extra empty bays in a desktop computer, additional hard drives can be inserted into them, thus increasing the storage capacity of the computer. Any additional drives can work in conjunction with the first drive in terms of backup or redundancy, or it can completely work alone as you desire. As you might imagine, adding additional drives to a laptop is not as easy because there is rarely any extra space to do so.

External hard drives are exactly what you would guess they were. They are portable drives that exist outside the computer and can be quickly attached by connection port, such as FireWire, USB, and in rarer cases SCSI. Serial ATA external drives have also become a recent option. Because of their portability, external hard drives can easily be added to any desktop PC or laptop computer for easy data storage or transfer. External drives tend to be used only as secondary drives. They are not designed to be a primary drive, meaning that you don't want to run your operating system off of one. External drives are also much friendlier toward laptops than additional internal drives might be because they can easily be connected.

In our ultimate gaming PC, we are opting solely for internal drives. We plan to have enough storage in our machine to cover all our needs. The reason we are mentioning external drives here is to let you know what your choices are. If you have another computer with which you share data—perhaps a laptop—you may want to think about picking up an external drive to help you transfer large files between them. External drives are useful in transferring data from one computer to the next, but they can also be used to back up important data off your main computer as a protective form of file storage.

We briefly mentioned the different types of interfaces for internal hard drives, so take a look at them in slightly more detail.

Internal Hard Drives

The following sections discuss several types of internal hard drives.

IDE

IDE has been the industry standard for years. IDE is the slowest of the interfaces listed only because it is the oldest, but that also makes it the cheapest of all the interfaces we mention. This is part of the reason most desktop computers you come across have their hard drives connected to the motherboard by an IDE connection. IDE, also known as Parallel ATA, is a parallel connection with a maximum throughput speed of 100 Mbps, but in bursts it can reach 133 Mbps. IDE is an interface that uses a 40-pin cable connection. IDE being parallel is great for performance. Parallel means that data can be sent simultaneously with other data as long as there is a communication path for each piece of data being sent. That is where the 40 pins, or 40 wires, come in. IDE is a lot of needle-thin, low-bandwidth, parallel data paths.

A downside of IDE-type drives is that connection cables only go up to 18 inches. This can make it a difficult to attach your drive to your motherboard if you have a large case or many other devices you have to work around.

SCSI

Next comes the Small Computer Systems Interface (SCSI, which is pronounced "skuzzy"). It has been around even before IDE and is still going strong since its birth in 1986. SCSI is a high-speed parallel interface that comes in many forms with a much faster transfer rate IDE of a maximum of 320 Mbps. The high-end 320 Mbps SCSI drives are very, very expensive, and are designed currently for servers. The average you are likely to afford and use in terms of SCSI drives is about 160 Mbps.

Because SCSI drives are built for enterprise class servers and are both very reliable and extremely fast, they're much more expensive than IDE drives. Where IDE drives are almost guaranteed to be found on sale, likely with rebates, every week in a Sunday flyer, SCSI is not. This seemingly increases the price difference even more.

Each form of SCSI requires a different connection to the motherboard, such as Ultra2 SCSI or Wide Ultra2 SCSI. Also, most motherboards do not have SCSI interfaces for the 160 Mbps and 320 Mbps built in, so you have to buy an intermediary card that allows them to communicate. This costs even more money. You really don't need to consider SCSI unless you're building a server.

SATA

The next interface type we want to mention is the SATA (Serial ATA). It's the newest interface on the market and offers a high-speed serial transfer rate of 150 Mbps. Some newer drives support 300 Mbps. It took SCSI a long time to get where it is and many revisions. If SATA is this fast first time around, its future capabilities should be incredibly impressive. Another benefit for SATA hardware, besides price, is that it uses a much thinner serial cable that can go up to a meter in length or more, making it much easier to work with. The thin cable increases the airflow internally of the computer; both SCSI and IDE use fat wide ribbon cables that are cumbersome and most of the time unwieldy in the small confines of a computer case.

The future has SATA written all over it. IDE is nearing its limits after a very good and respectable run. A lot of SATA fans love it is because many motherboard are coming out with onboard RAID controllers or interfaces for it. RAID (Redundant Array of Independent Disks) allows multiple hard drives to be combined in various ways to improve both speed and data security. Normally you would have to buy a separate controller card for this, but the motherboard manufacturers are making it easy for SATA.

SATA II

In terms of future tech, SATA II is worth mentioning. Just like SCSI, SATA is going to have its iterations. One of them is already starting to makes its appearance. In addition to doubling the speed to 300 Mbps, second generation SATA supports more robust cable connectors, external SATA drives, and more sophisticated connectivity options, such as SATA port multipliers. That speed is double what generation one SATA could do, making it an impressive leap in technology. Future roadmaps for SATA increase throughput to 600 Mbps.

With SATA II, it may be harder to find motherboards that support it with onboard technology. Luckily the motherboard that we choose in Chapter 2 does support it, so we do have the option to try SATA II if we like. Being that at the moment there is only one manufacturer, we may wait a bit on SATA II and upgrade to it later. By choosing a motherboard that can handle SATA II we are future-proofing ourselves in regards to faster hard drives we can buy when the prices are cheaper.

Controller Cards

With all these different types of hard drives you need different types of connections to the motherboard for them. Each drive type has its own specifications and requirements. Fortunately these interfaces are usually built into the motherboard these days. A PCI expansion card that supports additional interface connections allows you to connect your new technology to a motherboard that wasn't prepared for it. For example, if you were using a SATA hard drive and it was not supported by your motherboard, you would need to buy a SATA controller card that would likely fit into one of your empty PCI slots. Fortunately, if you plan ahead, you can now find motherboards that hold the interfaces you need.

Whatever the type of drives you decide to buy, make sure your motherboard has an interface for it or you will have to buy a controller card for it. Unless you are making a mass storage system with many hard drives, you probably don't need to buy additional controllers if your drive type is supported by your motherboard.

Additionally if you buy an external drive for your ultimate gaming PC, you need to make sure your motherboard has FireWire or USB/USB 2.0 ports built in. If you do not, you need to buy a controller card for it. And on top of the fact that external drives are already more expensive, you can increase your total budget more than you may have wanted.

How Much Storage Do I Need in My Ultimate Gaming PC?

You can only answer this question based on the full usage model for your computer. Are you only going to play games, or do you plan on storing digital music and photos? Are you also using the system for recording music performances? When deciding on how much space you need, a general rule of thumb is that you can never ever have too much storage space. If you were just running general applications, such as MS Office, Firefox, and your Blackberry Desktop Manager, a single 20GB hard drive is probably more than enough. General applications are not your goal here, though. This is a gaming rig. If you do photo editing, or collect MP3s and movies on a massive scale, that 20GB drive would deplete rather quickly. If you wanted to do video capture or editing, that would also fill up a 20GB drive rather quickly regardless of the compression you use on the files.

You are building the ultimate gaming PC, however, and you can bet whatever space you have will fill up pretty quickly. Some of the newer games or games with all their added expansions have 3GB or more installations sizes. What does this mean for a gaming PC in terms of needs? At the low end, 80GB hard drives are the smallest we recommend. This gives enough space for games and allows you a little growth in terms of MP3s and movies. Even if you don't use it right away, it is there when you need it. On the safer side staying above the 100GB+ mark is where you should be thinking of going if you can fit it in your budget. This amount of space gives you all the room to grow in terms of multiple games installations and file archiving.

If at all possible, supersize your purchase. It is always wise to purchase a larger capacity hard drive than you think you need at the moment. Because this is a powerful machine and not likely to be relieved of service any time soon, try to think of what future needs you might have.

The good news is that the price of smaller drives is so crazy-high that it's silly not to spend a few more dollars to get a larger drive. A few dollars more really does increase what you get in terms of hard drive space. On the current market it would be safe to say that if you shop around, you can find IDE hard drives of 40GB/80GB/120GB/160GB sizes with the price difference between sizes a mere $10 of less. It can be well worth squeezing a few extra dollars into your drive size so you don't have to worry about running out of space.

You also don't need to stick with just one drive. You could buy several smaller drives, if you find them on sale, and potentially end up with more space than you would have with one larger, more expensive drive.

Warning

Whenever you buy multiple or extra drives, make sure there are enough empty bays in your computer case to hold them. Depending on which computer case you decide to buy, it is likely that there will be at least one or several internal hard drive bays for you to place your additional drives. If that is not the case and you still need more storage space, you have to upgrade your main drive to a larger one or buy an external drive that you can attach from the outside of the computer.

What Happens If I Don't Have Enough Storage?

The main drawback of not having enough space is that you have to juggle what programs you have on your computer at any one time to make sure it can do what you want it to do. If you don't have enough storage space, you end up removing programs so that you have space to add others. This is not a huge chore, but it can get annoying when you get the sudden desire to play Neverwinter Nights and realize you have to wait 20 to 30 minutes to do the complete install — but only after you remove Doom 3. Meanwhile, your friends are waiting impatiently online for you to join their party.

Your other choice is to delete files, MP3s, or movies to make space, which you might not always be inclined to do. That means you have to make the choice of playing the game or keeping your files. You also have to worry that if you install games to make room for others that you don't lose your saved games as well. Most games actively leave your saved games behind, or ask you if they should be removed. It's just something to keep in mind because nothing is worse than losing 40 hours of gameplay because you forgot to click one button or forgot to make a backup before you removed the game.

Also, when you start to run out of hard drive space, Windows can get angry. It needs room to breath and work, and the room it uses is free hard drive space, otherwise known as Virtual Memory. When that space is not there for it to use as if it were RAM, everything slows down — and in the worst-case scenario, Windows crashes. As an example of how much space is needed, Windows 2000 Professional requires a minimum of 384MB of Virtual Memory space and

4096MB maximum. The rule of thumb is your default pagefile, or space used by your computer on your hard drive to work, is 1.5x your installed RAM. Also, the pagefile should not be located on the boot or application partitions if at all possible to help performance. As you learn later on in Chapter 12, it is wise to increase that number as close to the maximum as you can afford to give up. That comes out to about 4GB of space you need to have handy for Windows.

How Many Partitions Do I Really Need?

Need? Well you only need one, but it can help to have more for a couple of reasons. Partitions are nothing more than a way of dividing a hard drive into many smaller, logical drives. For example, if you have a 100GB drive, you could break it into four partitions — the first of 4GB, another of 20GB, yet another of 30GB, and the last of 46GB. Each of these sections would are considered its own drive by your computer, but would actually all be from the same physical drive.

We said partitioning helps, and the first reason you want to partition is organization. It is convenient to have separate places for all your different types of files. It is common to divide hard drives into several partitions. You might have one partition for games, one for backups, and one for files and OS. Using the partitions mentioned earlier, you could use the 20GB partition for your OS and files, the 30GB for your backups, and the 46GB partition for your games. When each file type has its own location, you have a much easier time managing and finding what you need.

Do I Want Multiple Drives?

The reason behind multiple drives is similar to wanting several partitions, except that each drive you make is not a section of one physical hard drive. Rather, it is a physical drive in itself. For example, you could have three partitions — one for your OS, one for your pagefile, and one for games — and then have an entirely second separate drive for your backups. This is a safe way to protect your data because if one drive dies, you still have all the information you need on the other one. That is the main reason people want extra drives because the chances of both drives dying at the same time isn't the most likely, though not impossible.

Multiple drives serve multiple purposes. They can save you money because you can buy a small-sized high-speed drive to use your OS and software, and a slower secondary drive for your data. Overall the price can be cheaper than two average-high speed drives.

Multiple drives also tend to mean more space and, as we said, it is rare to ever have too much storage space. You will be surprised at the ways you can find to grow into it. Of course we are not saying you need several 400GB drives, but two 200GB will likely suit your needs for quite some time.

The next point you should know about is mixing and matching different types of drives. By this we mean different speeds or interfaces. As an example, your computer has a primary boot drive that is IDE, and you purchase a second drive that is SATA hoping to increase your computers speed and performance. What is important to know is that your total computer only runs as fast as your primary boot drive can run, which is the drive containing your OS.

When you install a program or game onto a second hard drive, not all files are always installed to that particular drive. Some of the files get stored by the OS in the Windows directory on your primary drive. What this means is that when you play a game, it runs a lot off of your OS drive—maybe even more than the SATA drive after the game is loaded. Games also need Windows files such as the registry and DirectX to run, which are again loaded on the first drive—the IDE. The problem is that even though the SATA drive can dish out information as a super rate, the IDE drive cannot, and the whole system only works as fast as the slowest piece. To get full use of your fast SATA drive performance you need a second SATA drive for your OS, and run them on separate SATA channels.

Some people even buy an additional little drive just to hold their pagefile, which can really help the performance of a system. A hard drive dedicated to just the pagefile saves a lot of work from your other drives, giving them more time to run your games at, hopefully, a faster rate.

The final reason you may want multiple drives is so that you can use them in a RAID. We go into further detail just under the performance section of this chapter. Basically, RAID is a collection of two or more disks that work together to preserve data after a casualty and increase performance. When we finally build our ultimate gaming PC you can be sure that we will be using RAID to get its performance increase.

Is There a Cheap Way to Save Money on Hard Drives?

Some more goods news is that competition among hard drive manufacturers is fierce. What these companies do to help swing you their way is offer deals that allow you to buy a new drive at a very affordable price. This is normally done through rebates. Most companies that offer rebates hope you don't cash in for it, but if you want to save money on a hard drive make sure that if you buy a hard drive with a rebate that you mail it in for your money. It may take nearly two months for you to get your money back, but it's well worth the 10 minutes of effort it takes you to send off the information by mail.

Larger hard drives tend to have weaker bargains in terms of sales, and normally sell pretty close to list price. The cost of cutting-edge technology is rarely made more affordable because the manufacturers are trying to get as much of a return off the new product as they can—especially after all the money they spent on developing it.

Take a look at the simple fact that the price ranges for hard drives generally depend on the amount of storage space of the hard drive and who the manufacturer is. We already mentioned that prices between 40GB/80GB/120GB/160GB are in the range of $10 between sizes. One way to save money might be to buy the next drive-size down. The savings won't be huge, but if your budget is a concern that is one way to save some cash.

You can also buy a slower model drive. This is not something we recommend, but you could buy a 5400 RPM drive instead of the 7200 RPM model you had your eye on. This slightly slows your computer down, but this is something you have to consider when you are looking to buy.

Look for bargains, not just the rebates, but sales on hard drives. A rebate will often be included as well. Every Sunday grab the weekend flyers from your newspaper and look at the advertisements for the large retailers like BestBuy, CompUSA, and Circuit City. They always seem to have some sort of hard drive sale going on. Compare their prices and see who has the best deal for you.

Buy only IDE drives. SATA is new and fast, which makes it more costly. SCSI should also be looked past in terms of price savings. IDE is still respectable and gets the job done as well as it needs to be. SATA and SCSI are higher and you can see a performance difference, but it is up to you whether spending the extra money is worth it.

How Can I Get the Best Performance from My Hard Drives?

If you want to get the best performance out of your hard drives, you need to RAID them. RAID means several disks work together in regards to preserving data redundantly, and increase performance in terms of speed. There are several forms of RAID, but the one to concern yourself with here is the one that gives up the best performance speed, and that is called RAID0, also known as Disk Striping. Make note that RAID0 is actually NOT redundant, and doesn't preserve data. So if one drive dies, all your data on both drives goes with it. All that RAID0 is doing is taking two or more separate drives and locking them together to act as one drive.

Instead of one hard drive doing all the work—seeking and finding information, copying and moving it—you actually have two or more drives sharing the workload. This greatly increases the speed of your ultimate gaming computer. As data comes to the hard drives they each take what they can, splitting it up and writing it down on themselves. The drives work very fast. The drawback of RAID0 is that because they split up the data among them, half a file might be on one drive and half on another. If any one drive happens to die, you lose all your information because having 50% of a file is not enough to make it work.

Imagine two 74GB Western Digital Raptors and put them in RAID0. These RAIDed drives can be used to run the OS, your games, and all your other applications. You could then use a third, separate 120GB IDE drive for important file storage, MP3s, movies, or other big files you have that you want backed up. This gives you 140GB of super-fast storage for the performance intensive stuff in the RAID0.

For the best performance you also want to partition them. Your partitions don't have to match exactly as long as you follow the guidelines we listed earlier in this chapter. Don't worry if you don't know how to set up a RAID or the partitioning of hard drives. We cover both of them in step-by-step detail in the Assembly chapter.

Some current motherboards support RAID 1 and RAID 0+1. RAID 1 makes one of the two drives a redundant copy of the first. You never lose any data, but you gain no additional performance. Also, you have only as much disk space as the larger drive. For example, 2 Mlti 120GB drives set up as RAID 1 look like one 120GB drive to the system.

RAID 0+1 lets you combine up to four drives as a striped, redundant array. You get better performance, and your data is backed up. But like RAID 1, you need four drives, and they appear to be just two drives to the system.

Our Chosen Setup

When it comes down to it, our design goal has always been about speed and it's no different here. How do we achieve that with our hard drives based upon what we have learned? We take the best of the best. We take two SATA hard drives and put them in RAID0 to run our operating system and all our glorious games. This gives us an incredible amount of speed both from the SATA interface and from the benefits of the RAID0. When shopping for our SATA drives we find ones that spin at 10,000 RPM. This further increases the speed and performance of the computer. They also have as much built-in cache as we can find available.

SATA is no doubt worth it if you can afford it because it is new and faster and that makes it cost more than IDE. At the end of the day, it's your money and you really have to feel comfortable with where you spend it. SATA drives are faster and really do deliver what they promise in regards to speed, and the slender cables they use allow for better air flow in the case. Going with SATA is also a way to future-proof your machine, which is always a good goal to keep in mind when constructing a new computer.

The SATA drives help us boot faster and run games at lightning speeds. They won't help with burning a CD or DVD, however, because a hard drive is already 5 to 10 times faster than an optical drive, making the CD or DVD burner the bottleneck and not your hard drives. But for everything else SATA increases your total power.

Besides the two SATA drives we have in RAID0, we also put another drive — a 250GB IDE drive — in the computer for storage of movies, audio, and anything else we can find to store. All that storage together comes to about 390GB of space that we can use as we need. We will not likely run out of space on the RAID for games or programs any time soon, and that 300GB of storage goes a long way even if we pile everything we come across onto it.

What Are the Things to Look for When Buying Hard Drives?

Here are a few considerations when shopping for your new hard drives. The top consideration is use. You already know you are using a hard drive for games, so that helps a bit. When you know what you want to use the drive for, you can surmise the size and speed you might need.

As we keep saying hard drive storage space is pretty cheap or reasonably priced these days. Get a little more than you think you need in the coming future. It's cheaper to buy a little extra now than to buy a new drive later on because you need more space.

If you want good performance, look for drives with 8MB of cache. Almost all of today's drives have at least 2MB, and a few have 16MB.

Try to buy drives with at least 7200 RPM. We said before you can save money by buying the 5400 RPM models, but that should only be as a last resort to save money. Try for the 7200 RPM or the 10,000 RPM drives if you can swing it financially. Note, though, that the 10,000 RPM drives are usually much smaller than the larger 7200RPM drives.

Before You Buy Storage

- Make sure it is an interface type that is compatible with your motherboard, SATA, SATA II, SCSI, and so on.

- Make sure you look in Sunday flyers for the best sales.

- Make sure if you are going to RAID two drives that you buy identical ones.

- Make sure you are buying the largest drive(s) you can reasonably afford with your future needs in mind.

- Make sure the hard drives you are looking at have as large a cache as possible.

- Make sure the hard drives have a fast seek time.

- Make sure the hard drives are 7200 RPM or more.

- Make sure you're shopping at a reliable source.

Make sure that the hard drive you buy has a good warranty. As always, this is an important thing to think about.

Avoid all hard drive with a one-year warranty. You are using it for gaming, which means a lot of intense use, and if the manufacturer does not want to stand behind a product for a long duration, there might be a good reason. You will push those limits rather quickly. Find hard drives that have a least a three-year warranty, or even better a five-year warranty. Remember that a warranty only means you receive a free drive replacement if your drive fails. All your data is still lost and there is no warranty for that from any company.

Don't buy no-name brand hard drives for all the obvious reasons, such as quality and reliability. In the computer field everybody has their favorites of the standard hard drive manufacturers and everybody has a different story or reason why. There is no real guide for any of that other than people's preferences. Your best bet is to just make sure the hard drive you buy is one of the main brands available, or one that you already have had a good experience with.

And make sure you are getting a good price through a sale or rebates, if at all possible.

What Are Other Types of Storage Devices That I Need in My Ultimate Gaming PC?

Besides hard drives there are other types of drives you need in your computer, and some that you don't need but you may want. Hard drives hold all your information and programs, but that data has to get on them somehow. Currently that tends to be from CD and DVD drives. CD and DVD drives can read audio, data, and video from CDs and DVDs, and with the right drive can create new discs, allowing you to play back music and movies, install programs, and transfer data. The following is a list of the other types of drives you may want to include in your computer:

- Floppy drive. Older technology that is still being used, usually for very small files.
- CD-ROM (Compact Disc-Read Only Memory). Plays only CDs.
- CD-RW (Compact Disc-Read/Write). Reads and writes/creates CDs over and over again on the same disc.
- DVD-ROM (Digital Video Disc Read Only Memory). Plays back CDs and DVDs.
- DVD+RW or DVD-RW (digital Video Disc Read/Write). Reads and writes/creates DVDs over and over again on the same disc. (The "-" and "+" refer to competing standards for DVD recording. You can buy drives today that do both, so you don't have to worry about media types.)

You need a floppy drive if you are planning on doing the RAID0 setup as we mentioned. A floppy drive is needed to load the drivers for the hard drives during the Windows installation. Beyond that you won't need it. If you are opting for another route besides RAID0, you may do perfectly fine without a floppy drive. It really depends on your needs and if you like the luxury of a drive that can help you move small files around quickly. Floppy drives are relatively inexpensive and there is no particular manufacturer for them that is better than any other. The technology behind them has become pretty standard. The floppy drives' long lifespan is slowly coming to an end because manufacturers are trying to phase them out.

As for CD-ROMs the truth is that you don't need a CD-ROM drive anymore, simply because a DVD-ROM drive can do everything that a CD-ROM drive can and more, such as plays DVD movies. CD-ROMs can only read CDs and DVD-ROMS can read both CDs and DVDs. So if you had to only buy one of these devices it would be a much wiser use of money to purchase a DVD-ROM instead of a CD-ROM.

The only time you may want a CD drive of any sort is if you want to burn CDs, in which case you may want a CD-RW. This again does everything a CD-ROM does but it can also create and burn discs with up too 750 MG of information. Blank CDs are becoming cheaper by the day and can often be found on sale with rebates, making this is a great way to back up and transfer small or large files. CD-ROM+RWs are more expensive than a standard CD-ROM, but not by a whole lot.

Your last option is a DVD+/-RW drive. If you like the fact that the CD-RW can write discs that hold up to 750 MG of information, you will very much like the DVD+RW that can create DVD holding up to 4.7GB of data. There are even dual-layer drives that can write 8.4GB. Basically DVD is the CD-ROMs newer, faster, more mega-sized sibling. Everything a CD-ROM or RW can do, the DVD versions do it bigger and better. Blank DVDs are more costly than the blank CDs because they hold more information and are a newer technology, but they can also be found on sale if you take the time to look around.

When shopping for DVD and CD-ROM drives it would be good to understand what the specifications mean. The format may look complex, but when you learn the structure it is easy to understand. Take a look at the following drive specifications:

- 16X DVD+R
- 4X DVD+RW
- 48X CD-R write speeds

It looks like this drive can do a lot, and it can. The 16x DVD+R means that the drive has a DVD recording speed of 16. The 16 is for the speed of recording DVD+R media, which can only be burned once. The higher this number, the faster the drive spins — and the better it performs. The DVD is for the type of disc it can play at that speed, and the +R means it can also record a DVD disc at that speed.

Next is 4X DVD+RW. The RW stands for rewrite, which means this drive can write to DVD rewriteable media 4X speed. Finally, you have the 48X CD-R specification. This means the drive can record CDs at a 48x speed.

Which Ones Do I Need?

You may find that you are fine with just one DVD-RW to cover all your needs. It can read and write both CD and DVD formats, and also write the largest discs possible. Being the best choice also makes it the most expensive, but it's a solution that gives you everything you might want in one simple drive.

One instance where you might want an additional drive beyond a single DVD-RW is perhaps a secondary plain DVD-ROM so you can copy information from disc to disc. That means you put a CD-ROM or DVD that is full of data into your DVD-ROM drive and burn that information directly onto a blank disc in your DVD+RW. This is disc to disc copying. The benefit of it is that it is fast and easy, but if you want to save money it can be done without the extra ROM drive. It just takes a little more of your time and effort.

You can place the CD or DVD that is filled with information into your DVD-RW drive and then copy that data onto your hard drive. You can then remove the CD or DVD from your DVD+RW and replace it with a blank DVD. From there you can proceed to write the data from your hard drive onto your blank DVD. So you are basically paying a little more for convenience if you opt for a second drive because this way works just as well, but takes a little more time and effort from you.

Our Top Three Hard Drive Choices

Throughout the chapter we explained exactly what you need to know regarding hard drives for your ultimate gaming PC. Here come our choices based upon those theories. Picking the best hard drives or manufacturers was difficult because there are a lot of excellent products on the market by manufacturers like Hitachi, Maxtor, Samsung, and more.

To help us narrow down the field we went over the factors of what our goal is now and in the near future in terms of games. If you recall we mentioned our basic plan was to use two SATA drives in a RAID0 and a tertiary SATA for storage. What does this mean? Well, it means that all of our top three picks will be SATA drives. They are the latest and greatest drive on the market, and it would be a shame not to take advantage of their performance power.

Table 6-1 lists and details the top three choices we have come across. We chose these drives because they meet all of our requirements, including and most importantly being from respected manufacturers.

Table 6-1   Competitive Comparison of Hard Drives

	Western Digital	Seagate	Western Digital
Name	Raptor WD740GD	Barracuda	WD2500SD
RPM	10,000 RPM	7200.8 RPM	7200 RPM
Capacity	74GB	250GB	250GB
Cache	8MB	8MB	8MB
Seek or Access Time	4.5 ms	8 ms	8.9 ms
Interface	SATA (Serial ATA)	SATA (Serial ATA)	SATA (Serial ATA)
Transfer Rate	150 Mbps	150 Mbps	150 Mbps
Location	Internal	Internal	Internal
Warranty	5 years	5 years	3 years
Newegg Lowest Price:	$172	$143	$138

Our Pick as the Best Hard Drive

Looking at the chart you can tell we had some interesting decisions to make. In the end, though, we actually have two winners in this category! Because we are doing a two-drive RAID0 plus an extra storage drive, we need a total of three drives. And this allows us to pick more than just one drive.

So our choice for our ultimate gaming PC is to buy two Western Digital Raptor WD740GD drives and put them together in the RAID0. This gives us 140GB of super high-speed performance because these drives, though not overly large in size, run at a crazy 10,000 RPMs. With their high speed they are the logical choice for the RAID0, which we are only doing for speed anyway. Uber gaming, here we come!

Also 140GB of space should be more than enough for all the games and applications we want to run. And along with a nice, long warranty, we should be all set for our RAID0.

For our third drive that is to be used for storage of all kinds, we chose the Western Digital WD2500SD. As you can see from the chart, the differences between the Barracuda and the Western Digital WD2500SD are minimal. Seagate is a well-respected manufacturer of hard drives, and the table leans toward them slightly with their impressive Barracuda 250GB drive, but we decided to get all our drives from just one manufacturer, making the WD2500SD our second winner.

We chose two Western Digital Raptor WD740GD 10,000RPM 8MB cache SATA hard drives to use in a RAID0 shown in Figure 6.1.

We also chose to have an additional drive for storage, which is a WD2500SD. This is also made by Western Digital and is shown in Figure 6.2.

FIGURE 6-1: Our pick as best primary hard drives for the ultimate gaming computer: Western Digital Raptor WD740GD 10,000RPM 8MB cache SATA hard drive.
Picture courtesy of Western Digital.

FIGURE 6-2: Our pick as best secondary hard drive for the ultimate gaming computer: Western Digital Caviar RE WD2500SD.

Picture courtesy of Western Digital.

Our Pick for the Best DVD/CD Drives

CD-ROM and DVD-ROMs are different than most other computer parts except for floppy drives. What they have in common is that most any old drive can usually do the job. This means that the differences between the drives currently on the market are so minimal that no matter what you get, any name brand should suit your needs.

With that said we still do have to pick a CD-ROM and DVD-ROM drive for our computer. Some of the common and popular brands are LiteOn, Plextor, NEC, Sony, Pioneer, TDK, and TEAC. If you came across any of these and decided to buy it, you made a safe purchase.

When shopping for any type of drive that also writes information to a disc and is not just a ROM drive, you want to be a little pickier. Some are definitely better than others. Again the names we just listed are all reputable and quality brands.

When searching around for the drive for our ultimate gaming PC, we wanted a drive that could do everything—read and write CDs and DVDs, and rewrite over them as needed. We wanted it to be fast and trustworthy. What we found was the Memorex 16x Dual Format Double Layer Internal DVD Recorder.

This internal Memorex drive received rave reviews from numerous online Websites and magazines; more importantly, it can do everything that we want it to. The specifications are

- 16X DVD+R
- 2.4X DVD+R double layer
- 4X DVD+RW
- 8X DVD-R
- 48X CD-R write speeds

We also wanted a second plain DVD drive to aid us in copying information from disc to disc. We chose the LiteOn. It is inexpensive and runs well. The specifications are

- 16X DVD EIDE Drive
- 48X CD-ROM
- 512KB buffer

What's Next?

Now that you have picked your ultimate hard drives, you need to keep moving because technology waits for no man or woman! Next you will choose your sound card and speaker system. So here we go to Chapter 7, "Choosing the Ultimate Sound Card and Speakers."

Choosing the Ultimate Sound Card and Speakers

I n the early days of PC games, music and sound effects were nothing more than a string of different-pitched beeps emerging from your internal PC speaker. Eventually, programmers were able to coach a few catchy jingles out of the computer, and maybe a cool sound effect or two. Regardless, PC sound was not something that would be confused with music from your stereo or speech from your TV.

With the birth and evolution of the sound card, PC sound has taken on a life of its own. The latest generation of sound technology has brought the world of music and movies to your PC. Game soundtracks are expertly played by symphony orchestras rather than created by a series of beeps and buzzes. Professional actors who were once only seen on the movie screen are now lending their voices to bring game characters to life. But what does your ultimate gaming PC need to take advantage of these advances? Read on.

Sound: A Two-Part System

Unlike other components in your ultimate gaming PC, your sound setup is not dependant on a single component. A high-quality sound card works in tandem with an excellent set of PC speakers to create a field of sound that truly immerses you in a game. When the best card in the world is teamed with an inferior set of speakers, your music and games can sound more like someone plucking on a rubber band than a symphony orchestra. The reverse is also true. The ultimate pair of speakers reproduce and amplify the clicks, buzzes, and static that leak into the music and sound effects produced by a lesser sound card.

To understand what you're looking for in your sound card and speakers, take a look at the benefits gained from our gaming experience.

The Basics: Why Do I Need a Sound Card and Speakers?

Adding quality sound options to your PC is not inexpensive. An above-average sound card can cost between $75 and $200, with speakers setting you back twice as much. This significant price tag may make you question spending so much in this category, but it's important to realize that you are not just trying to improve your PC sound; you are really improving the entire gaming experience.

A game designer works very hard to ensure that you are immersed in the world he or she has imagined. A significant part of this immersion is dependent on graphics, but a deceptively large amount is dependent on a game's sound effects. Clear voice reproduction can give the illusion that game characters are actually conversing with you, much more than lines of text appearing onscreen. Ambient sound effects also add to the game illusion. Games that take place in a modern city have sounds of cars and trains mixing with the loud murmur of human voices as a sonic background. Cities in a fantasy setting are similar, except the sounds of cars and trains are replaced by the voices of merchants hawking their wares and livestock running through the streets. The deafening roar of the waterfall drowns out all other sounds around you, while the complete silence of an abandoned building is broken only by the footsteps of your game character.

Background music serves an important role in gaming, setting the mood that fits the game at a particular point. With designers spending significant amounts of money on music alone, it is an experience that should not be missed. Fast-paced musical scores create a feeling of tension for the most dangerous moments in a game; soothing tones are played in safe areas. With the right amount of subtlety, changes in the game music can assist the gamer in sharing the emotions of a character or emphasizing a sudden shift in a story's plot. All of these things help bring the gaming experience to life.

Of course, there are many games out there that do not focus on setting an "emotional tone." Playing an online, multi-player, first person shooter (FPS) game is not about sharing the emotions of your character. It's about pulling the trigger faster than your adversaries and pumping them with enough bullets so they can't get back up. Even though character emotions don't play a significant role in games like these, the experience still benefits from quality sound.

Multi-channel surround sound can be the greatest advantage to gamers, as this allows players to use their other senses to gain a tactical advantage. For example, imagine teammates in an FPS that become separated in a particular area. If one player gets into a firefight with the enemy, it can be difficult to pinpoint his or her location, especially if they are behind obstacles or inside a structure. Positional audio isolates the noise of the battle to one particular direction. If this battle is behind the in-game character and to the left, the sounds of the gunshots only come out of the speaker or speakers that are behind the player and to the left. Even though the player cannot see the enemy onscreen, he or she knows exactly where the gunshots are coming from due to positional audio, and heads off in the right direction in an attempt to assist their teammate.

Take a look at how a sound card and speakers work together to achieve these wonders. First, review the key terms that add clarity to the discussion.

Key Terms

- EAX: Name of technology invented by Creative to adjust sounds within computer games to reflect the virtual environment in which their source is located (i.e., add echoes to a sound source within a cave or canyon).

- Surround sound decoder: Audio tracks for surround sound must be compressed to fit on a DVD. For the sound to be replayed, it must be decompressed in a particular manner by a decoder. The two primary standards for encoding and decoding sound are

  - Dolby Digital: Surround sound compression technology developed by Dolby Labs, and commonly used in DVD movies.

  - DTS (Digital Theater Systems): An alternative to Dolby Digital, DTS uses different compression techniques, yielding higher bit rate audio streams. Many people claim that less compression results in higher-quality playback.

- THX certification: A certification program developed by Lucasfilm THX that indicates a device meets particular standards, including aggregate amplifier output, sound pressure levels, and certain types of audio equalization.

How the Tech Works

In basic terms, the sound card translates music, voice, and sound effects from a particular source (PC Game, DVD, and so on) into the appropriate sounds that come out of your speakers. Of course, it's not as simple at it sounds. To examine the entire process and the role your sound card and speakers play in it, take a look at how surround sound from a DVD is played back on your PC.

Decoding Surround Sound

Before your PC ever gets involved, the soundtrack for a movie is encoded on a DVD. In its raw form, the surround soundtrack would be too big to fit on the DVD. To solve this problem, the soundtrack is compressed with a particular method, shrinking its size and allowing it to fit on the disc. For this DVD to be played back by the end user, the sound has to first be decompressed. This decompression is performed by home audio devices, such as your DVD player or a home theater receiver, or by your PC.

Compression and decompression can be completed through one of two different processes created by separate companies. Dolby Labs created Dolby Digital, and DTS (Digital Theater Systems) created DTS Digital Surround. Each process has its own unique method for compressing the sound onto a DVD, and each method requires its own decoder to be present in your PC to decompress it.

When you pop this DVD into your PC, it begins to decode the soundtrack by using the Dolby Digital or DTS decoder built into your soundcard, or by using decoding capabilities of the software playing the DVD. The uncompressed soundtrack can then be divided into specific channels, causing signals to be sent to specific speakers. The speakers then reproduce the sound, allowing the soundtrack to be heard by the listener.

To hear surround sound, you need a surround speaker system. A typical surround sound speaker system consists of five speakers and one subwoofer. This setup is usually called a 5.1 speaker system, where the 5 indicates the number of speakers in the system, and the .1 indicates the presence of a subwoofer for added bass.

During the playback of sound, all five speakers are not necessarily active at the same time. Depending on the type of sound playing, it is sent through a specific channel and select speakers are activated. The following are the channels into which a surround soundtrack is divided and the roles that the surround speakers play in the process.

Center Channel (One Speaker)

This channel is used primarily for speech. Isolating character voices to a single channel keeps speech separate from sound effects and other noises that may overpower the dialogue. The single center channel speaker is almost always placed above or below the monitor or TV on which the video is playing. This placement creates a connection between the characters seen on the monitor or TV and the speech coming from the speaker, generating the illusion that the onscreen characters are speaking to the viewer.

Front Channel (Two Speakers)

This channel is used for music and sound effects, the primary non-speech sounds that you focus on during a movie. The front channel connects to two speakers placed on opposite sides of the monitor or TV, thus creating the illusion that the music and sound effects are surrounding the onscreen characters.

Surround Channel (Two Speakers)

The channel is used for ambient noises that provide environmental effects but are not sounds that the listener needs to focus on. The chirping of crickets in a field at night or the roar of the crowd at a baseball game are great examples of noises that might be sent to the surround channel. This ambient noise is not meant to remove the focus from an actor's voice or the musical score that is setting the tone of the scene.

In a typical 5.1 system, two surround speakers are positioned behind the listener—one to the left and one to the right. Because the sonic area in front of the listener is filled with sound from the front speakers and the center speakers, these surround speakers fill in the sonic area behind the listener with background sounds. This placement completely envelops the listener in sound from all sides.

Subwoofer Channel

The final channel connects to a subwoofer. A subwoofer generates low-frequency effects (bass) that are common in special effects such as explosions. Your front speakers normally handle the sounds of special effects. Because they must also reproduce other sounds, such as music, they cannot be designed to focus on floor-rumbling bass. This is where the subwoofer comes in.

Each subwoofer has a particular point where it takes over bass reproduction from your front speakers, enhancing these low-frequency sounds. This point may be controlled by a knob on the subwoofer labeled "crossover," by a setting on your computer, or in another manner. If you have access to this control, use it to balance the bass coming from your speakers and subwoofer in a way that fits your personal preferences.

Unlike the other speakers in your system, the subwoofer does not need to be placed in a particular location for you to hear its bass. Basic low-frequency sounds are reproduced somewhat by the front speakers, anchoring some of the bass to the primary viewing area. The more powerful bass from the subwoofer simply enforces the bass from the front speakers, allowing you to place the subwoofer away from the other pieces of your system.

 Note   Many sources indicate that the best location for your subwoofer is in the corner of a room that is closest to your viewing position. The corner walls work to amplify the bass from the subwoofer.

Figure 7-1 shows all of the typical components in a 5.1 surround speaker system and how they are usually arranged in relation to your monitor or TV.

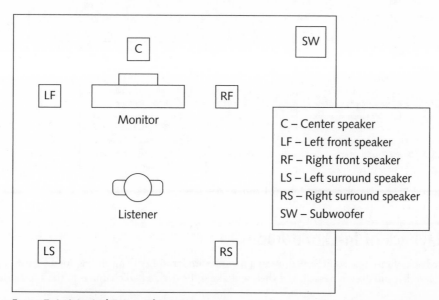

FIGURE 7-1: A typical 5.1 speaker setup.

You're Surrounded: More Advanced Surround Setups

A common complaint of the typical 5.1 surround speaker setup is that the rear sonic area doesn't quite live up to the task of surrounding the listener with sound. To solve this problem, Dolby and DTS adjusted their soundtrack encoding and decoding process to allow for additional surround speakers to fill in gaps in the rear portion of the sonic area. Dolby names their process Dolby Digital Surround EX, and the format adopted by DTS is called DTS Extended Surround.

A 6.1 speaker system, when matched up with a compatible decoder and a sound source encoded in a compatible format, adds an additional surround speaker directly behind the listener.

A 7.1 speaker system adds yet another speaker for a total of four surround speakers. In this setup, two speakers are set up behind the listener, as with a 5.1 system, and two are placed to the sides of the listener. These two alternate setups are illustrated in Figure 7-2.

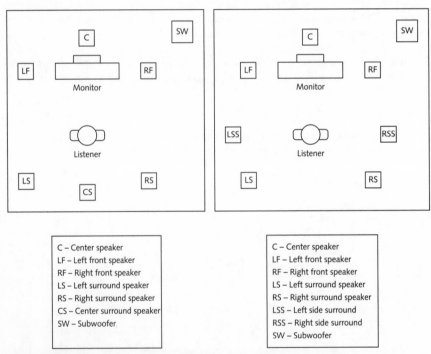

FIGURE 7-2: Speaker placement for a 6.1 and a 7.1 system.

Playback of In-Game Audio

Playback of in-game audio functions in a manner similar to DVD playback. Sound must be decoded and decompressed, and then sent along the designated channels to the appropriate speakers. However, unlike a DVD, sound in games is not limited to Dolby Digital or DTS; it can be encoded in a wide range of formats. These formats can vary from common file types such as .WAV or MP3 files to some lesser known formats such as OGG Vorbis, an open-source audio encoding format. Windows can easily decompress common file type for playback, but additional codecs may be required for the playback of these files.

Because DVD players have a limited method of input (the DVD) and plays media that only has a small number of sound encoding options, they provide a standard method of playback for movies. As mentioned, game designers have a larger variety of sound formats available to them for encoding audio. They must also contend with the different designs of the various brands of sound cards on the market. Because of these variations in the play device (PC), there is a need to provide game programmers with a standard way to trigger the playback of sounds from within a game no matter what sound card is installed. Microsoft has provided this capability through their DirectX API.

DirectX is an API (Application Program Interface) that is built into Windows. It works as the link between game programming and the drivers for the components installed on your PC. This enables developers to write code for hardware such as video cards, sound cards, and network cards without having to specifically tailor them for every brand and model of component that is currently available. Standardized DirectX code can be passed on to the manufacturer's drivers for each component, allowing them to determine how their hardware can best complete the assigned task.

Each component that can be programmed with DirectX has a specially named set of commands. In the case of your sound card, a game programmer can use the DirectMusic and DirectSound set of commands to designate a particular audio effect for playback and pass it on to the drivers for the sound card installed in the system. At that point, the sound card drivers take over, allowing the card to handle the actual playback using the specifications set by the card manufacturer.

Positional Audio

The power of DirectSound also allows a game programmer to associate a specific point of origin within a 3D world with a sound effect. In this case, the game, utilizing the capabilities of the processor and the sound card, compares the position of the in-game sound source to the position of a player's character. As a result of this comparison, the volume of the sound can be adjusted based on distance, and the direction of the source determines the speakers from where the sound is heard.

Take an example of a player's character (PC) in a 3D game that is listening to the speech of a computer-controlled character standing directly in from of him. Because the source of the sound is directly in front of the PC, the voice of the computer-controlled character comes out of the speaker directly in front of the player. If the PC rotates clockwise until the computer-controlled character is on the left, the sound then comes out of a speaker or speakers to the left of the player. If you continue this test, the sound rotates counterclockwise around the player as the PC turns clockwise within the game. Figure 7-3 illustrates this effect.

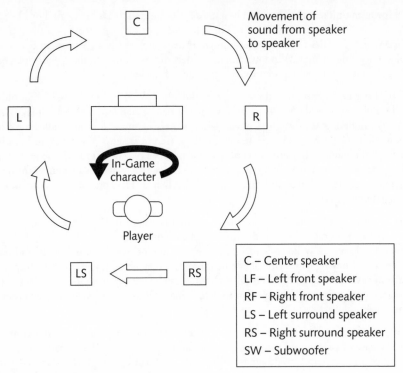

FIGURE 7-3: The effect of positional audio.

EAX

Originally introduced in 1998 by a company called Creative Labs, EAX (Environmental Audio Extensions) has changed the way sound is experienced in gaming. EAX is an extension to Microsoft's DirectSound API, and layers on top. The underlying concept for this technology is simple — noises sound different depending on their environment. Noise from deep within a cave sounds different than it does on a mountaintop, which sounds different than noises originating deep underwater. EAX offers game designers the capability to reproduce sound that simulates different environments. It also allows for sound to be modified by any walls, floors, or similar objects that are in the way of the source of the sound.

Decoding sound into discrete channels creates the illusion that the movie viewer or game player is actually in part of the show. Positional audio simulates the way sound travels in the real world and adds it to the virtual world onscreen. EAX modifies game sounds to reflect how they would be heard due to the environment of the source. Just because a PC game has these features, however, does not mean your computer is able to take full advantage of them. It's time to look at the qualities of sound cards and speakers that allow you to use sound to bring your games to life.

Sound Card Qualities

Great PC sound starts with the sound card. The best cards are able to handle every effect and musical score that a game designer has added without affecting system performance. It should also be able to connect to some of the best speaker systems to reproduce those sounds with fantastic clarity. Here are some of the things to look for when shopping for sound cards.

Strong Sound Processing Capabilities

The most important factor when purchasing a sound card is to find one that has the capability to decode and reproduce sound using the power of the card itself, and not relying on the PC's processor to pick up the slack. A good sound card has a DSP (digital signal processor) on the card, which offloads most of the audio processing from the main CPU. If a sound card is able to handle all of the tasks with its onboard capabilities, the power of processor is left free to handle other important tasks, like running your game. The less the card hardware is able to handle, the more has to be emulated by your computer's software, taking up valuable system resources.

For example, most of the audio capabilities that are built onto modern motherboards use the CPU for all audio processing. During intensive gameplay, frame rates can suffer if the audio processing hits the CPU too hard. Surprisingly, not all PCI sound cards have onboard DSPs. Some actually still use the host CPU for much of the audio processing.

To illustrate this point, let's revisit the positional audio example that was discussed earlier. Once again, place your in-game character in front of a sound source, causing sound to come out of your center speaker, as seen in Figure 7-4.

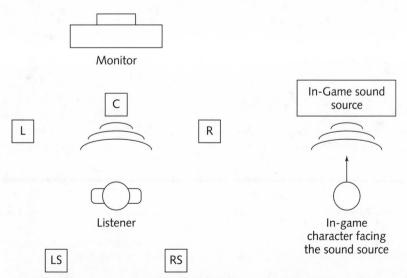

FIGURE 7-4: Comparison of positional audio effects to in-game character location.

If you slowly turn your character to his or her right, the in-game sound no longer hits your character head on. Instead, your character's left ear starts to face the in-game sound source, and sound comes out of your left speakers. As the character turns, the volume in the front left speaker should increase. At the same time, the volume from the center speaker should gradually decrease until all of the sound is coming out of the left front speaker, as seen in Figures 7-5 and 7-6.

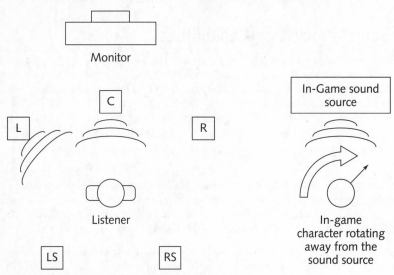

FIGURE **7-5: Beginning of a smooth sound transition.**

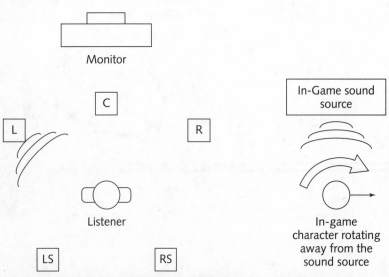

FIGURE **7-6: A smooth sound transition is complete.**

A quality sound card is able to handle this transition smoothly, subtly adjusting the volume in each speaker until the transition is complete. During the transition period, sound should come out of both the center speaker and the left front speaker. A poor-quality sound card is not able to perform this transition smoothly. Instead, sound comes out of the center speaker until half of the turn has been completed. At that point, there is a sudden jump to the left front speaker as the sound from the center speaker abruptly stops.

A similar test can be performed using games where there are many different sounds in one environment. For example, consider a game where a character is near a waterfall, shouting over a firefight. Can you make out the voice while still hearing the distinct sound of gunshots and the roar of the water? Do the environmental sounds abruptly cut in and out when the shouting starts and stops? A quality sound card is able to reproduce each of the sounds present in the scene in both volume and speaker positioning. A poor sound card may not reproduce the shouting without cutting some of the background noise.

EAX Compatibility

You've already learned how EAX settings within games enhance the illusion of the game experience by modifying sounds according to the game environments. To ensure that you are able to use EAX games setting, you need a sound card that is compatible with EAX. Check a card's specifications to ensure EAX compatibility.

Adding EAX effects via software and drivers can heavily tax a processor. The resources that are lost to handling sound effects are resources that are not available for other gaming purposes. To determine the effect that sound processing is having on your game experience, try turning off all sound. Sometimes this is an option in a game menu; other times you may need to configure your game or PC from Windows. If a game runs noticeably smoother with sound disabled, your sound card may not be shouldering the load that it should.

On top of that, some advanced EAX effects may simply be unavailable on sound cards that aren't made by Creative Labs. EAX 4.0, for example, is only available on Creative Labs cards, such as the Audigy 2 and Audigy 2 ZS.

This slowdown effect is not only related to the use of EAX. Simply enabling surround sound while using a poor 5.1 card could tax your processor. In the end, purchasing an inferior card may sacrifice more than sound quality. It can also strain your system, slowing down your favorite games.

Decoding Capability

If you plan to watch a lot of DVDs on your computer, or if you are just looking for another mark that denotes a high-quality sound card, look for one that has advanced decoding features. For example, the DTS logo indicates that the card is capable of decoding and reproducing surround sound according to the DTS specification.

Another seal to look for is THX certification. THX is a measurement of quality created by Lucasfilm, a company founded by George Lucas, famed director of the Star Wars movies. THX certification indicates that a card's performance measures up to the strict standards of sound reproduction set by the THX Corporation, formerly a division of Lucasfilm.

Connections

The connections that a sound card uses may be the easiest feature to look for and compare. At the very least, a sound card needs connections for a 5.1 surround speaker system. A separate headphone jack is great for late-night gaming because you can simply plug in a quality set of headphones to avoid disturbing your neighbor. However, you can always buy a line out splitter from Radio Shack that allows you to connect to speakers and headphones simultaneously. Some PC speaker systems also come with headphones, the connection usually placed near the volume controls.

Some online games allow for Internet chat, where you can speak into a microphone connected to your computer and allow other gamers to hear your voice. If this feature appeals to you, be sure that your sound card has a place to connect a microphone.

Even if your card has all of these connections, it can be inconvenient when they are located only on the rear of your computer. Headphone and microphones can be especially troublesome because their cords may not be long enough to reach from the back of the sound card to your desktop. Fortunately, some of the higher-end sound cards on the market take this into account and offer a form of front panel or external control boxes for your computer that makes all of these connections easier. Whether it's an external control box connected by a cable from the back or a front panel connected internally to your sound card, the added connectivity that these panels offer help you get the most out of your card.

Speaker Qualities

Just because you've found the greatest sound card ever made doesn't mean you experience incredible sound. It is vital that you pair your card with a great set of surround speakers to finish the job. Take a look at the components you need to watch for as you shop for speakers.

You Make the Call: Subjective Speaker Standards

Unlike sound cards, speaker systems can be difficult to judge through tests and benchmarking. Manufacturers can use statistics like "100 watts per channel" or "10-inch driver on the subwoofer" to claim superiority. In the end, the way they sound to the end user (that's you) is the primary method of judgment.

One of the best ways to judge speakers is to get a demonstration at a local store. See if someone at the store is willing to hook up the speakers to one of their computer systems on display. (In a perfect world, that computer is using the sound card you intend to use for your own PC.) If they have a game demo running, crank up the sound and judge the speakers for yourself.

If a game demo is not available, a common suggestion is to bring your favorite CD or MP3 file and play it on the test system. Unfortunately, this is not always the best method for testing gaming speakers because the demands that music places on your speakers is not the same as those of a PC game. When gaming, you primarily hear sound effects through your speakers, whether they are the sounds of a machine gun, footsteps echoing in a deep cave, or the voice of an in-game character. Speakers that excel at these types of sounds may need to be configured differently to reproduce the deep, satisfying sounds of your favorite CD. In short, be aware that if you test gaming speakers with a music CD, adjust your expectations accordingly.

If you are unable to have the speakers demonstrated for you, you might want to purchase your set from a store that has a very lenient return policy. If you are unhappy with the way they sound, the ability to bring them back for a refund or store credit can be extremely useful.

How Ultimate Can Speakers Be?

Looking for a set of speakers has become more complicated that it was a few years ago. Instead of buying two small speakers for your desktop, you now have to choose from 5.1, 6.1, and 7.1 systems, powered subwoofers, and a myriad of other features. The selection has also increased due to a blurring of the line between computer speakers and home theater speakers.

Originally, there was a distinct separation between computer speakers and those that you connect to your stereo or home theater system. The difference in size was the most noticeable because computer speakers were usually much smaller so they could fit on your desktop. Stereo speakers range from bookshelf models that were already bigger than your computer speakers, to floor-standing models that could be several feet tall. The connections were different, as well. Computer speakers used a mini-pin connection, similar to a pair of headphones, when connecting to the jack on your computer. Stereo speaker connections could range from alligator clips to bare speaker wire. Perhaps the greatest difference was in the selection of speaker manufacturers. Names that were very familiar to your stereo or home theater system like Bose and Onkyo did not cross the line and make computer speakers. They were reserved for music only.

Today, there is little separation between computer sound and that of your home theater. Bose and Onkyo are just two of many home theater speaker manufacturers that now make high-quality PC speakers. With the advances that have been made in sound card technology, you don't need separate speakers for your PC. With some additional cables, your computer can connect directly to your home theater receiver, utilizing the same speakers that you purchased for music and movies. Companies such as Logitech, who made their name in manufacturing high-quality mice and other input devices, now produce speaker systems, further erasing the line between computers and home theater.

Unfortunately, this blending of technologies complicates your speaker purchase. Spending several thousand dollars on a home theater setup and connecting it to your sound card definitely produces an ultimate sound experience; however, when comparing the sound experience to the amount of money spent, this setup is not very cost effective. You have to set some limits on your search to ensure that you're getting the set of speakers that match your ultimate gaming PC.

Limit your search to speakers specifically made for PC gaming, which are usually called multimedia speakers. There are two reasons for this. As mentioned earlier, the sounds from your PC games place different demands on your speakers than music. This search can get very complicated (and expensive) if you try to find speakers that excel in both areas. Because your focus is on gaming, you need to use that as the primary criteria when you select your speakers.

Also, it can be easier to shop for and select speakers that are designed for PC gaming. These speakers are carried by the same stores where you found your other computer components, and you should be able to find information on these speakers wherever you find PC information.

Speaker Features That You Can See, Not Hear

The sound that comes out of your speakers is their most important quality, but there are other useful features that add to their value. These features are seen, not heard, so check product descriptions for them when shopping.

Speaker Design

This one is obvious; you have to stare at these speakers on your desktop, so be sure that they are not eyesores. If you like their size and shape, it's easier for the speakers to blend into the background.

External Volume Control

When gaming, it can be great fun to shake the walls with sounds of gunshots and explosions; however, when pictures start falling and windows crack, it may be time to turn the volume down. Volume can be controlled with settings in your OS, but having a volume control knob for your speakers is the best way to do this. Simply reaching over and turning the knob is a lot easier than leaving your game to access the OS control panel.

Additional Speaker Inputs/Outputs

Some speaker systems have their own set of input and output jacks, independent of your sound card. If you want to play music from an outside source, like an MP3 player, you can bypass your PC and plug directly into your speakers using these additional inputs. Also, if your chosen sound card does not have a front panel with input and output jacks, being able to plug your headphones directly into your speaker controls can be a handy feature.

Wall Mounts

You can keep speakers and wires from cluttering your desktop by mounting them on a wall. If your speakers come with specialized hardware for wall-mounting, you will have a much easier time than finding an alternate solution.

Rear Mounts

Home theater speakers are often set up throughout an entire room, but your PC speaker system might be a little different. Often, your PC is restricted to a smaller space, such as a desk or a table. In these situations, you may not have a wall on which to mount each speaker. The center and front speakers can rest on your desktop, but your surround speakers could be hard to place.

To resolve this problem, see if your speakers system comes with a speaker stand on which you can mount your rear speakers. If the system does not come with them, they may be available as a separate purchase. Depending on your space limitations, these stands may allow you to get more out of your new speakers.

Selecting Our Ultimate Sound Card

Now that we've discussed all of the features you're looking for in your ultimate sound card, it's time to select one for our PC. After careful research, we've narrowed our selection down to three cards: the SoundBlaster Audigy 2 ZS Platinum, the BlueGears X-Mystique 7.1 Gold 8, and the Audiotrak Maya 1010. Take a look at their features in Table 7-1.

Table 7-1   Sound Card Comparison

	X-Mystique 7.1 Gold 8	Maya 1010	Audigy 2 ZS Platinum
Manufacturer	BlueGears	Audiotrak	Creative
No. of Channels	8 (7.1 surround sound)	8 (7.1 surround sound)	8 (7.1 surround sound)
Dolby Digital	Yes	Yes	Yes
DTS Surround	Yes	Yes	Yes
Dolby Digital EX	Yes	Yes	Yes
DTS Extended Surround	Yes	No	Yes
THX Certified	No	No	Yes
Front Panel	No	Yes	Yes
Remote Control	No	No	Yes
EAX Compatible	Yes (EAX 2.0)	Not listed	Yes (EAX 4.0)

All three cards are capable of handling a surround speaker system. The Audigy 2 ZS and the Maya 1010 have a version of a front panel for easy connections, a useful feature for a sound card. The X-Mystique 7.1 Gold 8 and the Audigy 2 ZS have specifications that seem to bend more toward the gaming market; the Maya 1010 seems to be designed to excel in the professional sound recording arena.

After careful comparison, we selected the SoundBlaster Audigy 2 ZS Platinum as our ultimate sound card. The capabilities of the card were the first selling point. Its support for 5.1, 6.1, and 7.1 speaker systems allows us to match it up with the best speaker systems available. Its DTS decoding capability and THX certification are signs that its sound quality is highly rated, features that pushed it ahead of the competition

The performance of this card is second to none. Test results from numerous online sources show that the Audigy 2 uses less processor power when compared to the other cards, leaving more available for gaming. The Audigy 2 also outperformed the other cards when EAX is enabled in a game, a result that you would expect because Creative was the originator of EAX.

The Platinum Drive that comes with the Audigy 2 ZS rounds out the package. This input/output panel is mounted in a drive bay in the front of the case. It is covered with all of the input and output jacks that we could possible need, with the headphone jack probably being the most useful. Volume control knobs on the panel allow the user to adjust headphone volume independently from the OS volume level and the volume of the speakers. A FireWire port is also available on the front panel, making it easier for us to plug in an MP3 player or external hard drive that utilizes this port. The Maya 1010 also had a front panel, but it was designed with professional recording in mind instead of gaming. A picture of our selected card is shown in Figure 7-7.

FIGURE 7-7: Our ultimate sound card, the SoundBlaster Audigy 2 ZS.

Selecting Our Ultimate Speakers

Our ultimate speakers are the final sound component we need for our PC. Keeping in mind the limitations we set for ourselves, we managed to narrow down our choices to the Logitech Z-5500 5.1 Digital Speaker Set and the Klipsch Promedia Ultra 5.1. You can check out their specs in Table 7-2.

Table 7-2: Speaker Comparison

	Promedia Ultra 5.1	Z-5500 5.1
Manufacturer	Klipsch	Logitech
No. of Speakers	5 speakers & 1 subwoofer	5 speakers & 1 subwoofer
Total Power	470 watts	505 watts
Subwoofer Power	170 watts	188 watts
Remote	Yes (wired)	Yes (wireless)
External Control Panel	Yes	Yes
Auxiliary Inputs	Yes	Yes
THX Certified	No	Yes

Our first impressions of these two systems can be summarized in one word: WOW! The sound from them was wonderful, making both systems a nice match for our sound card. Because we can only select one speaker system for our PC, we had to look a little deeper.

Both systems had excellent external panels for controlling the speakers, but we liked Logitech's design. A digital LCD makes it easy to see what settings are being adjusted. The ability to adjust not only the volume but also other speaker settings was a plus, as well. Both front panels have an auxiliary input jack that allows us to connect a portable music player without having to jack it into the sound card. However, the overall design and feel of the Logitech control gave it a slim lead.

We also noticed that Logitech's speaker system is THX certified, which pushed us a little further in the Z-5000's direction.

It wasn't until we looked around for the prices of these systems that we were able to declare a winner. With the Logitech system available for about $70 more than the Klipsch speakers, the Z-5500 was officially declared the winner. We have selected the Logitech Z-5500 5.1 digital speaker set as our ultimate speaker system. A picture of these speakers is shown in Figure 7-8.

FIGURE 7-8: Our ultimate speaker system, the Logitech Z-5500 5.1 digital speaker set.

How to Save Money in This Category

Using today's sound technology, it may seem as if the "all or nothing" approach is your only choice. Either match the best sound card with the best speakers, or suffer in silence. Luckily, there are some alternatives in this category to which you can turn to save some money.

Use an Alternate Model Sound Card

The SoundBlaster Audigy 2 ZS that we selected is definitely one of the top cards that Creative offers; however, with the included Platinum Drive, it can also be one of their most expensive. If you need to save some money on your card, Creative offers several different versions of the Audigy 2 that cost less. These versions won't offer you the front panel input and output ports, but you'll still have the performance of an Audigy 2 for all of your gaming needs.

Cut Back on Your Speakers

Choosing a different speaker set is also an opportunity to save some cash. The premium speaker systems that we looked at can cost between $300 and $500; however, it is possible to find some decent systems between $100 and $150. Creative makes affordable speaker systems that are a good compliment to their Audigy cards; take a look on their Website to see what they have to offer.

What's Next?

With the selection of your sound card, you've completed the shopping for all of your internal PC components. Now it's time to find a computer case for all of them. While you're at it, you might want to find a power supply, too. After all, the ultimate gaming PC doesn't run on sunlight! Move on to Chapter 8, "Selecting the Ultimate Case and Power Supply."

Choosing a Case for Your Ultimate Gaming PC

It's late. After spending all day shopping for computer components, you're almost finished. You're worried. You can just imagine what next month's credit card bill is going to be like. Suddenly, you remember that you need one last thing: a case for your PC. You quickly look at the selection that's available, pick the cheapest one you can find, and throw it in your shopping cart. You don't even bother to look at any cooling accessories.

After all, who cares about the case, right?

Unfortunately, this scenario happens to many people who are building their first PC, if not their second and third as well. After spending months of research on the newest video card or the fastest processor, the computer case is an afterthought; however, the computer case is an important part of your PC, and it should be given the same priority as your other computer components. Let's take a look at what your case does for your PC.

The Basics: What Does a Case Do?

Believe it or not, your case is more than just a metal box that sits under your desk. The computer case serves several purposes, all with a common theme: safety.

Structure

The first role of your computer case is to provide structure for all of your computer components. If you wanted to, you could assemble all of your computer components without a case. When you were done, you would find that your expansion cards would wiggle in their slots, causing a poor connection between the card and the motherboard. Cables connecting all of the components would be everywhere. CD and DVD drives could be obstructed, preventing them from opening. Without a case, you would just have a big mess.

This situation is very different when you have a computer case. When installed properly, your motherboard is securely fastened to your case, preventing any bending and twisting motions that could damage the board. Your expansion cards connect to your case as well, ensuring a secure connection and allowing your cards to function properly. The connection protects cards from damage, similar to the protection offered to the motherboard. CD and DVD drives have bays perfectly sized for them, holding the drives steady as a disc spins inside. The case keeps the computer components safe from damage, dust, other air pollutants, and helps them function properly.

Safety: Yours and Your Computer's

The second function of your case is to keep you safely away from your computer's internal components and vice versa. When it is turned on, your computer has a tremendous amount of electricity flowing through it. Accidentally touching some exposed circuitry can give you a nasty shock, if not worse. In addition, touching, jiggling, or removing computer components while power is flowing through them could damage your computer beyond repair.

A case also keeps dust and dirt from easily accumulating in your PC. Dust can interfere with your components, especially fans and other cooling devices, increasing the internal temperature in your case.

Key Terms

- Bezel: The front panel(s) of your case that gives access to bays behind it. Power buttons and LEDs are often embedded in the bezel.

- Bay: Pockets in the case structure where a device can be inserted and secured to the frame of the case. Common bays are

    - 5¼" Bay: Primarily used to secure CD and DVD drives. An opening in the bezel allows access to the front of these drives.

    - 3½" Bay: Sometimes referred to as a floppy bay, these are primarily used to secure disk drives. An opening in the bezel allows access to the front of these drives.

    - Hard drive bay: Primarily used to mount a hard disk drive to the computer frame. Often, this bay is secured behind the bezel or in another part of the case, preventing direct access to these drives.

- Tower case: A case in which front bays are stacked vertically and the motherboard is secured to the side of the case. Towers come in multiple sizes.

- Desktop case: A case in which front bays are often placed horizontally across the bezel. The motherboard is secured to the bottom of the case, laying flat.

Is It Hot in Here?

When your computer is running, the individual components give off heat. Heat puts added strain on your computer components, reducing their lifespan and making them prone to malfunctions. Some people think that a computer case only serves to trap heat, exacerbating the problem. In truth, a case with a good internal layout is one of the most important parts of an effective cooling system. When combined with some PC cooling fans that mount to the case, you can easily reduce the effect of heat on your system.

Before you take a closer look at case features, review the key terms to clarify the following discussion.

The Tech: Case Technology

The title of this section may seem a little odd. Exactly what technology is involved in making a metal box? Actually, well-designed cases are a great example of the principles of thermodynamics in action. In fact, a lot of research has been done in recent years by case manufacturers to reduce heat and increase airflow inside of their products. Take a look at some of these basic concepts.

Heat Transfer

Heat is the enemy of all things electrical, placing excessive strain on electronics. Unfortunately, it is a byproduct of running electricity through electrical components. For example, when flowing through the wires of your PC, some electricity is converted to heat as a result of its own resistance. In addition, heat is generated by the electrical components in your computer parts as a byproduct of whatever job they perform. Taking into account all of the electrical components that can be crammed into a computer case, it is easy to imagine heat becoming a problem for your new PC.

Under normal conditions, heat leaves the components and dissipates into the air in the case. This transfer causes the air to heat up and the component to cool down. This process continues until the air in the case is the same temperature as the components inside of it. As this air absorbs the heat, it doesn't have any place to go and becomes trapped in the case. Although some heat has left the components, the air temperature inside this case rises to unacceptable levels.

To cool the system down, the hot air inside the PC case has to be removed and replaced with cooler air from outside of the PC. The most basic way to accomplish this is with case fans. An intake fan is installed over an opening in either the rear of the case or the front of the case. This fan brings cooler air from outside of the case, pushing the hot air away from the intake fan. On the opposite side of the case, an exhaust vent offers an exit to the hot air, allowing it to leave the case. An exhaust fan can also be added to suck the hot air out of the case, assisting the flow of air.

The case enters the heat dissipation process by either helping or hindering the flow of air. A well-designed case creates a direct path for the airflow to follow from the intake fan, over the computer components, and finally out of the case. The basic diagram shown in Figure 8-1 is an example of a well-designed case facilitating the flow of air.

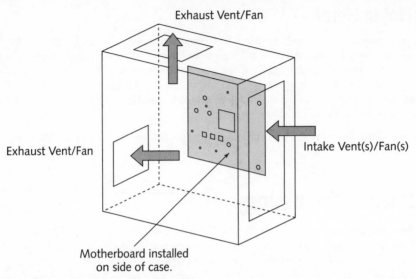

Exhaust Vent/Fan

Exhaust Vent/Fan

Intake Vent(s)/Fan(s)

Motherboard installed
on side of case.

FIGURE 8-1: Case design with good airflow.

A poorly designed case often has many obstructions between the intake area and the exhaust area. These obstructions could result from poorly designed panels and bays, or from a poor layout that causes components to overlap, restricting the flow of air. In addition, there are too few vents to allow enough of the heated air to escape, or they are poorly placed. Finally, these cases have no clear places to attach case fans, relying solely on the power supply fan to bring cool air into the case. Figure 8-2 depicts a case with poor airflow.

In general, larger cases like full towers offer more flexibility to the designer in determining the placement of components. This makes it easier to maximize the flow of air through the case. Conversely, smaller cases offer much less room for placement of internal components. With more components crammed inside a smaller space, it is much easier for airflow to be obstructed. Special consideration of heat problems is required for these small cases.

Immaterial Material: What's It Made Of?

The inner frame of computer cases are usually composed of steel, providing the rigid structure that is important to your computer components. The outer shell of the case may also be composed of steel, or it may be made of an aluminum alloy. Aluminum is lighter than steel, but more difficult to mold. As a result, aluminum cases are definitely easier to carry around.

Some manufacturers make note of the fact that aluminum cases conduct heat better than steel cases, which may help cool your PC. It is true that aluminum conducts heat better than steel, but you probably will not see any significant thermal benefit to your system. With proper ventilation and cooling, there should not be enough heat remaining in the PC to be transferred to the aluminum case. Don't let claims regarding the heat dissipation of an aluminum case be the primary factor in your case selection.

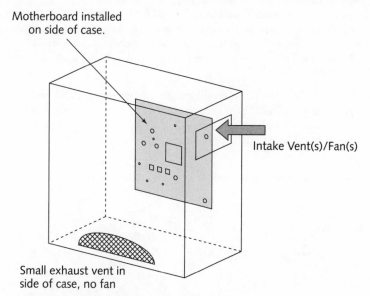

Motherboard installed
on side of case.

Intake Vent(s)/Fan(s)

Small exhaust vent in
side of case, no fan

FIGURE 8-2: Case design with poor airflow.

What to Look for When Shopping for a Case

Now that you've looked at some of the underlying concepts for case design, it's time to put them to good use. Here are some thoughts to consider when shopping for the ultimate computer case.

Size

Size is a basic yet important factor to consider when shopping for a new case. With many different sizes available, it is important to pick one that is appropriate for your PC. Not only must the case be of a reasonable size in terms of its dimensions, it must also have enough bays to allow you to install the storage drives and control panels that you've collected.

Cases can be oriented in two different ways — towers and desktops. Towers have the drive bays stacked vertically with the motherboard secured to the side of the case. Bays can also be stacked horizontally with the motherboard secured to the bottom of the case. These types of cases are called desktops.

Towers can usually be subdivided into three categories. These subcategories are more of a reflection on the number of bays that they offer than their physical size, but we can estimate their dimensions to give you an idea of what to expect if you shop for a tower.

The first subcategory is the mini-tower. These towers are often designed with space-saving in mind. They only offer one, possibly two CD/DVD drive bays, and one floppy bay. They are constructed to take up as little space as possible, with a typical height between 14 and 16 inches, and a typical width starting at 6 inches.

The second subcategory is a mid-tower. These are often used for a generic PC that has two CD/DVD drives for disc copying and a single floppy drive. They usually include an additional bay, but it often goes unused. These cases can be as much as 20 inches tall, but usually hover around 16 inches. They tend to be a little wider than the mini-tower, with a width as small as 7 inches, but are often a little wider.

The third subcategory is the full tower. These towers are great for customized PCs and some smaller servers. They offer at least five CD/DVD bays, but they often include many more. They usually have three floppy bays, although some smaller fan controllers can occupy these spaces. Cases such as these can be as tall as your desk, depending on the number of bays. Expect them to be at least 2 feet tall.

We've summarized this case information in Table 8-1 for easy reference.

Table 8-1   Case Sizes

	Full Tower	Mid-Tower	Mini-Tower	Desktop
Typical Number of 5¼" Bays	5 or more	3	1 or 2	1 or 2
Typical Number of 3½" Bays	2 or more	1 or 2	1	1
Typical Height	20 inches or more	16 to 20 inches	14 to 16 inches	6 to 8 inches
Typical Width	8 inches or more	7 inches or more	6 inches or more	16 to 18 inches
Typical Depth	21 inches or more	17 to 19 inches	15 to 17 inches	17 to 19 inches

Bigger Is Better

Generally speaking, a bigger case is usually a better case. Unless you have space constraints in the area where you are going to place your PC, you get more benefit in purchasing a variation of a full tower than a smaller type.

A bigger case gives you more room for installing components. This is a bonus for all computer builders, but it is especially appreciated by novices. To fit the necessary PC components in a smaller case, manufacturers have to build the drive bays so they hang over your motherboard. This can make physically installing your CD, DVD, and hard drives a real challenge. Running cables to the drives from the motherboard can be equally difficult. After the power supply is installed, entire sections of your motherboard will probably be blocked. Larger cases have the power supply and the expansion bays off to the side of the motherboard, giving you an unobstructed view during and after installation.

A larger case usually offers better airflow between your components. Because drives and cables are not hanging over your motherboard, there are fewer objects to block the flow of air. This aids in heat dissipation inside of your PC.

Finally, a large case offers many bays for future expansion. You never know when a new fan, drive, or expansion card will come with a control panel that needs to be mounted in a 5¹/₄" or 3¹/₂" bay. Having these bays available prevents you from having to choose between your new component and one of your DVD drives.

One trend for mid-tower cases is that they're getting deeper. This somewhat minimizes the internal clutter and small space. Of course, you need to make sure that a deeper case will fit where you want it.

Match Your Motherboard

Be sure to check that your motherboard fits inside your new case.

If you recall from Chapter 3, the size and shape of your motherboard is called its form factor. The motherboard we chose for the ultimate gaming PC is an ATX form factor, one of the most common.

Be aware that there are other form factors available, with many of them smaller than ATX. Cases that accommodate these smaller boards may be too small for an ATX board. Your case specifications list the form factors that it can accommodate, so check them before you buy.

A new form factor, BTX, will soon be available. If your case can accommodate both ATX and BTX form factors, you can still use it for future systems, increasing its value.

Material

The material from which a case is constructed may play a role in your case selection. Some older and cheaper cases have both a steel frame and outer shell. This can make the case significantly heavier than one with an aluminum casing. This extra weight can add to your shipping costs if the case is purchased online. It can also make it more difficult to move and lift. You may not think that your PC will be moved often, but you will appreciate the weight reduction during the initial assembly process. It also makes it easier to get access to the back of your computer for plugging in cables and to work in the case if you need to diagnose a hardware problem.

Aluminum cases may be more stylish than its steel counterparts. Aluminum cases are more likely to have useful features like additional vents, and some aesthetic features like transparent panels that show off the insides of your PC.

Cooling

With heat becoming a greater concern as computer components become more advanced, it is important to identify cases that promote cooling and avoid cases that are heat traps. Low-quality cases have fewer vents to promote cooling. They do come with any cooling fans to bring cool air into the case. They may also be smaller in size, creating a cramped interior that inhibits airflow.

Conversely, a quality case has vents on opposite sides of the case to allow air to flow through the interior. It comes with a preinstalled intake fan, and possibly an outtake fan as well. It has a larger interior with all the components laid out in a manner that promotes airflow. If components are set apart from the motherboard, removing them from the path of the intake fan, the case has another set of vents and/or fans to accommodate these components.

More recent case designs offer ducted fans that sit atop the CPU, which lets the case bleed heat from one very hot component almost directly to the outside. This means that the heat generated by the processor isn't simply circulated inside the case.

Ease of Use

The greatest improvements in case design are changes that make them easier to use. No longer will you feel that you need a blowtorch to get access to the inside of your PC. Keep an eye out for some of the following features when looking for a case.

Thumbscrews

Instead of the small flat heads that normal screws have, thumbscrews have oversized heads that can be grasped by hand. Grooved sides allow for easy tightening and loosening without the need for a wrench or screwdriver. Of course, thumbscrews often have a Phillips groove in the head if a screwdriver is needed. Overall, thumbscrews are an easy way to secure items such as the side panels of the case and often-removed parts inside of the case.

Tool-Free Drive Installation

Some cases come with small rails that attach to the side of your optical drives, either by snapping them in place or by securing them with small screws. After these rails are in place, the drive can simply slide into the appropriate bays in the case. They either lock in place automatically, or are secured by lowering a lever or panel on the case itself.

Depending on how difficult it is to attach the rails to the drive, this system can make it much easier to install your CD, DVD, and hard drives. Cases without tool-free drive installation can require drives to be secured with small screws. The holes for these screws can be behind large panels, where access is available only through small openings. Performing the installation through these small access holes can be frustrating, especially if you have large hands.

Warning

If you don't use all of your bays after initial installation, be sure to save your extra rails! Often, these can be difficult if not impossible to replace, especially if a year or two has passed since your last upgrade.

Expansion Card Clip

Another tool-free innovation is the expansion card clip. It can take many forms, but its purpose is always the same. When installing an expansion card, it must be secured to the case to prevent movement and ensure stability. This is usually accomplished with a single screw that connects the bracket on the back of the expansion card to the rear of the case. An expansion card clip replaces this screw with an arm or brace that is preinstalled in the back of the case. An arm or brace is lowered into place, covering the tops of the expansion card brackets. When this arm is locked into place, it secures the cards without the need for screws.

Warning Some of the newer expansion cards, especially video cards, can be very bulky. The expansion clip can get in the way of these larger cards, making installation difficult, if not impossible. You may need to remove the clip during installation.

Removable Motherboard Tray

In an attempt to make motherboard installation easier, some cases feature a removable motherboard tray. Depending on how cramped the interior of your case is, it can be a useful feature for the initial installation. Simply remove the tray, install the mainboard without being obstructed by the surrounding case chassis, and reinstall the tray.

Smaller cases benefit the most from this feature because the power supply and disk drives often hang over the motherboard, making it difficult to work with. However, this feature loses some of its effectiveness in larger cases. These cases have ample interior space to install the board. In addition, after the motherboard has been completely installed, you have to go into the case to remove the power cables and screws securing the expansion cards before you can remove the motherboard tray. Because you're working in the exterior of the case anyway, it's just as easy to remove the board that way instead of removing the motherboard tray first. Also, motherboard trays often don't fit with the same tolerances as a fixed platform, so you may need to fiddle with it a bit to make sure that slots and connectors align properly.

Warning Be wary of flimsy motherboard trays. Motherboards must be secured to the case to prevent bending that can cause damage. If the tray is not very solid, you may inadvertently damage your board during installation.

Easy Open Side Panels

Often overlooked features in cases are easy open side panels. Both during and after installation, you will find yourself tinkering with the components of your PC. It can be time consuming to install a part, replace a side panel and secure it with screws, only to find out that the new component is not working properly. Cases that have a simple latch or button to release a panel can take some of the tedium out of this process.

Removable Hard Drive Cage

Some cases require hard drives to be installed in the front of the case, near the floppy and CD drives. When your computer is fully assembled, access to the hard drives can be blocked by expansion cards, power supplies, or other large objects. This is where a separate hard drive cage comes in handy.

This cube-shaped cage snaps into place somewhere in your case, usually on the top or the side. To install a hard drive, simply pop out the cage, secure your drives, pop the cage back into place, and connect the cables. Upgrading your storage requires only the cables to be disconnected and the cage to pop out, instead of removing expansion cards to access front-mounted drives. If you're worried about having enough hard drive space when building your PC, get a case with this feature. It saves you some headaches during future upgrades.

Easy Access Panels

Many cases come with USB ports or FireWire ports preinstalled in easy access positions. Often, these ports are found on the front of your computer, but they can sometimes be found on the top of the case as well. Not having to reach around to the back of the computer every time you want to plug in a peripheral is a wonderful thing. These ports, however, are not always compatible with your motherboard. If these ports are a primary consideration for you, check with your motherboard manufacturer to ensure that you can use them.

Who Are These People?

Whether they know it or not, most people have a little bit of PC knowledge hidden in their brains. If you ask someone to name a computer manufacturer, brands such as Dell and Gateway are popular answers. Not only have they been around a while, their TV commercials over the years have added to their name recognition. If you try to research video cards, the names NVidia and ATI show up immediately. But can you name any computer chassis manufacturers?

Because computer cases do not advertise heavily outside of computer-specific magazines and similar publications, it can be difficult to start a search for a good case. In addition, computer case manufacturers do not often branch out into more mainstream products. For example, Dell not only sells computers, but they now sell printers and HDTVs. This increases the exposure of the Dell brand name.

Sometimes these other products that a manufacturer produces can give us some insight into their case design and quality. Consider Antec, a case manufacturer. They have a reputation of making solid power supplies in addition to cases. Because a power supply is not exactly a component that you need to upgrade every six months, Antec may not be a familiar name to most people; however, because Antec understands power supplies, they may also have unique ideas about cable management inside the case. Power supplies have to have a cable that fits every product in your PC. Because cooling and exhaust fans are a vital part of any good power supply, Antec may also have insight toward designing a case that promotes cooling.

Speaking of cooling, Thermaltake, a company with a great reputation for making cooling products, also produces computer cases. Because of their expertise, you can expect a Thermaltake case to have considered cooling in their design, whether that means including some quality fans or designing the case to promote airflow that effectively cools the PC.

Of course, there are some great companies that focus solely on computer cases. Lian-Li, a Taiwanese case manufacturer, has produced several excellent case designs in recent months. Because they don't make other products, their name may not seem as familiar as some others. Even so, they remain one of the top case manufacturers around.

You may be a little more familiar with the names of some case manufacturers now than you were when this discussion began, but you should also realize that name doesn't tell the whole story. When shopping for cases, don't be afraid of manufacturers that you do not recognize; just because you haven't heard of them doesn't mean their products aren't of a high quality. Simply check a case for the qualities discussed earlier in this chapter. Unlike processors and memory, it is easy to examine a computer case for yourself to see if it fits your needs.

To Mod or Not to Mod; That Is the Question

Some people can shop for cases forever and not find the one they really want. It could be something as simple as not finding one in electric blue or hot pink. Some people want something a little more complex. Lights that pulse in time with cooling fan speed show some imagination; fitting an entire PC inside of a model of the Millennium Falcon shows a little more.

If you consider case modding (modifying to suit your tastes) to be the final step in your ultimate gaming PC, you're not alone. If you plan to mod your case, have your imagination ready when shopping. Instead of looking for great features that the manufacturer has incorporated into the case design, look for parts on which you can make your own mark. A plain case without a window or an expensive paint job may appear incredibly ugly to some, but appears as a blank canvas to a case modder. A case with beautiful colors and clear windows may cramp a modder's style because it may not fit the image in their mind.

If you find the perfect case to work with, but you need a little help making your vision come true, consult Extreme Tech's book "Going Mod," written by Russ Caslis. This book gets you started on the road to modding and gives you some great pointers to bring your vision to life, covering many topics that we don't have the space to discuss here.

If modding is not up your alley, that's okay, too. Case design has come a long way since the days when all computers were just beige colored steel boxes. If you look hard enough, you should be able to find something that appeals to you.

Case Closed: Selecting Our Ultimate Case

Now that we know what qualities to look for in a case, it's time to browse all of the brands and models available and select one that fits our needs. When we picked our case, we didn't exactly go about this task in the same way we approached our other component. Online photos helped us find a case that looked great, but we wanted to judge their internal layout as well. In our experience, one of the most frustrating aspects of assembling a PC is not having enough room to work inside a case. If a part malfunctions or is installed incorrectly, a cramped case only increases our ire, making us prone to mistakes. As a result, we took a trip down to our local computer store to inspect their case selection first hand.

Because there were so many case designs from which to choose, we looked for features that were the most important to us, starting from the inside. We wanted space — lots of space. We also wanted a case that was laid out well for cooling and came with some good fans to increase airflow. Finally, we wanted as many bays as possible so the parts we would install in the future weren't limited by available space, or lack thereof.

In terms of the exterior, we wanted something relatively simple. We didn't want too many flashing lights or other random gadgets. They would simply add to the already large amount of wires and cables inside of our case, and we wanted to spend our time installing cool gaming things, not flashing LEDs. As for color, we were looking for something black. Nothing says "Ultimate Gaming" like a shiny black case. An aluminum chassis would be nice, too, reducing the overall weight of the system. After all, because we're shopping in a brick and mortar store, someone would have to carry it to the car.

After spending an hour or so debating, we settled on the Thermaltake Armor VA8000. It has lots of space inside, perfect for our needs. The power supply and hard drives are installed near the top of the case without overlapping the motherboard. The drive bays on the front of the case don't hang over the board, either.

It's clear that Thermaltake's experience in creating quality cooling products definitely came in handy when designing the case. It comes with three fans — one intake and two exhaust — enhancing an intelligent layout that promotes airflow through the case.

It has 11 front bays for future upgrade options. The bays are interchangeable, meaning we aren't locked in to installing our floppy or DVD drives in specific places.

It has some features that make it easy to use, like thumbscrews for the side panel and a removable hard drive cage. It also has tool-free installation for the 5¼" drive bays, and an expansion card clip for securing cards without the use of screws.

Its aluminum shell makes it extremely light, considering its size. And, most importantly of all, it comes in black!!! Take a look at it in Figure 8-3.

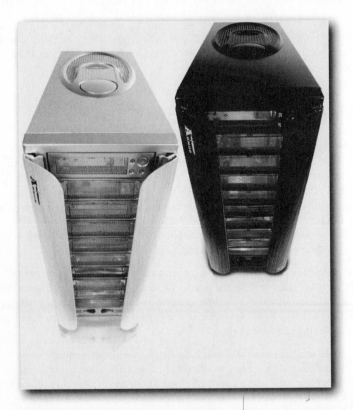

FIGURE 8-3: The Thermaltake Armor VA8000 — in black and silver.

Other Ways to Approach the Situation

Of course, not everyone has access to a computer store with a wide selection of cases to choose from. In that case, here are a few tips to help you find cases online:

- Start your search by browsing for cases from the three manufacturers we mentioned earlier in this chapter: Antec, Thermaltake, and Lian-Li.

- Use a shopping site that has several pictures of the case from different angles. Look for additional photos on the manufacturer's Website.

- Use the methods outlined in Chapter 1 to do a little online research. There are many Websites that publish computer case reviews. These reviews can give insight into features that are difficult to judge online, such as how easy it is to install parts.

- Find a case that has the size and features that are most important to you; then use the photos to decide if the style and color of the case is the right one for your desk.

How to Save Money in This Category

Top of the line computer cases can cost you between $150 and $300. For many people, this may be too much money to spend on the metal box that sits under the desk. Just because you don't have that much money to spend doesn't mean you have to be stuck with a terrible case.

For between $30 and $60, you can find a decent mid-tower case for your PC. Because tool-free features are often the most expensive to implement, don't be surprised if cases in this price range don't include them. You can still find a case with good cooling, front panel inputs, and many other features that we have discussed. The tips mentioned in the previous section will still come in handy for shopping online. Because selection can vary from store to store, the best tip we can offer is to shop around.

What's Next?

Now that you've got a case in which to install your ultimate gaming PC, you need to worry about supplying it with power. You're almost finished; let's quickly move on to Chapter 9, "Selecting the Ultimate Power Supply."

Selecting the Ultimate Power Supply

Similar to the PC case, your computer's power supply is an often over-looked component. In fact, many people think the power supply is part of the case, and not a standalone device. This is a result of many case manufacturers adding a power supply into every case they sell as an additional selling point. These "throw-in" power supplies may not be sufficient to power your ultimate gaming PC, causing more harm than good in the long run. To tell a good power supply from a bad one, you need to understand the role of the power supply in your PC.

The Basics: What a Power Supply Does

Some people know the power supply is that metal box with the black plug on it, usually found in the back of the computer. You simply plug your power cable into that box and then into the wall socket to provide your PC with power. However, your power supply is not just passing the electricity from the wall socket into your PC. It has a lot of work to do before you hear the pleasant sounds of a system booting up.

The first job of the power supply is to pull in electricity from your wall socket. Unfortunately, this electricity is not in a form that can be used by the internal components of your PC. The power supply must convert it to the proper form and then split it to provide power to every part that needs it.

Wall current is AC (alternating current); the internal PC circuitry runs on DC (direct current). So the first conversion is to convert from AC to DC. Next, internal voltages for PC components range from as little as 1V (volt) up to 12V, but draw differing amounts of current, so the power supply must also step down the voltage. Note, though, that power regulators on the motherboard convert voltages and route power to the expansion slots, CPU, memory and onboard devices.

Key Terms

- Voltage: The force that causes energy to flow. It is usually measured in volts (V).

- Current: The rate at which energy flows or is produced. It is usually measured in amperes (A).

- Rectification: The process by which a power supply converts AC power to DC power.

- Power: The amount of work that can be completed in a given period of time.

- ATX: A particular set of specifications that dictate how a power supply must be built, both in terms of size and in terms of the power it produces.

The third role of the power supply is to meet the power needs of the PC. When the demand for power is high, the power supply increases its production to meet that need. Similarly, when the demand is low, the power supply lowers its production. This saves money on electric bills because the power supply uses only the amount of electricity needed to do its job.

As a result of the power conversion process, a power supply generates a tremendous amount of heat. This heat is as dangerous to the long-term health of your power supply as it is to the rest of your system. The power supply must act in some way to remove the heat that it has generated from your PC, preventing overheating.

This is just a basic overview of how a power supply works. To truly understand how a good power supply benefits your PC and how a poor one can damage it, you have to examine the job of the power supply in closer detail. Before you do that, review the key terms (see sidebar) that will be useful in the discussion.

The Tech: How a Power Supply Works

To understand how a power supply works, take a brief look at the type of power your computers use internally as compared to the type of power your local power company supplies to your home.

As mentioned earlier in this chapter, a PC uses DC power. In this form of power, electricity flows at a constant voltage, never varying as it is supplied to the device using it. For many heavy-duty machines such as trains and elevators, this DC electricity is supplied at relatively high voltages. For your PC, the power supply creates DC electricity at much smaller voltages.

An easy way to visualize the concept of DC power is to consider electricity as water flowing from a garden hose. To supply your PC with "water," the hose pumps it out in a steady, constant stream. This stream can be very forceful or very gentle, but it is always constant.

The electricity provided by your power company is in the form of AC power. Unlike the steady, constant stream of your garden hose, AC power is similar to ocean waves. The "water" arrives in these waves, with a small amount of time between the arrival of each wave. Power utilities use AC power because it is easier to transmit long distances and can be modified by electrical devices to be used for many different purposes. This versatility and ease of transmission doesn't help you power your PC, though. This is where your power supply comes in.

The first task a power supply performs is to take the high-voltage AC power that come from the wall outlet and convert it into lower voltages that are easier to manage. In the water analogy, this changes high oceans waves into smaller, more manageable ones.

Next, the power supply converts this AC power to DC power, which is the type that your computer is looking for. In the water example, this is similar to a funnel on one end of a garden hose. The smaller waves that your power supply "shrunk" enter this funnel and become a stream of water coming out the other end of the hose.

Unfortunately, because the electricity is arriving in the form of these "waves," the other end of the hose is spitting water in an irregular, pulsing manner. The power supply now works to regulate this stream. Using capacitors, it quickly stores some of the electricity from each arriving wave. When the wave starts to recede, it releases that energy, filling in the gap in time before the next wave arrives. The result is a less noticeable pulsing that very closely resembles the DC "garden hose" that your computer needs to operate.

Now that your DC "garden hose" is releasing a relatively steady stream of power, you need to adjust its voltage to be used by the internal components of the system. In the water analogy, voltage is equivalent to the force or the pressure with which the water is flowing from the hose. If you need to water delicate flowers, you use low pressure to avoid damaging them. Conversely, if you are watering a large tree, you can use a higher pressure without fear of damaging the tree.

The power supply splits this DC electricity into three different voltages, with each powering different parts of your computer:

- 3.3 Volts: This voltage is used to power older CPUs, your system memory, and some video cards.
- 5 Volts: This voltage powers your motherboard.
- 12 Volts: This voltage powers newer processors, hard disk drives, CD and DVD drives, and any other devices that have a motor.

Nobody Likes Leftovers: Byproducts of a Power Supply

Thanks to the power supply, you now have electricity in the exact form that you need to run your PC. However, this conversion process creates a very nasty byproduct that we now need to deal with: heat.

As part of the power conversion process, the power supply must lower the voltage of the incoming electricity to smaller amounts usable by the PC. It accomplishes this by converting this excess voltage into a significant amount of heat. The process by which the power supply regulates its DC output is also a major heat contributor.

To combat this heat generation, all PC power supplies are equipped with some form of a cooling system, usually a cooling fan. This fan pulls cooler air into the power supply and the computer case where it absorbs some of this heat before being pushed out of the case. As a result, a power supply not only works to power the system, but it helps to cool it as well.

Power

The whole point of having a power supply is to produce power for your PC. But what exactly is power? And how much of it do we need?

Power is a measurement of how much work can be done in a given period of time. Electrical power is measured in watts (W), and all power supplies list the number of watts they produce. A higher wattage means the power supply can run more devices simultaneously, producing more work in a given period of time.

This leads to another question: how much power do you need for your ultimate gaming PC? Considering that today's processors can consume 100 watts of power, and PCI Express video card can consume another 100 watts, you can tell that you need a significant amount. If you wanted to, you could try to calculate exactly how much power your PC needs, but this is of limited usefulness. You never know when you might buy another drive, a different video card, or even a new processor. Each of the components brings new power requirements, throwing off your calculations.

To be best prepared for the power needs of today and tomorrow, use a power supply with a maximum power of at least 500 watts. Grabbing a supply that is capable of generating this much power ensures that your ultimate gaming PC has all of the power it needs to run today's best hardware. It should also be sufficient for any upgrades you make in the near future.

Why Is a Cheap Power Supply Bad?

If you're like many people out there, your PC case came with a power supply already secured in place. Why not just use this power supply? After all, it's free. All power supplies power a PC when they are plugged in, right? To answer these questions, take a look at what a bad power supply can do to your system.

The Ripple Effect

When we discussed how a power supply converts AC power to DC, we mentioned that the power supply regulates the pulsing effect of converted DC power, releasing a relatively steady stream of electricity. Of course, the stream is not perfectly steady; there is still a slight pulsing effect. The AC "pulse" that is left behind in DC power is often referred to as the ripple.

A quality power supply reduces this ripple greatly, preventing your PC components from noticing it. A poor power supply does not reduce this ripple as much, letting a larger AC pulse reach your PC. If this pulse exceeds the tolerances of your components, it can cause them to malfunction or destroy them completely.

Brownouts

It's hard not to notice a blackout. When the lights go out and everything shuts off, it's bound to get your attention. But do you know what a brownout is?

When electrical demand becomes very high, your power utility may reduce the voltage of the electricity that is being transmitted. This can be noticed by flickering lights, or by lights being dimmer than normal. These visual signs make brownouts easy to identify, but can your computer tell when one is happening?

The power supply attached to your PC expects the power coming from the outlet to be a specific voltage. If the electricity is of a slightly higher or lower voltage, that's okay, too, because it's probably within the tolerances of your power supply, preventing it from affecting the DC power being produced. When a brownout occurs, the voltage being supplied falls well below these tolerances. At this point, a power supply should turn itself off, preventing any irregular DC power from reaching your PC. A poor-quality power supply will not shut itself off cleanly, letting some of this potentially damaging power through to your components.

Heat

It's impossible to build a power supply that doesn't generate heat. Some form of cooling must be used to prevent a buildup of heat in the power supply that could damage it beyond repair. Because most power supplies have at least one cooling fan built in, this is not usually a significant problem.

Unfortunately, one way for a manufacturer to lower costs of their power supply is to use low-quality cooling fans in its construction. These fans may not cool the power supply effectively, reducing its lifespan, or they may not last long themselves, burning out after a year or two of operation.

Power Good Signal

After a power supply first starts up, it takes a few moments before it is generating power at the correct levels for your PC. After it is ready, it sends a signal to your motherboard, telling it to start the computer.

Poor-quality power supplies may not use this signal. Instead, it simply sends the signal to the motherboard immediately, or after a short delay. This can cause your motherboard to try to boot up when proper voltages are not available, resulting in malfunctions or damage to your equipment.

These are just a few of the reasons why you shouldn't be satisfied with the free power supply that came with your case. Instead, try and find a better power supply that will power your ultimate gaming PC for many years.

What to Look for When Shopping for a Power Supply

Exactly how do you pick the best power supply out of the many choices available to you? Take a look at some of the qualities to keep in mind while shopping.

Outstanding Performance

Exactly how do you determine if a power supply offers outstanding performance? Many Internet review sites answer this question by hooking up multimeters and oscilloscopes to various power supplies and measuring the voltage, the "ripple," and more. Afterward, they will not hesitate to tell you that a particular brand outperformed another by .01 volts, or that one power supply was 2 percent closer to specifications than another. Do you really need this kind of information to select a power supply? Put that oscilloscope away; the answer to this question is no.

The truth is, a quality power supply meets or exceeds all of your computing needs. And while some people determine a quality power supply using high-tech tools, you can do it in a much easier way: brand name. Companies like Antech, Enermax, PC Power & Cooling, and Thermaltake consistently produce quality power supplies. If you stick with well-known manufactures like these, you know you're getting outstanding performance.

Note that each power supply has a set of rails that can deliver current independently. However, in a poor power supply, the sum of the current loads on individual rails may actually be greater than the rated power of the power supply. You could then run into intermittent stability problems.

Power Connectors

Each component in your PC requires power. As a result, they need a corresponding plug on your power supply. Every power supply has the main power connector necessary to power your motherboard; however, if you have two DVD drives, three or four hard drives, and three case fans in addition to other power components, you can start to run out of plugs very quickly. There are extension cables that can add an extra plug or two to your power supply, but you don't want to rely on these to meet your needs. Be sure that there are a sufficient number of connectors to fit every component in your system.

In addition to the number of plugs, be sure to check that you have the right type of plugs. SATA hard drives have introduced a different type of power connector that not every power supply provides. If you use drives that require this connector, be sure that it's part of your power supply.

Cable Management Systems

If you've ever worked with a power supply before, you know that it can be very difficult to work with its power cables. This multi-colored spaghetti that reaches into your case can get tangled with other cables. If you don't use every connection, wires not in use just dangle in the case. In short, it's a big mess.

Some power supplies now utilize cable management systems to solve some of these issues. Cables can be sheathed in a mesh covering, helping to reduce that multi-colored mess. Other power supplies have cables that can be removed when not in use, keeping extra cables from cluttering your case. Buying a power supply with some sort of cable management system only serves to make your life easier.

Fan Noise

Power supply fans help to keep your computer cool, but they can be very loud. Well aware that a noisy power supply can turn away customers, power supply manufacturers are working to keep things silent. They are now using high-quality, quiet fans in their power supplies. Innovations in fan speed have also been a great help. Some manufacturers have added sensors that run the fan only as fast as necessary to cool the power supply. At times of light use, the fan runs slower and quieter. As load increases, the fan speed increases only as much as is necessary, keeping the corresponding increase in fan noise to a minimum. Other manufacturers have added fan controllers that can be mounted to an empty bay in your case, giving you complete control over fan speed and noise. Also, look for 120mm fans in the power supply that can move the same amount of air, but turn more slowly and are (usually) quieter than power supplies with smaller fans.

Warranty

As with all computer components, see how well a manufacturer supports their product by checking the warranty that comes with your power supply. If you see a guarantee that your product will be free from defects for two or even five years, you know that the company backs their workmanship. Be sure to consider warranty length when choosing your power supply.

Selecting Our Ultimate Power Supply

Now that you know what to look for, it's time to select our ultimate power supply. With so many quality candidates, it looks like this could be one of the hardest choices we've had to make yet. After much research, we've narrowed our choices down to the Thermaltake PurePower TWV500W and the PC Power and Cooling Turbo-Cool 510 SLI. While we try to make this decision, take a look at some of their specifications in Table 9-1.

Table 9-1   Power Supply Comparison

	PurePower TWV500W	Turbo-Cool 510 SLI
Maximum Power (Watts)	500W	650W
Molex Power Connectors	9	8
Floppy Power Connectors	2	1
SATA Connectors	4	6
PCI Express Connectors	2	2
Warranty	2 years	5 years
Cable Management	Removable cables, covered cables	Covered cables
Extras	Case fan, fan controller	None
Estimated Price	$120	$220

If you take a look at the specifications, the Turbo-Cool 510 SLI definitely scores some points, especially in the maximum power department.

The PurePower TWV500W comes out ahead in the connectors department when matched up with our system. The extra power connector helps us out with the multiple fans that came with our case. The extra floppy connector is needed to power our Sound Blaster Platinum Drive.

In terms of warranty, we would have liked to see a few extra years out of Thermaltake; however, any warranty pales in comparison to the five years offered by PC Power and Cooling, one of the best warranties in the business.

The cable management system began to tip the scales in favor of the PurePower TWV500W. The fact that we have to use only the cables that we actually need is a great feature, especially when you consider that our SATA drives utilize regular molex power connectors. The idea of having the 6 SATA connectors of the Turbo-Cool 510 SLI clogging our case was not appealing.

The fan controller that came with the PurePower TWV500W is a nice bonus feature. The ability to control not only the speed of the power supply fan but of the included case fan as well is a nice extra.

Finally, with the PurePower TWV500W coming it at $100 less than the PC Power and Cooling model, Thermaltake's power supply offers a little more value for the money spent.

In the end, we selected Thermaltake's PurePower TWV500W as our ultimate power supply, although either brand would have made an excellent choice. A picture of our chosen part is seen in Figure 9-1.

FIGURE 9-1: The Thermaltake PurePower TWV500W.

How to Save Money in This Category

Similar to a computer case, it can be difficult to save a great deal of money in this category. You definitely don't want to settle for a low-quality power supply, especially when you consider the amount of money being spent on your other system components.

You might be able to save a little money in the category by changing the focus of your search. Begin by finding power supplies with a maximum power of 500 watts or more at your favorite store or Website. From these choices, isolate the reliable brands that we mentioned earlier in this chapter. There should be at least a $20 or $30 difference between the highest-priced brand and the lowest. Just be aware that this savings may be a result of the power supply not having a cable management system or other such features.

Before you buy a power supply that you find on this bargain hunt, be sure that it has enough power connectors to meet your needs; otherwise, that $30 savings may prevent you from running an extra DVD drive or case fan.

What's Next?

Now that you have a way to power your PC, you're done with components that fit inside your case. That doesn't mean the next part isn't any less important. On the contrary, it could be one of the most vital pieces of your ultimate gaming PC. It's time to find your ultimate monitor!

Choosing Your Ultimate Monitor

In this chapter we discuss the possible choices for monitors and what might be best for your ultimate gaming PC. With only two core choices out there, either CRT or LCD, it may be pretty simple to narrow down the field to the type of monitor you want. But just because you decide what type of monitor is ultimate enough for you doesn't mean there are not a bunch of decisions still to be made.

Monitors are a very important part of the gaming experience. How bright or lush the colors are onscreen can affect how the game looks. Even the size of the monitor screen can make huge changes in the feel and enjoyment of a game. When monitors are small, you don't see a lot of detail; however, on a large screen, those models and textures really come to life. Basically, in a monitor, you want nothing but the best in color, brightness, resolution, and size.

Some people might think that a monitor is a monitor is a monitor, but that is far from the case. The difference between a high-quality monitor and some low-end no-name one can be just like watching your favorite movie on a really expensive television and then watching the same movie on a television that has been sitting in the attic for 20 years. It could be near appalling.

In the following pages we go over all the ins and out of monitors to help educate you on their important factors. Through the monitor is where you see the results of your computing power. If you can't see it well, and with quality, you undermine all the other work you have done in building your super computer.

On top of all that, monitors aren't just monitors anymore. Wait until you see some of the accessories they can come with these days. These aren't the days of your father's monitor, so come along as we find out what is the ultimate gaming monitor.

Key Terms

- CRT (Cathode-Ray Tube): Monitors essentially using the same technology as a standard television (one with a picture tube and not a newer LCD or Plasma). It works by scanning a continuous beam from top to bottom of a large vacuum bottle that excites the individual phosphors onscreen, collectively producing a picture. The CRT electron beam excites phosphors that combine to form individual pixels.

- Pixels (Picture Elements): Individual points of a screen or graphic. Basically, the pixels are what make the "picture" by blending thousands (if not millions) of individual points of colored light into a collage that appears to be one smooth image.

- LCD (Liquid Crystal Display): Screens used in most laptops and becoming "the norm" for many home computing screens. One of the original uses of this technology was for "digital" watches but has evolved to include the computer industry and beyond. This technology uses two sheets of polarized material with a liquid crystal solution between the layers. Rather than having a continuous beam scanning the screen, the crystals act as individual pixels that allow only the color band of light designated to them to pass.

- DVI (Digital Visual Interface): Allows the data transfer from the computer to remain in digital form instead of converting it to analog. DVI allows the digital signals to pass directly to the display, bypassing the DAC (digital-to-analog converter) on the graphics card. Most graphics cards with DVI outputs support the DVI-I version of the standard. This also lets you attach an analog, VGA display if you have the correct adapter.

- VGA (Video Graphics Array): An IBM-developed graphics interface that is so widely used that it has become the standard monitor or display interface of many computing systems. A standard VGA connection has 15 pins (3 rows of 5 staggered pins) and has a trapezoidal shape. If a monitor is VGA compatible, it should work with most new computers. VGA has become a "catch-all" phrase mostly denoting the analog, 15-pin connector rather than the actual resolution of the display.

- Response Rate: The rate of time it takes for a pixel to react after it's activated. This is usually rated in milliseconds (e.g., a response rate of 16 is equivalent to 16ms). This can directly translate to frame rate—a 16ms response time equates to 60 frames per second. LCDs tend to have a slower response rate than CRTs, although they are rapidly improving.

- Resolution: Refers to the total number of pixels used to create an image.

The Tech: How Does the Monitor Do What It Does?

In this chapter we discuss the important aspects of monitors and what points to consider when purchasing one for your ultimate computer. With that said, what is a monitor? The monitor is the "window to the soul" of your gaming computer. It does not help your computer run faster, leap higher, or think quicker, but it does allow you to see your new computer doing many of these activities. (Well, maybe not the leaping.) Without a properly chosen monitor, you may not be able to see all the benefits of having your own super computer. The monitor must be able to display the benefits of the speed, color, and detail for you to appreciate all the work you have done to build your computer.

The first aspect of monitors to know about is size. How much room do you have for a monitor? This is important not just for height and width, but for depth. The size of a monitor is determined much like that of your standard home television. It is measured diagonally across the screen from corner to corner. Note that CRT measurements vary more than LCD. A 19-inch CRT may have 17.5 inches to 18.5 inches of actual diagonal viewing area, where 19-inch LCDs are pretty much all 19 inches. The 17-inch monitor is the minimum standard of what is available.

Now that you have the size of the monitor fresh in your head, think about its resolution. Resolution refers to the number of pixels that the monitor can support. This is determined by the number of pixels of the monitor (individual points of colored light that, when looked as a whole, produce a picture), the capabilities of those pixels, and the spacing between them. Each monitor screen is made up of thousands, if not millions, of pixels, depending on the model.

Monitor resolution is usually given as a horizontal resolution times a vertical resolution, such as 1280x1024. Note that a smaller display that can generate a 1280x1024 pixel image is denser than a large display that can do the same. You may see references to DPI (dots per inch), which refers to the pixel density of the display. Mostly, though, gamers are concerned with resolution rather than pixel density.

This is important because a 15-inch monitor with a resolution of 1024x768 is much clearer and sharper than a 24-inch monitor with the same rating. But the quality of the display also is a factor. Although no 24-inch monitor would have that rating, we hope, it is serving here as an example. The reason being is that the dot pitch (the space between the pixels) is much smaller or more compact with the smaller monitor, allowing a cleaner, sharper image. For this reason, it is important to note that with larger monitors, you want a higher resolution rating if you wish to achieve the same crispness as its smaller counterparts. For instance a 24-inch widescreen monitor would look best at 1600x1024 or higher resolution. Because it is bigger in screen size, it requires more pixels to make it look as clear.

Always look at a monitor's "native resolution." This is the resolution that the monitor is rated for, will work best with, and is mainly a factor with LCDs. You can set the resolution to anything you want, but it might look blurry or pixilated if you use anything other than the native resolution of your specific monitor. Because the pixel positions are fixed on an LCD, they have one optimum resolution. CRT pixels are made up of clusters of phosphors, and the phosphors tend to bloom together, making lower resolutions look less pixilated.

Modern LCD displays have sophisticated video scaling circuitry that actually allows images to look pretty good at resolutions lower than the display's native resolutions. In a few cases, some can even scale down higher resolutions and still look fairly good.

Because high-quality video cards let you play games at 1600x1200 with all the settings turned up, you may want a monitor with 1600x1200 as its native resolution. However, when your video card ages and doesn't perform as well, you can do two things to improve the frame rate: lower the detail setting of your card, or lower the resolution. A CRT owner could choose to lower either one. The LCD must interpolate two or more pixels on a lower resolution to generate the same effect as simply lighting up one pixel on a higher resolution.

Now let's talk about refresh rates. CRTs and LCDs build their images one line at a time. They go through processes until the entire screen is drawn, and only then do they start to draw the next frame of information. How fast a CRT can redraw the frame per second is called its refresh rate, and refresh rate is measured in hertz (Hz).

Sometimes with a CRT, refresh rates below 70 Hz be can seen by the human eye as flickering because the phosphors need to be constantly excited by the electron gun. The larger the monitor, the more obvious the flickering. For this reason, many computers have their refresh rate set at a minimum of 75 Hz. Because they are a completely different technology, LCDs don't have the same problem. If you put up a still image on an LCD, the pixels are simply on all the time with no flicker at all.

So, how does your computer talk to your monitor? This is where we get into the aspects of VGA and DVI interfaces. These are the two most common forms of cable technology designed to get the information from the computer onto the screen of your monitor. Over the years, the VGA cable has become the standard cable connection from computer to monitor. It is a 15-pin, trapezoidal array that was developed in 1987 by IBM. This interface is so common that it is unlikely that you will find a system that does not support this connection. This is truly one of the benefits of the VGA system. VGA is analog, and so the graphics cards have DACs (digital to analog converters) built onto the GPU.

DVI is different because the data is actually transmitted digitally from the computer to the screen. With VGA, the digital data from the computer gets changed from digital to analog because the VGA is analog. When that change occurs, a bit of degradation of the data takes place. DVI transmits the data from its core digital form and keeps it that way to make the most out of the information being sent. A DVI connection provides sharper, clearer, and faster refresh rates if your video card supports DVI technology. This, of course, is provided that both the monitor and the DVI interface on the graphics card comply properly with the DVI standard. The digital information allows more information to be processed to the monitor, at a rate of up to 165 MHz, and can vastly improve the quality of the picture. With a DVI connection, you can also use HDTV and UXGA, both of which greatly improve resolution even more, just to put into perspective the increased capabilities of DVI.

There are two main divisions of monitors now on the market — the CRT and the ever-increasingly popular LCD. The CRT (Cathode Ray Tube) monitor is the same monitor type that was first used with home computers. LCD (Liquid Crystal Display) monitors are the next evolution in the computer market. They are the thinner, flatter monitors that are dropping rapidly in price.

No longer is a monitor just like any other monitor. There can be a huge difference in what you get and what you see, depending on which brand and size of monitor you have. For a long time with computer monitors, you really didn't have a choice of what type of monitor you wanted. You could decide on the brand and size, but there were only CRT monitors out there. In the past years, however, a new type of monitor has been making its rise in a big, big way.

When the first LCD, or flatscreen, monitors hit the market, they were barely affordable, even at a measly 15 inches in screen size. Now they are everywhere and working hard to become the new standard. So much so that Sony has nearly decided that they will not make CRTs any longer, and are devoting their efforts on the flatscreens. This tells us that CRTs may be on their permanent way out, making LCDs the new and perhaps only monitor standard. Time will tell, but the CRT had a good long run.

The CRT versus LCD war is similar to the new flatscreen televisions versus the regular old standard large box televisions. More and more, people want bigger and bigger televisions. To get that, they are buying the flatscreens because they save size in a large way, and the screens are actually larger. This is the same concept and the same technology that is powering the LCD monitors to take over the CRT market.

The LCD monitor had a slow start. The technology was new, and it certainly wasn't perfect. People expected the same type of color and quality that came with the CRT, and they weren't quite getting it. The screens could be really dark, especially for gaming, thus making dim, murky dungeons nearly impossible to see. That was a big a drawback. The good news is that times have changed and so has the technology. LCDs have evolved and become much better.

The following sections take a look at these monitors in more detail.

CRTs

We mentioned that CRTs have had a good long run, and it's true. The technology used to create CRT monitors has been around since 1897. It is also the same technology that makes televisions functional, which is why they have a similar shape. A big difference between televisions and computer monitors is that the television monitors are designed to be looked at from across the room, and the computer monitor requires a much closer feel. It creates an interesting dilemma as the size of monitors is rapidly growing to meet the smaller-sized televisions.

CRT monitors have been the industry standard since the beginning of computers. They may not have been as lavish back then with the black background and ugly green text, but they have proved themselves over the years. With that in mind, it is easy to understand why they are also the most common type of monitor in the world. CRTs are everywhere. The technology used to make them is now so cheap that sometimes when you buy a packaged computer, they toss in a 15-inch monitor for free.

One of the problems causing the CRTs to loose the battle with the LCDs is that even small CRTs are heavy. And the bigger they get, the heavier they get. This makes them difficult and troublesome to move. Another reason for the CRTs' loss of popularity is that like any tube monitor, be it television or a monitor, the bigger the screen size you want, the bulkier the device becomes. A 21-inch CRT monitor can nearly take over an entire desktop. They have a wonderful picture that is clean, crisp and bright, with superior black levels, but if you have nowhere to place your keyboard or mouse pad, the monitor becomes slightly less functional.

The good news about CRTs is that with the rise of LCDs, the price on these has gone down a little. You can get a nice-sized monitor, if you have room to hold it, for a fair price — much less than what you would pay for an LCD. Just think of the cost for a flatscreen television, and what it costs for the ones with picture tubes. It's a similar comparison.

The last point to understand about CRTs is that they seem to be limited in size. Sony did come out with a 24-inch monitor for a short while, but that looks as though it may be the limit of how large manufacturers want to go. Beyond that size, it is easier to make LCD monitors.

LCDs

The CRT is the old standby, but you want to build the ultimate gaming PC. And to do that, you need fresh, new, and overpowered technology. In terms of monitors, that means having extra features and capabilities that are not the standard any more. So, of course you are leaning toward LCD monitors. Why, you ask? Well, because with an LCD monitor, you can get a larger-sized screen that is not reasonably possible with a CRT as well as getting it in widescreen format.

One of the best selling points that LCDs have going for them is that from a viewpoint of a common appraisal, a CRT monitor takes up about three times more space than an LCD monitor. That is a huge savings of space. Instead of a CRT monitor being 1 foot thick, an LCD monitor is perhaps 3 inches thick. Now you have room on your desk for all your extra peripherals. Your joysticks, Wacom tablets, extra speakers, and driving wheel because your monitor isn't taking up all the room.

LCD technology works by using a different principle than CRT. It doesn't use an electron beam to excite phosphors, but instead uses the crystals in conjunction with a backlight and color filters to create the image. Essentially, they block all the colors except the color that the pixel is supposed to be, and this creates the image on the screen.

One "gotcha" of the LCD-type monitor is that the response time of pixels isn't as fast as a good CRT. The faster the pixel response time, the faster the maximum frame rate. Table 10-1 shows response times versus maximum frame rate.

Table 10-1: Response Time Versus Maximum Frame Rate

Pixel Response Time (ms)	Maximum Frame Rate (FPS)
25	40
20	50
16	62
12	83
8	125

You can get an LCD that has close to the response time of a CRT, but you end up paying a significant amount for that. For gaming — and that's all you care about — you really need that fast response time or you may get what is called "ghosting." Ghosting is when the previous image sent to your monitor for the slightest fraction of a second remains there as the new image is sent to the monitor. The effect is that you see both at the same time, but only for a fraction of a second. Some people can't even see it, but it can be annoying to others.

Unless you've been gaming on CRT for a long time, you probably won't notice a difference on LCD. The bottom line is that when buying an LCD for the purpose of gaming, you don't want to skimp on response time. The drawback of spending a lot on an LCD with a great response time is that you could get a really good and likely larger-sized-screen CRT for the same price.

In a little more detail the common response time of an average CRT is around 4ms; the response time for an average LCD is 25ms. That's a substantial difference, so you generally see very little ghosting on CRTs. However, newer LCDs have response times of 16ms or lower. We've even seen a few 8ms panels announced. And this brings up the question, "why not just go for the monitor that saves space?"

Brightness is another important factor regarding LCDs. The larger the LCD becomes, the more brightness seems to become a factor. When understanding brightness in regards to LCDs, just remember that you want all that you can get. Brighter is better. Brightness on an LCD monitor is gauged in candela per meter squared, also known as cd/m2. This is the amount of light that filters through the liquid crystals and is then seen by you. A good brightness is 500 cd/m^2. Note, however, that very bright LCDs may also have uneven backlighting, so you may want to actually turn the brightness down a bit.

Unlike CRTs, LCDs have the native resolution factor to contend with. The image quality on some LCDs suffers at non-native resolutions, but the advent of sophisticated video processors is making that less of a problem. CRTs don't have this problem. Ideally, you want a video card that offers solid performance at the native resolution of the LCD, but it's still good to have an LCD with a good video processor. Some games may simply not have the option of running at the native resolution.

LCDs have become substantially better over the years. Ghosting is disappearing, or is already gone. The dimness they had in darker-toned games is gone. LCDs have come a long way and are a prime choice for a gaming computer.

How Big Is Too Big for a Monitor?

How big is too big? Well, like most things, that really depends on you. But I can't think of any gamer we know who would turn down a larger monitor if they were offered one. Monitors are how you get to visually realize the intent of the game makers. It is your lens into their work and your fun. You are supposed to be immersed in games. They are designed to draw you in, and the better you can see the game, the more involved and overwhelmed you will likely be by its brilliance.

Monitors are now coming in all shapes and sizes, and they are still growing. The bottom of the chain, or at least the absolute minimum you would want as a gaming monitor, is probably 17 inches. You would be hard-pressed to find a smaller size nowadays as the 15-inch monitors are slowly dying off with everybody wanting bigger and bigger.

With 17 inches of viewable space you could play all your games. The art of the characters might be a bit small, and you would probably miss some of the little details the game designers put in there, but you would be able to play and enjoy the core essence of the game. On the other hand, competitive players of RTS (real time strategy) games prefer the smaller size because they can take in the entire screen without moving their eyes.

The next step up is 19-inch monitors. Now we are getting into some flavor. Just 2 inches bigger than the 17-inch monitor, but the difference can be rather astounding. Details begin to come to life. You might even see the little insignias drawn onto your swordmaster's leather armor. As a serious gamer who is building the ultimate computer, if at all possible financially, 19 inches is the minimum you want to have.

The next jump up in size gets a bit messy, at least in terms of LCD. You can get a 20-inch, 20.1-inch, and 21.3-inch monitors. There might even be more in the mix, but you get the idea. You have a lot of choices, and as you get close to this size you are already getting big enough in terms of size that any little difference really won't be that great. CRTs are a little different than LCDs; with a CRT, you jump straight from 19-inch monitors to 21-inch monitors. That is a substantial difference. It is like watching a baseball game from the nosebleed bleacher seats and then watching the same game from much closer and nicer box seats. With monitors, you get what you pay for in terms of size, very much like televisions. Televisions can never be too big.

Admittedly, some people who get really large monitors actually find them too big. They don't like the fact that they have to turn their head to take in the whole scene on the monitor. They can no longer see it all at a glance. Some people who get the next size up have mentioned they get slightly motion sick when playing first-person shooters on the 23- or 24-inch wide screen monitors. These things are beautiful, a monitor that eclipses the horizon. But as we said, it's only beautiful to those who don't mind a vast expanse of visual space and don't feel queasy fragging their friends on Doom 3 while playing on it.

Continuing with the baseball game analogy, going up to a 24-inch flatscreen LCD from a 19-inch monitor is similar to going from the box seats to right behind the dugout. You are there, you are in the game, you can see it all, and it's clear, perfect, and crisp.

The level of detail gets to be incredible. The characters and enemies become larger, proportional to the size increase of your screen. Along with the insignias on your leather armor, you might also see the stitching that holds it together as you hack your way through the legions of the dead. All the little details come to life and that's when you need to be careful because it is just about then that you get sucked into the engrossing landscape and never leave the house again.

The size of a monitor does matter in the end. Your best bet is to buy the largest monitor while still retaining quality that you can afford on your budget. You won't be disappointed.

Warning If you buy a big CRT monitor, make sure that you have room for it on your desk or table. They can be rather large and very heavy to move, even for those people who are fit. Also, make sure your desk can bear the weight of the heavy load. It would probably not be a happy experience to buy a monitor that you couldn't fit into or on your desk, and then have you desk crumble under the weight of the monitor.

Are There Ways to Save Money on Monitors?

There are actually ways in which you can save money while shopping for a monitor, though none that are great. If you really needed to cut down the cost of your ultimate gaming PC, you could buy a lower-quality monitor. This means putting that 24-inch Sony CRT back on the shelf. It may be a very valid and large savings. Not going with any of the extreme top brands can save quite a bit of money, but only if you don't mind the reduction in visual quality.

You can pick up lower-end brands for hundreds of dollars less, but the problem with this is that the quality and reliability of the monitor is likely to significantly decrease in direct correlation with the financial savings.

Another way you can save money on your monitor is to keep the same brand you had in mind, but buy the next screen size down. Not buying the cutting-edge size, which is currently about 24+ inches, can save you quite a few precious pennies. Here's an example we just pulled off of Newegg.com. You can buy a Samsung 24-inch LCD flat screen monitor for $1,600. If you need to save money, you can buy a 21.3-inch monitor, also by Samsung, for $644. That's nearly a $1,000 in savings for buying the next size down and not buying the cutting edge technology. Prices fluctuate and will probably decrease by the time you read this, but the premise is the same and will still be in effect as the 26+-inch monitors get rolled out into the world.

The next option for saving money on monitors is buying them used. Monitors are really the only component, except maybe for a case or a mouse, that you can chance by buying used. All the other parts are so delicate that you are best off getting them new. But monitors are a bit more durable as long as they are taken care of properly.

Chances are you won't get the warranty on a used monitor, but it can be a bit of a savings. eBay is one place you might look for a good deal, but remember if you buy it from a place like eBay you will likely have to pay for the shipping costs that could hit around $50, depending on the size, type, and weight of the monitor you purchase. On average, shipping an LCD monitor is cheaper than a CRT because they weigh substantially less.

You can also look in the newspaper or any online site that you know of to find a good deal. You might just get lucky and come across somebody moving, who has just upgraded, or has decided they don't need a computer anymore and is trying to get rid of their equipment quickly but at a fair price. You just never know when a good deal will pop up, and only those who are looking get to take advantage of them.

And of course, buying a CRT monitor rather than an LCD can save you money. It all comes back to buying the latest technology. If you want it, you have to pay for it. A Viewsonic 22-inch CRT monitor costs only $529, whereas the 21.3-inch Samsung LCD that we mentioned earlier costs $644. Admittedly, the brands are different, which isn't really a bad thing, and you need more space for a CRT monitor of that size, but it is a way to save money.

How Can I Get the Best Performance from My Monitor?

The answer to this is similar to asking about optimizing your television. You basically want the same things — a clear, bright, and sharp picture that is pleasing to the eye.

So what does that mean regarding a monitor? Well, actually, the same things. You want the brightness set so you can see blacks as true lightness black, and whites as bright as they can be. You want the image completely in focus, altered by adjusting the sharpness just as on a television. You also may want to adjust the contrast to something that better suits your eyes.

All of this, and a little more, can be done by using the menu on your monitor, normally accessed by pressing a button or turning a dial that brings up the monitor settings. Each monitor is different, and you have to figure out how to scroll through the menus with a series of button presses, but eventually you find all that you want and can tune you monitor into the exact look that you desire.

Note If you have a problem navigating the settings of your monitor, reference your user's manual for a little more help on the subject.

You can adjust the position of the viewable content on a monitor, but the viewable area on a television always remains in place. Monitor settings enable you to adjust the height and width of the shown screen as well as move it up, down, left, and right. You can also choose your screen resolution, and adjust the screen so it stretches to the absolute limits without the picture disappearing off the screen. Some monitors have auto-adjust features that automatically perform these settings for you.

Note If you connect via the DVI port, you may lose most of your adjustment options. You can use the graphics control panel on your PC to make similar adjustments.

What Should I Consider When Buying a Monitor?

Here are a few points to keep in mind when shopping for your monitor. Your first consideration, like any purchase, is how much can you spend. Before we talked about how big is too big for a monitor, you should assume any monitor you can't afford is too big.

CRTs are the old standby. They are reliable and get the job done for many years. CRTs are larger in size and have nearly reached a limit of 22 to 24 inches in screen size. Newegg.com doesn't even carry monitors that are larger than 22 inches in size.

LCDs, on the other hand, can be found reaching 30 inches. The 30-inch Cinema HD Display M9179ll/A is Apple's 30-inch monitor. It is very costly, but you won't find a comparison in the CRT market. So if extreme size is your goal, LCDs might be the choice for you. Beware, however, that you need a very high end graphics card with dual DVI outputs to support it.

CRTs take up more power than LCD monitors, and they generate more heat. A CRT monitor takes 50 to 70% more energy to run than an LCD. That equals near an additional 100 kilowatts of power a year to have a CRT monitor rather than an LCD. You save on electricity with an LCD, but it takes more cash to purchase one. So are the savings in electricity a huge deal? Probably not, but it's something to think about.

The average CRT monitor has only a VGA connector and not DVI. This limits you somewhat if you want the newer technology. The video card we choose has two DVI ports on the back, and there is no VGA connector. This is an example of how cutting-edge video cards are doing away with VGA technology. The good news is that a simple adapter allows you to connect from VGA to DVI without a problem. Most current LCD monitors have DVI connections that you can use.

LCD monitors are more compact than CRTs. If you have a large room with a large desk, a CRT will probably suit you just fine, and you can save a few dollars buying one. But if you are in a cramped room with meager desk space that is already cluttered with books and action figures, you might not have desk real estate available for a CRT. In that case, an LCD is a better choice. Plus the smaller the monitor, the easier it is to move. You won't have to ask your friends to come over and help you hoist your 21-inch CRT from the box onto your desk.

Dead pixels are a problem with LCD monitors. A dead pixel happens when one of the pixels on your screen no longer works, leaving it unlit and appearing like a black speck on your screen. Or you may have a "stuck" pixel that's always on. These can be just as annoying. Dead or stuck pixels can be a problem with any LCD technology. A good example is when Sony launched the PSP. Many consumers complained that they had anywhere from one to several dead pixels on their new toy. It's not the end of the world; you can return the monitor and ask for a replacement, but if you ordered your monitor online, you might have to pay shipping to return it. Dead pixels can be a problem, but it is by no means a rampant problem as long as the manufacturer cares about its product.

If you want a widescreen format monitor, you want an LCD. CRT doesn't offer much in widescreen, but many LCD models do. It is a great feature, especially on larger-sized screens. The screen is so wide that you can have several full gaming Web pages open at once, or a cheat code Web page and your email, or a Web page and Word document each sitting side by side. It makes toggling back and forth easier when you don't actually have to toggle, but rather just turn your head. It's also a great screen for DVD movies. Some of these monitors are larger than low-end televisions and can handle HD technology to give you a crisp image.

Monitors are not just monitors anymore — or at least LCDs aren't. While shopping around, look for monitors that have extra features. Some may offer FireWire, USB, Flashcard readers, and other useful interfaces that can make your life easier. These features are usually on the side of the monitor or underneath the screen. Having extra features like this could mean not having to buy a USB hub for all your extra gadgets, or not having to buy a card reader to download all the pictures off of your camera. This is a nice way to save some money on extras that you might have wanted anyway.

As always, regardless of what type of monitor you buy, get a reliable and lengthy warranty. With monitors, if you can get a one-year warranty, you've done well. Some companies, such as Dell, give only 90 days with their LCDs. Also, like every other product we mentioned, don't buy no-name brands. The likelihood that you will suffer in quality and reliability is just too big of a chance to take.

Make sure you shop around, and that you look at sale items. Try to find rebates or free shipping, if at all possible. The cost to ship a monitor can be significant — upwards of $50.

The great thing about monitors is that you actually have a chance to see them before you buy them. Generally speaking, you can't look at or even touch hard drives, memory, and video cards before you buy them. With monitors, however, you can go to your local BestBuy or CompUSA and actually see the monitors in action. You can see what size they really are and get a grasp of what might suit your needs.

One warning — the monitors in the stores are on all day every day. And tons of people play with and touch them, changing settings, making them dirty, and likely knocking them out of tune or calibration. So if you do look at monitors in the stores, take your initial impression with a grain of salt and know that these monitors have already been through the ringer.

Before You Buy a Monitor

- Make sure your video card can handle the native resolution of the LCD monitor.

- If the monitor is LCD, make sure it has DVI input on it, even if you don't have a DVI compatible video card yet.

- Make sure that you are buying at least a 17-inch monitor, if you can budget it.

- Make sure that the manufacturer or retailer offers free shipping, if at all possible.

- Make sure you have room on your desk for the size of monitor you want.

- Make sure that you're shopping at a reliable source.

What Are the Top Two Monitor Manufacturers?

With the information from this chapter under our belt, we are finally ready to scour the market and come up with some top picks for your monitor. What is a good monitor for gaming, we asked ourselves. Not only in terms of size, but of quality, price, and options. After a bit a research, we found we didn't have many reliable choices from which to choose. After all, our goal is to find the ultimate monitor, and that means it has to be big — as big as possible but still somewhat reasonably priced. We have to go with the LCD monitor, in part so we don't have to hire a forklift to move it around.

By choosing the LCD, we can go larger than a CRT, but we can save space at the same time. And potentially we can get a few of those extra built-in options we mentioned.

We found there were only two prime choices in the LCD marketplace, thus making our decision process easier than it has been in other chapters. It took only a quick look before we made a decision.

Table 10-2 lists and details the top two LCD monitor choices we found. We chose these two monitors because they met all the criteria that we desire in a gaming monitor.

Table 10-2: Comparing Monitors

	Dell	Apple
Name	UltraSharp 2405FPW Flat Panel	Cinema HD Display M9178ll/A
Type	LCD Flat Panel	LCD Flat Panel
Screen Size	24 inches	23 inches
Native Resolution	1920 by 1200	1920 by 1200
Aspect Ratio	16:10	16:10
Video Inputs	Component, Composite, DVI, and S-Video	DVI

	Dell	Apple
PC Interface	Analog VGA and DVI	DVI and Vesa DDC
Pixel Response Time	16 milliseconds	16 milliseconds
Rated Contrast Ratio	1000:1	400:1
Brightness	500 cd/m^2	270 cd/m^2
Height Adjustment	Up to 3.93 inches	None
Screen Rotation	Yes	No
TV-Tuner	No	No
Built-In Flashcard Reader	Yes	No: but has two FireWire ports
Built-In USB Ports	Yes: 4	Yes: 2
Warranty	90 days	1 year limited
Lowest Price	$1,199	$1,499

Our Pick

Looking at Table 10-2, you can see that the two monitors have a great deal in common, or are at least are on par with each other. But after we examined and compared the factors that are different, the final decision seemed obvious.

So without further ado, our choice for monitor on our ultimate gaming PC is the Dell UltraSharp 2405FPW flat panel. Across the board it beat Apple's M9178ll/A Cinema HD Display. The Dell is a bigger monitor — an inch over the Apple's 23 inches. The 2405FPW Ultra offers more options for video inputs, and it also has the Picture-In-Picture feature.

The contrast ratio is probably the biggest difference between the two monitors. The Apple has only 400:1 while the Dell achieved 1000:1. This means that on the UltraSharp 2405FPW, the range in blacks and whites is much more significant. The Dell's 12ms response time also makes it a better monitor for PC gaming.

The stand for the UltraSharp 2405FPW lets you adjust the height of the monitor. Because people are not all equal in height, this is nice feature that allows you to comfortably adjust the monitor so you don't have to crane your neck up or down to view it.

When you add up all the features and options, along with the extra ports and flashcard reader, then throw in the $300 price difference, we are positive we have a winner. Dell is a strong force in the monitors market, in part because they have cut their prices beneath that of their competitors and still offer a reliable product.

We choose the Dell UltraSharp 2405FPW flat panel because it is a large monitor that enables our games to come to life. All 24 inches of this beautiful piece of hardware allow us to see the full glory of all our games, whether they be RPGs, FPSs, or the Sims. Plus it's a widescreen format! The Dell UltraSharp 2405FPW flat panel is shown in Figure 10-1.

FIGURE 10-1: Our pick as the best monitor for the ultimate gaming computer: Dell UltraSharp 2405FPW flat panel.

Photo courtesy of Dell Inc.

What's Next?

With the choice of an ultimate monitor, it's time to move forward. In Chapter 11, "Selecting the Ultimate Gaming Accessories," you learn about all the extra devices that you may not actually need, but probably really want to have. These include gaming keyboards, wireless laser mice, and incredible speakers that are as good as (or even better than) a home stereo system. Turn the page and keep moving because it's getting close to gaming time!

Color Figure 1: Our pick—The AMD Athlon 64 FX-55. Our choice was also based on the established 64-bit processing history of the AMD line, readying this processor for the Windows OS of tomorrow. We also chose this processor because it will allow us to use future AMD technologies without having to buy a new motherboard for our PC. Finally, the $200 price difference was a great plus. In the end, the AMD processor was exactly what we wanted, both now and in the near future.

Color Figure 2: We chose the Gigabyte GA-K8N Ultra-9 as the motherboard for our Ultimate Gaming PC.

Color Figure 3: With the small extra punch that the manufacturer's overclocking brings, and the excellent tech support, the BFG Geforce 6800 Ultra OC is the video card for our Ultimate Gaming PC.

Color Figure 4: Our pick as best primary hard drive—the Western Digital Raptor WD740GD 10,000RPM 8MB cache SATA hard drive. We chose two of the same hard drives to use in a RAID0.

Picture courtesy of Western Digital.

Color Figure 5: Our pick as best secondary hard drive for the Ultimate Gaming Computer: Western Digital Caviar RE WD2500SD. We also chose to have an additional drive for storage which was a WD2500SD also made by Western Digital.

Picture courtesy of Western Digital.

Color Figure 6: Our ultimate sound card, the SoundBlaster Audigy 2 ZS. The Platinum Drive that comes with the sound card rounds out the package. This input/output panel is mounted in a drive bay in the front of the case. It is covered will all of the input and output jacks that you could possibly need, with the headphone jack probably being the most useful. Volume control knobs on the panel allow the user to adjust headphone volume independently from the OS volume level and the volume of the speakers. A firewire port is also available on the front panel, making it easier for you to plug in an MP3 player or external hard drive that utilizes this port. While the Maya 1010 also had a front panel, it was designed with professional recording in mind instead of gaming.

Color Figure 7: After spending an hour or so debating, we settled on the Thermaltake Armor VA8000. It had lots of space inside, perfect for our needs. The power supply and hard drives are installed near the top of the case without overlapping the motherboard. The drive bays on the front of the case did not hang over the board, either. It was clear that Thermaltake's experience in creating quality cooling products definitely came in handy when designing the case. It came with three fans, one intake and two exhaust, enhancing an intelligent layout that promotes airflow through the case. It had 11 front bays for future upgrade options. The bays were interchangeable, meaning we weren't locked in to installing our floppy or DVD drives in specific places. It had some features making it easy to use, like thumbscrews for the side panel and a removable hard drive cage. It also had tool free installation for the 5 ¼" drive bays, and an expansion card clip for securing cards without the use of screws. Its aluminum shell made it extremely light considering its size. And, most importantly of all, it comes in black!!!

Color Figure 8: In the end, we selected Thermaltake's PurePower TWV500W as our ultimate power supply.

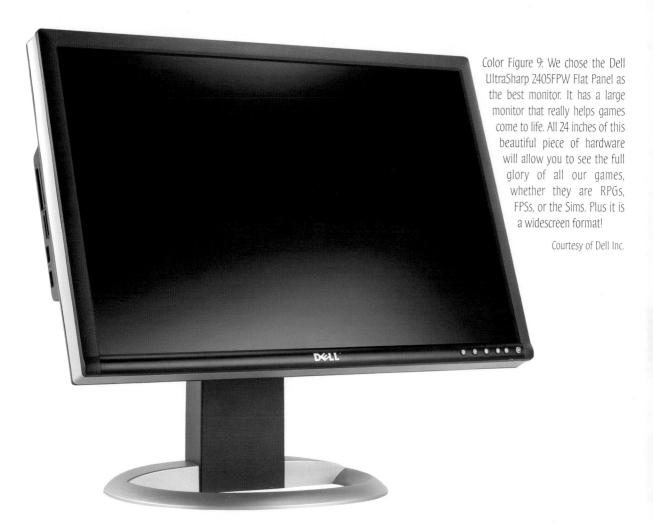

Color Figure 9: We chose the Dell UltraSharp 2405FPW Flat Panel as the best monitor. It has a large monitor that really helps games come to life. All 24 inches of this beautiful piece of hardware will allow you to see the full glory of all our games, whether they are RPGs, FPSs, or the Sims. Plus it is a widescreen format!

Courtesy of Dell Inc.

Color Figure 10: The Gamer's Keyboard by Saitek. It combines many useful features with some cool twists to make it a great device to add to our PC.

Color Figure 11: The Logitech Rumblepad 2 Vibration
Feedback Gamepad. For those who have never strayed from
PC gaming, keyboard and mouse controls are the only thing they've ever
known. In fact, they are probably very comfortable with any keyboard and mouse based control scheme that a game designer can come
up with. However, for those PC gamers who have crossed the line to console gaming, a gamepad can be the preferred method of control.

Color Figure 12: When playing a game, have you ever wished you
had a mouse for your left hand as well as your right hand? If so,
the Nostromo N52 Speedpad is the perfect accessory for you.

Color Figure 13: Apply the thermal paste that came with your heat sink to the top of the processor. Ours came in a little blue tube that looks like a tiny syringe. Simply pop off the blue cap. You want to put a small dollop of paste onto the center of the processor. It can be a rough estimate; try using an amount the size of the blue cap. The directions call for "adequate" amount—there are articles about this, but it equates to just about the size of a dime when flattened. You really want just a very thin layer, so it doesn't ooze out between the heat sink and the processor when you clamp down the CPU cooler. Spread paste around with the tip of the tube. Careful—the paste comes out quickly! Do not let it leak over the sides!

Color Figure 14: The Gigabyte Rocket Cooler Fan Controller after installation.

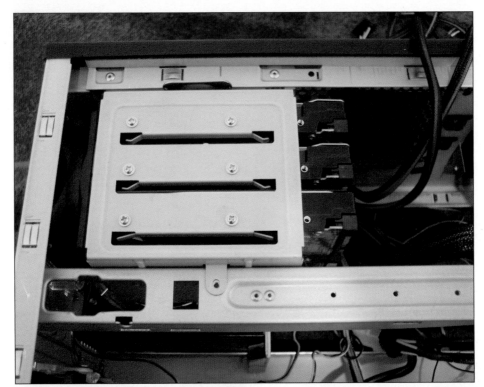

Color Figure 15: Once all three hard drives are secure in the hard drive cage, clip the hard drive cage back into place over the power supply and secure the cage with the thumbscrew that was removed at the beginning of the installation.

Color Figure 16: Connect your SATA data cables to the backs of your three hard drives. The cables are blue with black ends, and come with the hard drives.

Selecting the Ultimate Gaming Accessories

You've selected all of the components for your ultimate gaming PC. Your shopping cart is full, and you're heading for the checkout line, be it virtual or an actual register at the front of the store. But did you really get everything you need?

This chapter takes a look at some cool gaming accessories that we threw into our cart on the way out the door. Some of these items are improvements on the generic input devices that many people hook up to their PC. Others are additional game controllers that make games much more fun to play. Finally, we'll throw in an object or two, just because it looks cool. This is the fun part of shopping, so let's get started!

Improving on Basic Input Devices

How many people buy or build a powerful PC and then connect a generic keyboard and mouse? Far too many, in our opinion. It's time to spruce up these basic input devices, and maybe give yourself a game advantage at the same time.

The Gamer's Keyboard by Saitek

The first thing you might want to do is upgrade your keyboard. One of the best keyboard improvements is the The Gamer's Keyboard by Saitek. It combines many useful features with some cool twists to make it a great device addition to your PC. The keyboard is shown in Figure 11-1.

This keyboard looks great. The metallic gray base and the blue-gray keys are not going to hang in an art gallery, but the colors combined with its appealing shape make it a great improvement over the basic white keyboard most people use. After you plug the keyboard into your PC via USB, it looks even better when the electric blue backlighting begins to glow. This just adds to the keyboard's futuristic style, making a nice addition to your desktop.

FIGURE 11-1: The Saitek Gamer's Keyboard.

Of course, the purpose of a keyboard isn't to look good. As the primary input device for your PC, it has to get the job done. The solid feel of the keys gives the impression that the keyboard is very sturdy, and you won't have any concerns about pounding away on it for hours. The keys themselves are extremely quiet; frantic gaming with the keyboard won't disturb any roommates you may have.

A nice feature is the built-in volume controls above the number pad. You can make fine adjustments to PC volume without having to dig through your control panel. This also comes in handy if your speakers don't have an easy-to-reach volume knob of their own.

Of course, these basic features aren't enough to warrant its addition to the ultimate gaming PC. The Saitek keyboard's programmable Command Pad is what pushes it over the top. This small, external pad looks like nothing more than an extra number pad; however, Saitek's drivers allow you to map any keystroke to these buttons, giving you the power to group nine important keyboard commands onto one easily accessible pad. You can also string several commands together, creating macros that run a series of actions in sequence. This reduces the number of keystrokes required for complicated moves, preventing missed keystrokes that could cost you a victory. You can see the Command Pad in Figure 11-2.

The Command Pad also has a Shift key, allowing for another nine commands to be mapped. In total, you can link 18 different keystrokes or macros to this pad, giving you extreme flexibility in your gaming. This is definitely an improvement over a $10 generic keyboard.

The Logitech MX 1000 Laser Cordless Mouse

Gaming with a generic, corded mouse can be a miserable experience. The cheap, lightweight feel can make precise movements next to impossible. Dust inside of the ball can reduce the accuracy of your cursor, making gaming extremely difficult. Short cords that crimp and snag on different parts of your desk are just another issue that gamers have to deal with. It's time for something different. The Logitech MX 1000 Laser Cordless Mouse will keep your focus on the game, and not on the drawbacks of your input device. Take a look at this mouse in Figure 11-3.

The greatest advantage to this mouse is its lack of a cord. This wireless mouse can go anywhere on your desktop without you having to wrap, stretch, or run a cord around your other gaming devices. This may not be an issue for people who only have a keyboard and mouse on their desktop, but many gamers have several other peripheral devices plugged into their PC. These are just more obstacles to tangle up your mouse.

There are two main drawbacks to most wireless mouse devices. The transmission from the mouse to the base unit can be unreliable. Interference from other electrical devices in your home can cause the signal to be interrupted, resulting in a cursor that jumps around onscreen. In addition, slow transmission speed between the mouse and its base unit can reduce its responsiveness. These transmission problems are not an issue for this Logitech mouse because the speed of its transmissions matches that of a corded USB connection, resulting in responsiveness on par with a regular mouse.

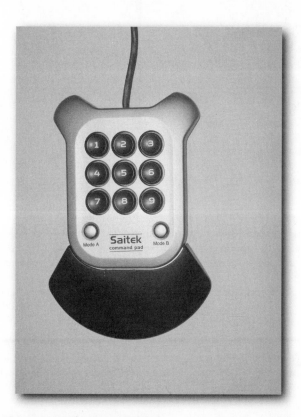

FIGURE 11-2: The Command Pad.

FIGURE 11-3: The Logitech MX 1000 Laser Cordless Mouse.

Another drawback to wireless mouse devices is that they typically chew through dozens of AA or AAA batteries a year, making it expensive to keep your mouse "fed." The Logitech MX 1000 Laser has a built-in rechargeable lithium-ion battery that never needs to be replaced. You just have to place it in its base unit overnight to charge the mouse to full power. This battery lasts for an extremely long time. In our experience, it wasn't uncommon for it to run an entire week without needing a recharge. In addition, the mouse turns itself off when not in use, saving battery power. If you want to be extra frugal with the battery life, an on/off switch on the bottom of the mouse gives you manual control over battery usage.

The Logitech MX 1000 Laser is comfortable to use, molded perfectly to fit your right hand. Even if you have large hands, you will find it easy to grasp comfortably. Lefties may have to look elsewhere, however, due to this righty-only contoured shape. You can see this design in Figure 11-4.

FIGURE **11-4: The right-handed contour of the MX 1000.**

The design of the mouse puts all of its buttons within easy reach of your fingers. The basic left and right buttons, along with the comfortable scroll-wheel are readily available. There are also Internet-browsing buttons within reach of your thumb, making the forward and back buttons on your browser obsolete. There is also an application switch button that some people may find useful, located between the browser buttons. It makes switching applications with ALT+ TAB a thing of the past.

The final piece of this package comes in the form of the mouse drivers. Logitech's new SetPoint drivers give you complete control over the sensitivity and acceleration of the mouse. In addition, you can change the assignment of any of the extra mouse buttons to other useful shortcuts, such as cut and paste. You can even assign keystrokes to the buttons, giving you even more customizing power.

The Logitech MX 1000 Laser is exactly what you're looking for in a gaming mouse. It keeps your focus on the game being played, not on any drawbacks of your input devices.

Taking Control

Just because you've upgraded the basic input devices of your PC doesn't mean you need to stop there. Many gamers are happy enough to settle for a decent keyboard and mouse, but you're not! You're going to take a look at some game controllers that can change the way you play.

Game controllers come in many different shapes and sizes. No matter how their appearance differs, their primary purpose is always the same — to provide the same method of control across all games. For example, many 3D games employ the ASDW systems of movement where these four keyboard keys move your character left, back, right, and forward. However, there may be some games that require the use of the keyboard's arrow keys for movement. Other games may utilize the number pad for character control. These varying control schemes can be confusing at best, annoying at worst. A properly configured game controller ensures that every game is controlled in the same exact way, unifying these schemes and making gaming more enjoyable.

Let's take a look at some of the game controllers that would be worthy additions to your ultimate gaming PC.

The Logitech Rumblepad 2 Vibration Feedback Gamepad

For those who have never strayed from PC gaming, keyboard and mouse controls are the only controls they've ever known. In fact, they are probably very comfortable with any keyboard- and mouse-based control scheme that a game designer can come up with. For those PC gamers who have crossed the line to console gaming, however, a gamepad can be the preferred method of control. For these gamers, we suggest looking into the Logitech Rumblepad 2 Vibration, shown in Figure 11-5.

This gamepad closely resembles the one from Sony's Playstation 2, incorporating the same M-shaped design. There are 10 programmable buttons, a directional pad, and two analog sticks, offering you many ways to control your favorite games. A USB connection to your PC is all that you need to get these controls up and running.

To make this controller more comfortable for intense gaming sessions, Logitech has included a rubberized texture to ensure the controller doesn't slip out of sweaty palms. The controller is also capable of vibration feedback, showing that Logitech put as much thought into the feel of their controller as they did they layout.

The Logitech drivers give you complete control over the functions of each button as well as the analog sticks on the controller. You can mix and match any setting, switch the functions of the left and the right stick, and even map keystrokes for added control.

Unfortunately, it appears that many first-person shooter game designers never played with their Xbox or Playstation very much; it can be difficult to find FPS games that support gamepads. You can map the corresponding keyboard commands to your pad, but its performance is often less than ideal. In addition, the force feedback of the pad requires support by the game as well, another thing that can be hard to find. If you like FPS games, especially if you play them on a console, you might be very disappointed with a PC gamepad.

FIGURE 11-5: The Logitech Rumblepad 2 Vibration Feedback Gamepad.

However, fans of sports games will not be disappointed by the performance of this gamepad. Games like EA Sports' Madden 2005 are perfect examples of how this Logitech gamepad improves gaming. From calling up passing windows to throwing the ball downfield for a touchdown, there are enough buttons to give you complete control of your quest toward the Super Bowl.

If you are playing a game that is gamepad compatible, we definitely recommend the Logitech Rumblepad 2 Vibration Feedback Gamepad. This is especially true if you're a console gamer who can never get the hang of an ASDW control scheme.

The Nostromo N52 Speedpad

When playing a game, have you ever wished you had a mouse for your left hand as well as your right hand? If so, the Nostromo N52 Speedpad is the perfect accessory for you. The Nostromo Speedpad is shown in Figure 11-6.

When you first look at it, the Nostromo appears to be some futuristic hand rest sitting on your desktop. When you place your hand on it, however, the design puts a mini keyboard with 14 programmable keys at your fingertips. Belkin took some pieces of other input devices and added them to this device, with both the scroll wheel from a mouse and the directional pad of a game controller in easy reach.

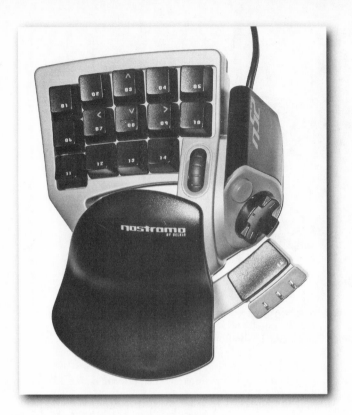

FIGURE 11-6: The Nostromo N52 Speedpad.

Using Belkin drivers, every part of the Nostromo is programmable, including the scroll wheel and the directional pad. Don't worry about not having enough keys to program. Using the Shift key located below the directional pad, you shift the Nostromo from normal mode into "Red Shift," "Green Shift," and "Blue Shift," essentially giving you three new sets of keys to program, as seen in Figure 11-7.

Each key is not limited to a single command. You can also program macros, storing entire chains of keystrokes including any necessary time delay between key presses. This is definitely a very powerful device.

By inputting all of the vital commands of your favorite FPS, you can increase the speed of your gameplay. No longer do you have to struggle to find the right keys in Battlefield 1942 or Medal of Honor, nor do you have to worry about timing the keystrokes just right. The Nostromo reproduces them the exact same way every time. Movement, selecting weapons, and crouching are just a few of the actions that are simplified with the Nostromo.

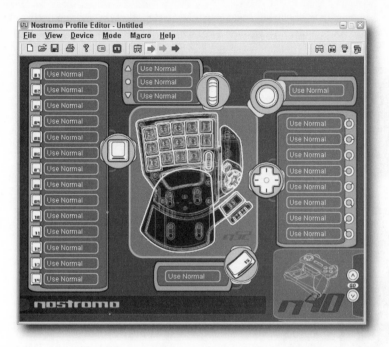

FIGURE 11-7: Assigning commands using the Nostromo's driver.

However, the power of the Nostromo can also be seen in real-time strategy games like Warcraft 3. Construction and placement of specific buildings usually requires two or three keys. Now, you can map an entire build order to a single key, helping you establish your first base or create your first squadron of troops in record time. In games such as these, every second shaved off your build time gives you an advantage over your adversaries, be they human or computer controlled.

If setting up all of these keystrokes and macros manually sounds like a lot of work, you're right. But it can be avoided by simply downloading pre-set profiles for your favorite games from the Belkin Website. These profiles get your Nostromo up and running in a matter of minutes, and you can be sure that all of the commands you need are mapped and ready to go.

Be warned: there is a bit of a learning curve for this device. No matter how much gaming experience you have, the Nostromo N52 is like no other controller ever created. It may take a few days to get the hang of it. After you do, though, you'll never go back.

The Saitek R440 Force Feedback Wheel

If you're a fan of EA Sports NASCAR SimRacing, or any other PC racing game for that matter, you know that the true feeling of racing down the track in excess of 200 mph is not conveyed by simply pressing keys on the keyboard. A gamepad helps with the controls a little bit, but it's still not enough. To really feel like you're behind the wheel of the car, you need a physical steering wheel in your hands. That's where the Saitek R440 Force Feedback Wheel comes in, as seen in Figure 11-8.

The R440 is more that just a game controller in the shape of a steering wheel. It is a two-piece device, consisting of a set of plastic pedals for the floor and a plastic wheel for your desktop. The pedals are attached to a plastic footrest. As you rest your foot on it to use the pedals, you are also securing them to the floor. This design ensures that the pedals don't slide away from you while gaming. The steering wheel has also has a no-slip design. It comes with a C-clamp that you use to secure it to the top of your desk, allowing you to turn the wheel quickly without throwing the device across the room.

Just because these pieces don't move around your desk doesn't mean they get in the way. They are both sized just right—not too big, not too small. The pedals can find a home under your desk no matter how much junk you have stored under there, and the wheel shouldn't take up too much desk space, either.

FIGURE 11-8: The Saitek R440 Force Feedback Wheel.

Of course, a great setup is nothing if its performance doesn't measure up. When it comes to racing, the R440 doesn't disappoint. The rubber-like grips make the wheel easy to grasp and turn. After you grab a hold of this device, you experience the wheel's precise control as you turn corners and move around other cars. The control of this wheel is definitely one of its best features

For games that support force feedback, the wheel really begins to shine. Racing games are fun, but part of that fun is feeling the bumps and crashes that are a big part of the racing experience. The R440 ensures that you feel each and every one of these events, really bringing the race to your desktop.

If racing is your game, you haven't truly experienced it until you've used a gaming wheel. For our racing games, the only wheel we use is the The Saitek R440 Force Feedback Wheel.

Fun with Cooling

Throughout this book, we've talked about heat being the enemy of your PC. We've told you about all of the horrible things it can do to the various components. We've even explained how having good cooling throughout the system is vital to keeping everything running smoothly. But have we mentioned how cooling can be fun?

We were turned on to the idea when we saw our power supply. Not only was the dual fan setup perfect for keeping things cool, the blue LEDs in the fan gave the power supply a little something extra. However, it wasn't until we plugged in the cooling fans that came with our case that we began to see the trend; they, too, had blue LEDs. If we turned out the lights, our cooling solutions had turned into a pretty cool light show.

Of course, there was still something missing. We had this nice window on the side of our case, but no light coming from inside. We set out to solve this problem while keeping our PC cool at the same time.

The 3D Rocket Cooler Pro from Gigabyte

When we picked up our Gigabyte GA-K8N Ultra-9 motherboard, one of their cooling products caught our eye. The 3D Rocket Cooler Pro is a cooling fan that replaces the basic fan that comes with your processor. Although your original processor fan is more than capable of keeping the CPU cool under normal conditions, you can run into heat problems if you try to overclock it. This is not our intention, but if you plan to do so, a powerful CPU cooler moves up from fun accessory to a definite necessity. The 3D Rocket Cooler Pro is shown in Figure 11-9.

The Rocket Cooler has a cool design, no pun intended. The cylindrical design with fan ducts on the bottom clearly shows the rocket-shaped design that gives the cooler its name. The cylinder is composed of aluminum with fins cut along the surface to draw in air and cool the CPU. The base of the unit that draws the heat away from the processor is made of copper, which is even better than aluminum for transferring heat.

The speed of the fan in this cooler is adjusted by an included control panel that can be installed into an empty 3.5" drive bay in the front of the case. You can use it to turn the fan speed low for normal operation, or to maximum while overclocking. This panel keeps the control of the cooler in your hands.

FIGURE 11-9: The 3D Rocket Cooler Pro from Gigabyte.

Everything you need for setting up the cooler is right in the box. The Rocket Cooler fits all of the latest processors, whether they're from Intel or AMD. Simply use the correct mounting clip based on your system. It also comes with a tube of thermal paste to apply to the surface of the processor. This ensures a proper bonding between the CPU and the copper base of the cooler, allowing heat to be drawn away from the processor much more effectively than simply placing the two surfaces in contact with each other.

Of course, we've save the best part for last. There are bright blue LEDs on the top of the rocket cooler that fill the inside of the PC with a brilliant blue glow. It's the perfect finishing touch we need for our ultimate gaming PC.

What's Next?

Your shopping is done! You finally have everything you need to assemble your ultimate gaming PC. It's time to leave this section and get your hands dirty. You have to figure out how all of the parts fit together and bring your PC to life. Onwards to Chapter 12.

Bringing Your Ultimate Gaming PC to Life

part

Assembling Your Ultimate PC

Finally, here we go! The best part of the whole process! Well, except for actually using the computer to play games, of course. This is where you begin to see the results of all your hard work. As you assemble your computer, it slowly comes to life, and that is all done by your own hands. There are many steps to take to make sure you get it right, but it is well worth it in the end. Don't worry if you don't exactly know what piece we are talking about at each point, because we have inserted photos to help clarify any questions you have. Hopefully, if all goes well, in a few short hours you can turn on your super computer for the very first time.

The first thing to do in this process is to get familiar with all the parts you bought. Parts vary greatly by manufacturer; every case, motherboard, memory chip, and so on is different. To save yourself time and heartache, it's best to look over your parts to make sure everything is there. Make sure that what the package said comes in the box is actually there, all the wires, screws, CD-ROMS, instructions, and such. It is very annoying to get halfway through a part's installation and find the connection wire that was supposed to come with it is missing. If you are missing anything, now is the time to contact your supplier and ask for a replacement. After you are sure you have everything, you need time to get the ball rolling.

Tip You may want to install all your devices first. Resist this urge! The more you have in the case, the less room you have to work. Because we chose a large case, we can go step by step to make sure everything works.

In this chapter, you set up your workspace and start going through all the parts. Then, you install each part. And we walk you through the process step by step. Here's the order of the installation:

1. Case

2. Power supply

3. Motherboard

4. Processor

5. Cooler

6. Memory

7. Fans

8. Rocket Cooler Controller

9. Video card

10. Hard drives

11. DVD drives

12. Floppy Drive

13. Sound Card

14. USB port

Ready to get started? Let's go!

Setting Up Your Work Space

You can't build a computer without a place to work. The more room you have, the better. Start by finding a flat surface to work on such as a desk or a table. We usually use the floor. The area should be big enough to hold your case and all the hardware, and allow you to work freely without knocking into anything. If you are working on a table, you may want to put a towel or sheet down to protect the table from scratches as you move the case around.

Don't overlook the value of good lighting. There will be times when you try to connect a wire deep inside the case; the more light you have to see the connection, the better you'll be. Although not necessary, you'll quickly see the benefit of having decent light in the area. Look for an area with bright overhead light and arm yourself with a small flashlight so you can illuminate those dark caverns of the case.

That's pretty much it for the workspace. You also need two non-magnetic screwdrivers — a Phillips head and a flat head. And finally, you need an additional computer that has a floppy drive and a CD-ROM drive.

During the installation of the OS that we discuss in Chapter 13, you'll need to create a boot disk. We'll go into detail on that topic later, but make sure you have this additional computer and a blank floppy handy.

As you start to take all the parts out of their boxes, try to keep each part with their original accessories; you won't be using all the parts for your computer, but you will be using the majority of the parts. Your task will be much easier if you remember what came with what piece — including the screws!

And that's it! You're now ready to work.

Starting with the Case

Taking the case out of the box, you get your first look at the Thermaltake Armor VA8000 you selected, as shown in Figure 12-1. The first thing you notice is that this case is HUGE compared to other cases you've seen. You may even wonder why you bothered to get such a large case. But you'll see as you start to pile all the hardware into the case that the case seems to get smaller and smaller as you go along, until in the end you have a beautiful tangle of wires and top-end hardware.

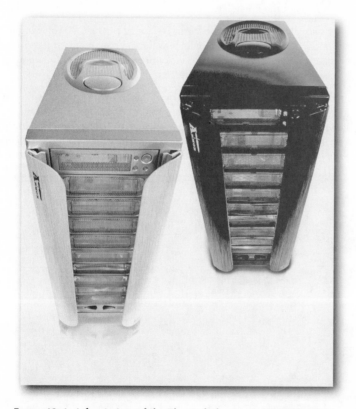

FIGURE 12-1: A front view of the Thermaltake Armor VA8000. We're using the case on the right.

Source: Used by permission.

Looking at the front of the case, you notice an expansion slot for a floppy drive at the top of the case next to the power button, followed by nine bays and one drawer closest to the floor. You can use the drawer to hold your extra screws, or even the remote control that came with the SoundBlaster Audigy 2 ZS Platinum sound card. You also notice two metal plates attached by hinges to the case. These plates are a great defensive mechanism that prevents you from accidentally hitting the power button or CD drive. This is the "armor" part of the Thermaltake Armor brand. As an additional bonus, the case comes with a soft cloth for cleaning!

One side of the case has a clear Plexiglas sheet. It's a nice bonus feature that you'll appreciate after all your fans are installed and the power turned on. Some of these components give off a blue glow that you can see through the Plexiglas.

Keys on the back lock the two release levers on the Plexiglas side of the case, so you can prevent unwanted hands from tampering with your valuable machine. We're going to leave our keys attached for now because we don't see a reason to lock our case; you can do the same, or if you do want to lock the case, just store the keys in a safe place.

The top of the case has a circular door that you can release and open by pressing down on it. Underneath the door is a FireWire drive, two USB ports, a headphone connection, and a microphone jack, as shown in Figure 12-2. It's extremely cool that Thermaltake included this feature, but they don't work with the motherboard. The good news is that your motherboard comes with a similar expansion slot that you will use later on.

FIGURE 12-2: Top-mounted USB and FireWire ports.

Warning Make sure to keep all sharp edges and objects away from the top and the sides of the case. This means no hardware, screwdrivers, or anything with hard pointy edges. The case can scratch very easily, and on the black case, scratches are extremely noticeable.

Now it's time to get to work.

1. Unscrew the two large thumbscrews located on the back of the case.

2. Lift the levers simultaneously to remove the first side panel—the one with the Plexiglas—and pull the back side of the panel toward you. It should come off rather easily.

3. The second side panel gives you access only to the bottom of the motherboard cage. Remove this panel by unscrewing two small screws. Swing the back end out, and it will come off just as easily as the first.

Note Removing both panels give you unlimited access to the internals of the machine.

4. Tied down inside the case is a brown box that contains screws, top exhaust fan, a padded lever, and some silicone gel to keep away moisture. Unfasten this and remove it from the case.

5. Lay the case on its side with the major opening facing up. Take all the cords in the case and drape them over the top of the case for now to keep them out of the way.

Note Inside the case there are several wires connected to the top mounted ports. Unfortunately, the cables attached to these ports are not compatible with the motherboard we selected. Because of this, we bound the cables together to keep them out of the way. If you purchased a different motherboard, check your documentation to see if these are compatible.

You're now ready to install the power supply.

Install the Power Supply

You're going to install the power supply now, but not connect any of the cords. After all the hardware is in place, it will be very difficult to get to this section of the case.

We chose the Thermaltake TWV500W – ATX 12V 2.0 Version power supply. The cables on this power supply are entirely removable, which is why we chose this; you'll only get the cables you want. Because there are no cables, it is easy to install the motherboard because no cables are in the way. The power supply came with a power cord and screw box, an adjustable fan speed function application for PC case, a PCI card-slot fan-speed control panel, 5.225 HDD fan-speed control panel, cable sets, and the huge power supply neatly packed in bubble wrap.

Note Because of its size, we're installing the supply now, rather than having to work around the motherboard. After the board is secure, we'll have to put the other cables in. Right now we're not putting any cables in.

Let's get started. Before you begin, make sure the case is still on its side. The power supply is installed just behind the hard drive case, at the top-left corner of the case (when looking down into it).

1. Which way does the power supply face? You can tell this by matching the screw holes on the power supply with those on the back of the case, as shown in Figure 12-3. The ones on the back of the supply have the power button on it, so those holes have to line up (and allow you access to the power button). For this particular model of power supply, the fan of the power supply must face upward.

FIGURE 12-3: Align the screw holes on the back of the power supply with the screw holes on the back of the case.

2. Rest supply in the case, fan up, and slide it to the back of the case so the holes align, as shown in Figure 12-4.

FIGURE 12-4: Position the power supply in the case.

3. Secure it from the back of the case with the four screws, one in each corner, as shown in Figure 12-5.

FIGURE 12-5: Secure the power supply to the back of the case with four screws.

Caution

You may be able to secure the supply with less than four screws, but it's a good idea to always use the maximum. The screws act as a ground to the power supply from random static charges.

Note

With this brand of power supply, we found that the screw closest to the button is slightly off, so we were unable to secure that screw in place.

It's in! That wasn't so hard, was it? On to the motherboard, which requires just a little more work than this. Grab your screwdrivers, and we'll see you there.

Install the Motherboard

Some people consider this one of the trickier parts of the process. It's normally the one piece that you purchase and don't change through the life of the computer. But regardless, it really isn't that difficult to install.

The Gigabyte GA-K8N Ultra-9 motherboard gets installed into the side of the case, or the bottom if your case is still on its side. Note the numerous screw holes and letters that are punched into the case. The case has outlines for positioning the motherboard. It has letters that indicate what type of motherboard goes where. In our case, follow the outline labeled A for ATX (M for MicroATX, B for BTX, and S for SSI).

Note The good news is that every motherboard that is an ATX form factor is the same size. And, because the outgoing ports on the motherboard have to face out the back of the case, you know how to orient the board inside the case. If you chose a different motherboard, these steps still apply to you.

The motherboard doesn't actually sit on the bottom of the case. Risers separate the motherboard from metal and allow air to circulate around the board, keeping it cool. The first step is to place the nine risers that you need to hold up your motherboard.

If, as we go through this step, you can't find the slots marked "A," you can lay the motherboard in the case gently to see how it would be positioned before you install it.

1. Take the nine brass rising screws that came with the motherboard. These screws are the risers. Insert the screws into the A slot on the motherboard. Figure 12-6 shows the placement in the case.

Note After you think you've found all the places for the risers, count the number of risers in the case and the screw holes in the motherboard just to make sure you have the right number. In this case, you need nine.

2. The punchout plate that came with your case, which mates to the motherboard ATX I/O port cluster, isn't compatible with our motherboard. Remove the punchout plate for the external ports; it's located at the back of the case. It's easy to remove — simply unscrew the two screws that secure it and remove it through the back of the case, as in Figure 12-7.

3. Replace the plate with the one that came with the motherboard. Secure it by pushing it in until you hear it snap. Be careful — the edges are sharp. Use the original screws to secure the plate. Figure 12-8 shows how the plate looks.

Screw holes

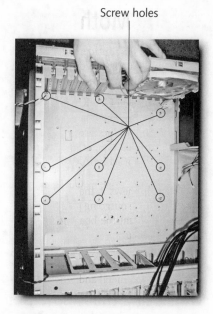

FIGURE 12-6: Screw the nine risers into the case, following the indents marked "A."

Figure 12-7: Remove the back punchout port plate that came with the case.

Figure 12-8: Installing the punchout plate that came with our motherboard.

4. Metal tabs on the back of the punchout plate cover the mouse PS2 port and the network port. Lift or bend these inward inside the case to allow port access and the motherboard to be installed.

Inserting the Motherboard

Now it's time to insert the motherboard into the case.

Note All the mounting materials came with the board; all the screws to fasten the motherboard to the case came with the case, and NOT the motherboard.

1. Insert the motherboard at a slight angle, gently pushing it toward the punchout plate and aligning all the outgoing ports exactly with the port openings in the plate. After they align, gently lay the motherboard flat on the nine risers, as shown in Figure 12-9.

2. Screw in the nine screws through the motherboard into the risers, as shown in Figure 12-10.

Warning Do not over-tighten the motherboard screw; if you do, you could crack the motherboard and destroy it.

Tip If you use an electric screwdriver with a built-in clutch, you'll never strip or over tighten a screw. Just set the clutch to the minimal setting.

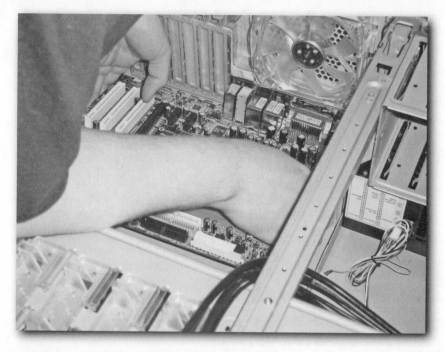

FIGURE 12-9: Position the motherboard inside the case.

FIGURE 12-10: After positioned, screw the motherboard into the case.

The motherboard's now in place. All the ports should line up neatly in the punchout plate, as shown in Figure 12-11.

FIGURE 12-11: All the ports line up in the punchout plate after the motherboard is installed.

Time to install the AMD processor.

Install the Processor

AMD FX-55 2.6 GHz, Socket 939 brand of processor comes in a big box for such a tiny item. The processor is protected in a molded plastic case. The heatsink is strapped into the foam casing to protect it. Because we have purchased a more powerful heatsink, we will not be using the heatsink that came with this processor. If you want to use it, the instructions are easy to follow.

There are two parts to installing the processor. The processor needs to be installed onto the motherboard, and then the heatsink is installed directly next to the processor.

Warning Do not touch the processor without grounding yourself first — you just spent a lot of money and you don't want to short it out and ruin it. Simply hold *unpainted* metal or touch a screw on a light switch plate before you touch the processor. Better yet, use a grounding strap and anti-static mat.

Installing the Processor onto the Motherboard

The first step is to install the processor onto the motherboard. The processor is installed in the upper-left quadrant of the motherboard, as shown in Figure 12-12.

FIGURE 12-12: The area on the motherboard where the processor is installed.

1. Gently remove the processor from the molded case. Open the plastic covering, and dump it gently into your hand.

2. Raise the ZIF (zero insertion force) bar on the motherboard that latches the processor socket, as shown in Figure 12-13. This is used to hold the processor in place.

FIGURE 12-13: Lift the bar covering the processor socket.

Warning **STOP** Just in case you jumped ahead and connected the power, MAKE SURE NO POWER IS CONNECTED TO THE MOTHERBOARD at this time — or you may short out the chip.

3. Line the chip up with the pins on the motherboard. To do this, match up the triangle symbol on the corner of the processor with the triangle symbol on the corner of the processor socket on the motherboard, and simply place the chip into place as shown in Figure 12-14.

Tip Chips are designed only to fit in one way; don't force it.

4. Lower the ZIF lever back to its original position, as shown in Figure 12-15.

FIGURE 12-14: Position the processor and gently put it into place.

Figure 12-15: Lower the bar back into place, securing the chip.

Wasn't that easy? With the chip installed, the next step is to attach the heatsink to the chip.

Installing the Heatsink

We opted not to use the standard heatsink that came with our processor. Instead, we'll use the Gigabyte GH-PCU22-VG (3D Rocket Cooler PRO) Processor cooler, which ensures we meet all our current and future cooling needs.

If you haven't opened it already, pop open the Rocket Cooler Pro and get ready to place it on top of the AMD processor. Notice the heatsink is significantly bigger than the one that came with the processor, but that is also why we chose a bigger case — so we could fit all this high-end technology inside.

Let's get the cooler ready for installation:

1. Hold the cooler so that the power cable is on the left, and the notched flanges face you and away from you.

2. Slip the retaining arm appropriate to your processor, in this case the K8 level arm, between the heatsink and the copper base, as shown in Figure 12-16. Make sure the plastic securing piece is on your side of the heatsink. For now, set the heatsink aside.

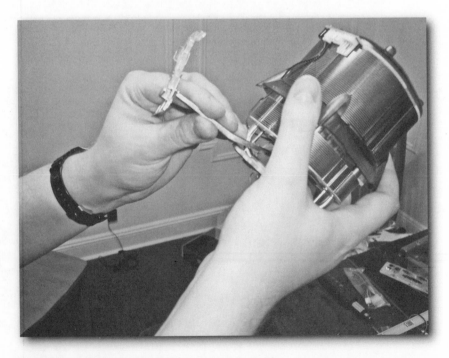

FIGURE 12-16: Install the retaining arm on your heatsink.

Tip If you're apprehensive about attaching the heatsink to the processor, you may want to test run the positioning before applying the thermal paste.

3. The next step is to apply the thermal paste that came with your heatsink to the top of the processor. Ours came in a little blue tube that looks like a tiny syringe. Simply pop off the blue cap. You want to put a small dollop of paste onto the center of the processor. It can be a rough estimate; try using the amount the size of the blue cap.

 Tip The directions call for an "adequate" amount — there are articles about this, but it equates to just about the size of a dime when flattened. You really want just a very thin layer, so it doesn't ooze out between the heat sink and the processor when you clamp down the CPU cooler.

4. Spread paste around with the tip of the tube, as shown in Figure 12-17. Careful—the paste comes out quickly! Do not let it leak over the sides.

FIGURE **12-17:** When spreading the paste over the processor chip, don't let it leak over the sides.

5. Quickly, before the paste dries, secure the far end of the retaining clip onto the three retaining posts on the far side of the processor base, as in the first image in Figure 12-18. On the near side, you must raise the clear plastic arm before the three posts will align (the second image in Figure 12-18). Rest the sink on the posts and secure the other end of the bracket onto the three retaining posts.

FIGURE 12-18: Secure the heatsink to the processor.

6. Make sure that all six retaining posts are firmly in the holes on the clip; then lower the clear arm as shown in Figure 12-19.

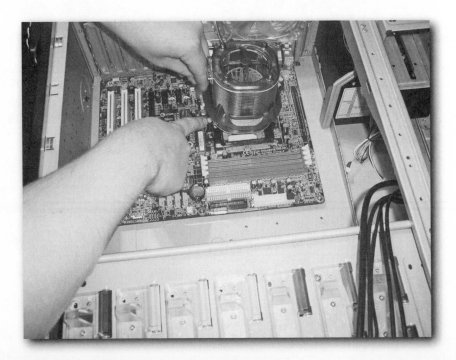

FIGURE 12-19: Lower the clear arm to secure the heatsink.

Note Don't worry if the clear clip is on a slight angle after you lower it; it's designed that way so it's able to fit underneath the wide center of the heatsink.

Now connect the heatsink to the motherboard for power. The heatsink actually requires several sources of power, but we're just going to connect one of them for now.

7. Connect the primary power cable power into the motherboard. The cord is a yellow three-pin connector cable, which goes onto the three pins on the motherboard labeled "CPU Fan." This is close to where the processor sits on the motherboard. See Figure 12-20.

Figure 12-20: Connect the primary power cable to the motherboard.

The heatsink and cooler are now in place. On to the memory!

Install Memory

Memory is one of the most straightforward pieces in terms of installation. It comes in a simple plastic case that you pop open. Ground yourself before pulling it out of the plastic case. This is probably one of the shortest and simplest of all the parts installations in the whole assembly process. All you have to do is take them out of the case and slide them into place. If they were all this easy, you'd be playing games by now!

It is important to read the installation instructions for the motherboard to determine what slots to use for the memory. Although you think that they should be installed in the slots next to each other, that may not be the case. In our motherboard, the memory modules must be placed in adjacent purple slots.

1. Lower the retaining clips on the memory slots.

2. Memory fits in one way only – do not force it. DDR Memory has one groove, off center, on the bottom of the RAM module. Align this notch with the socket, which has a similar hump or post, as we did in Figure 12-21.

FIGURE 12-21: Align the notch on the memory card with the socket on the motherboard.

3. Gently push down on both ends, applying force evenly, until it snaps into place. You'll know it is in position when the retaining clips rise and snap into place over the memory module.

4. Repeat the steps to install the second memory module in the DDR slot.

The next step is to do the first power test, but before you can do that you have to run the power to the elements in the case. It's time to install the second part of the power supply—the cables.

Connect the Cables

Begin the process of connecting the cables. We won't be connecting them all right now because we don't have all the devices installed. The following is a list of the power we'll connect now.

- Power supply to the motherboard
- Power supply to heatsink
- Power supply to the case fan and the hard drive fan
- Power button to the motherboard
- The case speaker to the motherboard
- Case LEDs to the motherboard

Don't worry—this is enough to keep us busy for now!

Connecting the Power Supply to the Motherboard and Heatsink

Start with the power supply. The power supply was chosen because it provides individual cables. You need to select the cables for your motherboard. In this case, we're using the following cables:

- One 24-pin main connector cable. This is a thick, multicolored cable housed in a black mesh. One end has two rows of 12 pins on one plug; the other has two rows of 10 pins and an additional plug with 4 pins (two rows of two). This is the biggest cable of all of them, so you should be able to spot it. (Your power supply may only have 20 pins, and that's okay. too.)

- Four-pin, 12-volt power connector. This black and yellow cable has a plug on one end, eight pins—two rows of four—and the other end has four pins, two rows of two. It connects to the processor power socket on the motherboard.

- Four-pin peripheral and floppy power connector. This cable has one end with a four-pin connector, two by two, and three female molex power connectors at the other end.

- Secondary power connector cable — This cable has two molex power connectors — one male and one female — and one four-pin connector that connects to the heatsink.

- A general power cord that runs from the back of the computer to the electrical socket.

Figure 12-22 shows all four cables. As you can see, all the cables are thin and wrapped in a nice protective wire mesh. This makes managing them much easier because they slide without getting tangled up.

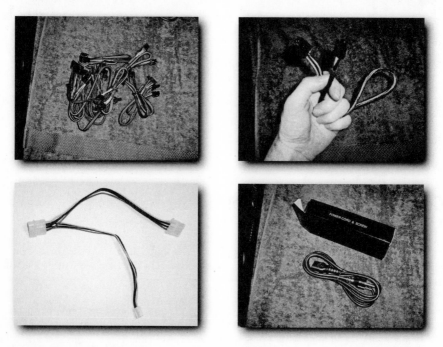

FIGURE 12-22: Four cables for the power supply.

The cables connect from the back of the power supply (inside the case) to the motherboard. Each socket on the back of the power supply is labeled. To help read these labels, you need to remove the hard drive casing. This also allows for easier access to the power supply because it sits right behind it.

To remove the hard drive cage, simply unscrew the thumbscrew located under the hard drive cage; push down on the tab, and remove the hard drive cage, as shown in Figure 12-23.

FIGURE 12-23: Remove the hard drive cage and put it aside.

Put the cage to the side for now.

The First Cable

The first cable you're going to install is the cable that reaches from the power supply to the motherboard.

 Warning When wiring the power supply, make sure you go through the case (as opposed to over the support bar) when connecting the wires. Otherwise, you'll have to rewire it all.

1. Start with the 24-pin main connector cable — the large multicolor cable. Plug the 24-pin connector into the power supply socket, shown in Figure 12-24. There's only one slot it can fit into.

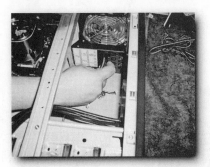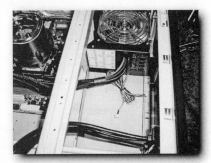

FIGURE 12-24: Connect the 24-pin main connector cable to the back of the power supply.

2. Plug the 20-pin connector into the motherboard main power slot, as shown in Figure 12-25. The four-pin plug remains unconnected.

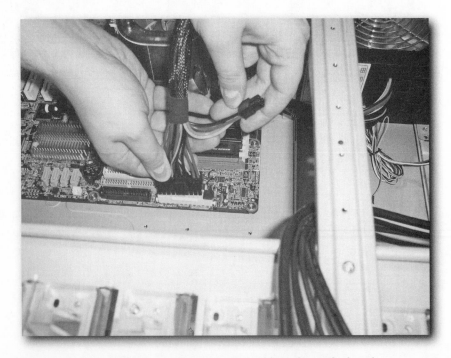

FIGURE 12-25: Connect the 20-pin main connector cable to the motherboard.

The Second Cable

The next cable is the black and yellow cable four-pin, 12-volt power connector.

1. The eight-pin end connects into the power supply. There is only one slot, labeled as "4-pin power connector" on the diagram on the back of the power supply (Figure 12-26).

2. The four-pin connector goes onto the motherboard's processor power socket, as shown in Figure 12-27.

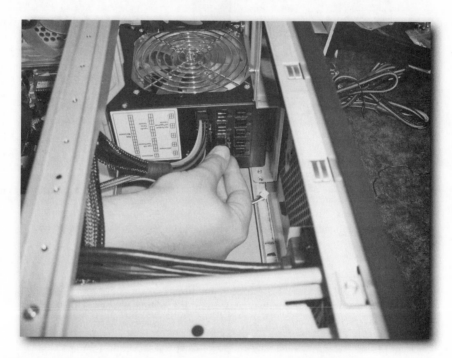

FIGURE 12-26: Connect the 12-volt power connector to the power supply.

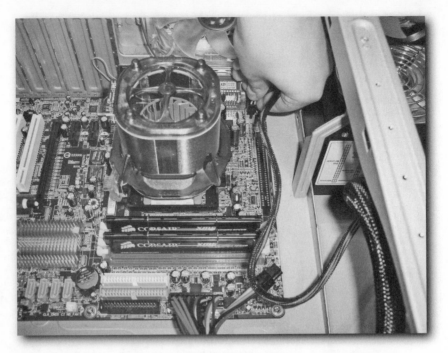

FIGURE 12-27: Connect the four-pin 12-volt power connector to the motherboard.

The Third Cable

The third cable is the four-pin peripheral and floppy power connector. This cable has one end with a four-pin connector, two by two, and three female molex power connectors at the other end.

1. The four-pin plug goes into the power supply as shown in Figure 12-28.

2. Locate the secondary power cable. Connect one of the molex connectors from the power supply to the male connector on the secondary power cable.

3. Connect the four-pin connector to the heat sync as shown in Figure 12-29.

The complete connection is shown in Figure 12-30.

FIGURE 12-28: Connect the four-pin peripheral and floppy power connector to the power supply.

FIGURE 12-29: Connect the four-pin connector of the secondary power cable to the heatsink.

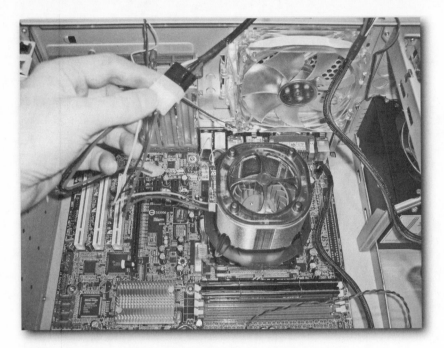

FIGURE 12-30: Full connection between the heatsink and the power supply.

Before you test the power, let's connect the power button, case speaker, and case lighting.

Connecting the Power Button, Case Speaker, and Case Lighting

You have to connect the power button from the front of the case to the motherboard. In the top bay of the case, cables extend from the front panel to the inside of the case. They are normally two colors — white and a color or black and a color. Unwrapped, they are long and can easily stretch across the case.

At the end of each wire is a black connector, which is labeled

- Red and black: Power SW (power switch)
- Red and black: Speak +- (case speaker)
- Purple and white: Reset SW (reset switch)
- Blue and white: Power LED (power light)
- Orange and white: H.D.D. LED (hard drive light)

These wires are shown in Figure 12-31.

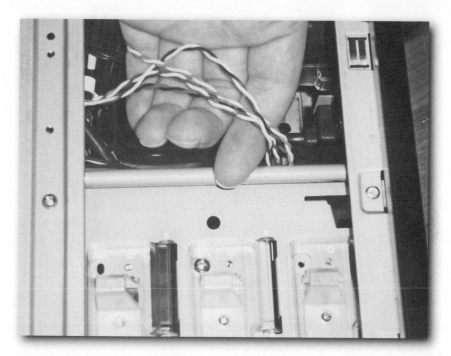

FIGURE 12-31: Cables for the power switch, reset button, case speaker, power light, and hard drive light.

Note Black is always negative.

There is an entire row of pin connectors in the corner of the motherboard, right next to three large yellow sockets. These cords connect into those slots.

Connect the power switch (power SW) to the motherboard. You need the cord labeled Power SW (red and black).

On the motherboard, locate the slot PW +-. The +- indicates the orientation of your pin connector. The black connector should go to the -; the red cable should go with the +. Figure 12-32 shows how the power switch should be connected to the motherboard.

FIGURE 12-32: Connecting the power switch to the motherboard.

Next, install the red and black speaker wire, labeled "Speaker." This is located in the bottom bay of the case. Connect these to the orange-colored pins located in the same section as the power switch button. These are labeled SPEAK+- on the motherboard.

These are the only ones you need for your first power test. But, while you're here, you might as well do the other three: Reset SW, H.D.D. LED, Power LED.

In the same area as the power and speaker cables, there is a two-pin male connector labeled HD+-. Connect the orange and white H.D.D LED wire to this connector with the white cable on the right if you are facing the front of the case.

Next to that, there is a two-pin connector labeled RES+-. Connect the purple and white cable labeled Reset SW to this connector with the white cable on the left.

The final light is the Power LED. Immediately above the connector to the power button is a black three-pin male connector. Connect this blue and white cable to that connector, with the white cable on the right.

The final connections are shown in Figure 12-33.

FIGURE 12-33: Cables for the power switch, reset button, case speaker, power light, and hard drive light connected.

Note There is a black and white cable that comes off the back of the bottom of the case. It's for the chassis alarm—an alarm that sounds whenever you remove the side panel of the case. Our motherboard does not have that feature—plus, we didn't think it was necessary for our gaming needs.

That's it! You're now ready for your first power test!

Perform the First Power Test

If you completed the last section correctly, you should have one last cable left over – the thick black power cord. This is the one that plugs from the computer to the power outlet in your humble abode. We'll discuss a little bit about the power test before we connect the cable.

Incredible Beeping Motherboard

We mentioned during the power test that the beeps you hear are the way the computer communicates with you. When you power up your machine, the computer does a self-test. During this self-test, it checks all the devices attached to the motherboard to ensure that all are there and functioning properly. If all are in place, the computer beeps once and boots up.

The problem is when one of the devices is not functioning properly. The beeps are like a Morse code — the length and frequency of the beeps tell you what device may not be functioning. Our guide to our beeping motherboard was in the manual from Gigabyte that came with the motherboard, in the Troubleshooting Appendix. If you have a different motherboard, check your manual for the key that works with your motherboard.

You're performing this test to make sure that the processor, heatsink, memory, and the motherboard are all installed properly. Doing a test now with only a few items attached lets you quickly evaluate your work up to this point. It's easier to see where you may have gone wrong with a few devices attached. After you have 20 devices attached, it can be difficult to find which were miswired or not connected.

When you power up the computer at this point, you should hear a series of beeps. The beeps are the computer's way of communicating with you. The sequence and length of the beep tell you what devices are attached and functioning. The beeps are just like the computer's version of Morse code.

Let's start the power test.

1. Make sure all the cables that have not yet been connected are clear of all the fans on the case — you don't want to accidentally cut the cables or burn out the fans by having a cable stuck in it.

2. Turn the power supply off at the back of the computer. Off is deNoted by the 0 as shown in Figure 12-34.

3. Plug the black power cord into the back of the case, and into the wall. (As long as the switch on the power supply is set to off, it doesn't matter what you plug in first.)

4. Switch the power supply to the On position.

The fan on the power supply should turn on, and the rocket cooler heatsink should glow blue, shining through the clear case. You should hear one long beep followed by two short beeps. This indicates the power test is successful! The three beeps indicate an error — on our board, it indicates that there is no video card connected. Despite the error, the test was a success!

The hardest part of the assembly is done — if you made it this far, it only gets easier! Well, with the exception of the RAID.

FIGURE 12-34: Make sure the power supply is turned off before doing the power test.

CHECKLIST for Power Supply Test 1

If you did not get the beeps you were expecting, check the following:

- Reseat all the connectors; check all connections to make sure you have all the wires connected to all parts.

- If the power supply turns off immediately after it turns on, check that you have power to your heatsink.

- If the power supply turns on but there are no beeps, check to ensure that the speaker cable is connected to the motherboard.

- If the series of beeps do not match the documentation of the motherboard, make sure the memory is in the right slots.

- Make sure you're plugged into the outlet.

- Make sure the power supply is on (1 and not 0).

- If you do see a light on the motherboard but the heatsink fan is not on, TURN ALL OFF and double-check the power to the heatsink.

Install All the Fans

The next step is to install or give power to all the fans. In the end there will be four fans:

- Case fan, located at the center of the back of the case
- Ceiling fan, located at the top of the case
- Front fan, located in the front, bottom side, of the case
- Hard drive fan, located behind the hard drive cage

You also install the controller for your heatsink's fan.

Also as you may recall, we chose a special fan and Thermal Watts Viewer and controller with the power supply, Purepower TWV 500W. We are going to use this to replace the main case fan.

Overall that is a lot of fan power, some might say over the top, but then again this is the ultimate gaming PC. We weren't going to skimp on anything!

Let's get to it!

Installing the New Case Fan

We're going to replace the case fan that came with the case, with the orange and black fan that came with the power supply.

1. Locate the fan on the back of the case. Clear white clips, two on either side, attach it. Pull the clips out and pull the fan upwards, out of the case, as shown in Figure 12-35. The fit is very tight, so it's okay to use pressure.

2. Take the new black and orange fan, which is identical in size and shape, and slide it down into the holder.

3. Re-clip both ends with the clear clips. The clips should snap fully in place. Snap one side in at a time; the other side goes in rather easily, as shown in Figure 12-36.

4. After the fan is set in place, connect power to it. Grab one of the free females black molex connector from the power supply and connect it to the male molex power connector, a thin red and black cable, on the fan.

FIGURE 12-35: Remove the clear fan that came with the case from the back of the case.

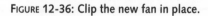

FIGURE 12-36: Clip the new fan in place.

Let's install the fan controller for this fan.

Installing the Case Fan Controller

Your new case fan came with a Total Watt Viewer that allows you to control the speed of the fan and view the wattage of two fans in your case. You'll connect this controller to the case fan, and to the fan on the power supply.

1. Make sure the knobs on the controller are turned all the way to the left, pointing to the minimum designation on the label; then pull off the knobs from the Total Watt Viewer.

2. Peel off the clear protective plastic covering.

3. Replace the knobs, making sure that the black lines on the knobs once again line up with the MIN designation on the faceplate.

Stand the case upright. Because the armor shields prevent you from working with the faceplate, you need to work standing up. You'll be putting this in the second full tray down, leaving one slot above it for the SoundBlaster controller (you install that later in this chapter).

4. Pop off the face of the second full bay from the top. Reach in, push out the face plate by raising the two black tabs on the side as shown in Figure 12-37 (left), and pull the face-plate off (right).

FIGURE 12-37: Release the clips inside the case to pop out the faceplate.

Note   This controller has to go in a bay close to the top because the wires are not long enough to stretch through the case in any other position.

5. Feed the wires through the bay, into the case, as shown in Figure 12-38.

6. On the side of the case, unclip the clear clips as shown in Figure 12-39 and slide the Total Watt Viewer into the front of the viewer.

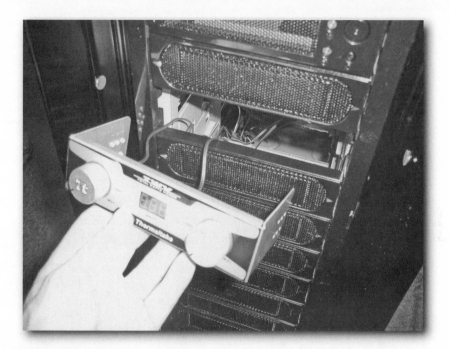

FIGURE 12-38: Removing the faceplate to feed through the wires.

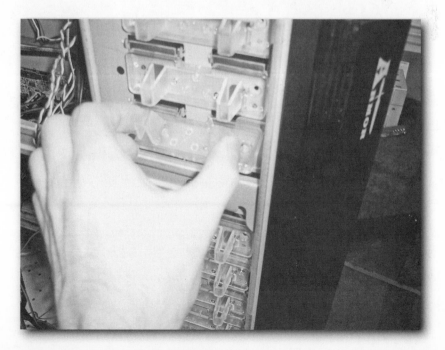

FIGURE 12-39: Unclip and lift the clear clips.

Note Make sure the arms on the face plate (off the back) are straight. You need to put the screws through this to secure the viewer. The holes won't align if they are not perpendicular to the case.

7. Push it in until it is flush with the case. On the side, under the clip, to the front of the case, two screw holes now line up — one from the case and one on the viewer.

8. Holding the clear plate up (Figure 12-40), insert the one screw into the top hole to secure the viewer in place. Reach your hand into the case to hold the viewer in place as you secure it with the screws. The arms of the viewer are flexible and may bend without additional support as you screw in the screws.

FIGURE 12-40: Hold the clear clip up and insert the screws.

Caution Even though you have two holes, you only insert the screw into the top right hole. If you insert both screws at this point, the clear clips won't fall back into place in Step 7.

Tip

If you have a hard time inserting the screws because the clear clip is in the way, simply lift the clear clip for the bay above the one you're working on. This allows the clip on the second bay to lift totally up, giving you clearer access and more room to secure the viewer.

9. There's one more screw to insert to secure the viewer in place. To access it, remove the remaining side panel from the computer by unscrewing two screws on the back of the computer and then sliding it toward the back of the computer to remove. Then screw in the last screw to the side of the viewer.

10. Put the clear clips back down and snap them into place.

11. Two wires extend off the back of the controller with two-pin female white connectors on the end. One attaches to the two-pin male connector on the power supply (the only all-yellow cable coming off the power supply). The other connects to the two-pin male connector on the case fan (black and orange) as shown in Figure 12-41.

FIGURE 12-41: Connect the controller to the case fan.

12. There is a three-pin female connector on the back of a red, black, and white wire on the back of the power supply. This connects to the three-pin male connector on the rear of the Total Watts Viewer controller.

Tip The wires off the viewer are not labeled, nor are the knobs. Make a Note to yourself for which wire attaches to which fan. This enables you to know which knobs on the front powers the fan for the case and which powers the fan for the power supply.

Note There's an extra yellow wire hanging off the case fan. It's unnecessary for the PC you're building, so you can disregard it for now.

Turn on your machine at this point. The Total Watts Viewer should light up, as shown in Figure 12-42. The wattage display should light up with the speeds of the fan. At this point, you can test both dials, one at a time, to ensure that the fans operate properly — the fans should move faster and slower as you turn the dials from minimum to maximum, respectively.

FIGURE 12-42: The controller panel should light up to display the wattage of the fans.

Note Why use fan controllers? You can adjust the speed of the fans to accommodate higher temperatures or overclocking. Plus, it's really cool!

On to the next piece — the Gigabyte Rocket Cooler Fan Controller for your heatsink.

Installing the Gigabyte Rocket Cooler Fan Controller (Heatsink)

The Gigabyte Rocket Cooler Fan Controller for the heatsink is similar to the controller you just installed for the case fan and the power supply fan. It, like the other controller, controls the speed of the fan on the heatsink. The steps for this installation are similar to those in the previous section. Refer back to that section if you don't recall some of the figures.

Note   We selected the fifth bay for this installation. This slot looks like a 5-1/4 inch bay, but has a tray built to hold an additional 3-1/2 inch drive, which is the size of the fan controller. We chose this spot also because the cable we have to run to the Rocket Cooler is not very long; this slot is the closest to the cooler.

1. Lift up the clear clips and remove the two screws from both sides (two on the front, one on the far).

2. Slide the 3-1/2 inch bay back as far into the case as you can, and push out the C clips that hold the faceplate in place.

3. Pop out the faceplate from the fifth full bay from the top.

4. The bay should now slide easily out the front, as shown in Figure 12-43. Put it aside for now.

FIGURE 12-43: Pull the bay out of the front of the case.

5. Flip the faceplate over and gently remove the black foam insulation. It's easy to pull out with your fingers.

6. Notice that the center part of the grating is secured with three tabs on both sides. Gently lift up the largest of the three tabs, the one in the middle, on both sides and remove the center grating. The faceplate is now ready to hold the heatsink controller.

7. Now grab the 3-1/2 inch bay that you set aside and insert the controller into the front of it, leaving an inch between the face of the controller and the face of the bay, allowing the holes on the interior of either side of the bay and faceplate to align

8. Use the two self-tapping screws that came with the heatsink to secure the controller to the bay as shown in Figure 12-44.

FIGURE 12-44: Leave about 1 inch between the face of the controller and the face of the bay, and secure with the self-tapping screws.

Tip

Take the fan controller and screw the screws into the holes before installing it into the bay. "Tapping" the holes in this way makes it easier to screw in the screws when attached to the bay.

9. Untie the red, white, and blue cables from the back of the controller.

10. Reinsert the bay into the case by lifting the clear clips on the side and sliding the bay into the case, as shown in Figure 12-45.

11. Snap the black faceplate back on the front of the bay, ensuring that the Gigabyte control panel is flush with the plate. You know the bay is in position when the screws line up with the case under the plastic clips and the face is flush with the faceplate.

12. Install two screws under the clear plastic clip, in the lower-left and upper-right holes.

13. Install two screws on the other side, lower-left and upper-right, as shown in Figure 12-46.

FIGURE 12-45: Reinsert the bay into the case.

FIGURE 12-46: Install two screws on the other side of the case.

14. Now it's time to wire up the controller. The back of the controller has one red, white, and blue cable with a thee-pin female connector. This connects to the three-pin male connector on the heatsink, shown in Figure 12-47. You may want to lay the computer back on its side at this point.

FIGURE 12-47: Connect the controller to the heatsink.

 The cable for the controller is very short. Make sure whatever tray you put it into that the wires can reach from there.

15. Remove the clear plastic protective film.

That's it! Your controller should now look like Figure 12-48.

FIGURE 12-48: Installed Gigabyte Rocket Cooler fan controller.

Installing the Ceiling Fan

On the top of the case, notice a fan in the center of the roof, directly in front of hard drive cage. The fan comes with a clear plastic base already attached. Off the bottom of the base are four tiny, squat legs. Installing this fan is rather easy, as long as you line everything up.

1. Locate the four legs on the inside top of case.

2. Center the fan in the top of the ceiling of the case, lining up the four legs with the four holes in the roof.

3. Push evenly in the fan, to get all four legs into the holes simultaneously, and slide it downward, about 1/8 of an inch, to lock it into place. Slide it over in one motion (similar to how you would open a child-proof medication bottle).

Make sure the fan is completely flush before sliding it over.

4. Locate an empty molex connector attached to your power supply. Connect the red and black power cord from the fan to the empty molex connector, as shown in Figure 12-49.

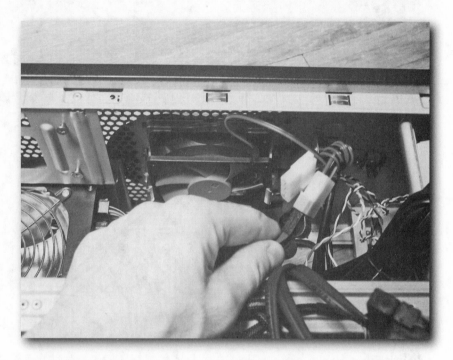

FIGURE **12-49:** Connect the molex connector from the ceiling fan to any free molex connector off the power supply.

That's it.

Connecting the Front Fan

The good news is that the front fan is in place when you get the case. It sits just in front of the secondary hard drive cage that's in the lower front of the case. For you to connect this fan, all you have to do is reach around the hard drive cage in the front and locate the male molex connector that comes off the fan. Simply attach it to any free female molex connector in the case.

Note If you don't have a free molex connector just yet, don't worry. As you proceed, there will be plenty to go around. Just make a Note to come back and plug these in when you have the chance.

Connecting the Hard Drive Fan

There is also a fan behind the hard drive cage that's in front of the power supply. It, too, is already in place. Simply grab its molex connector and attach it to any free connector available in the case for power, as shown in Figure 12-50.

FIGURE 12-50: Connect the molex connector from the hard drive fan to any free molex connector off the power supply.

Testing the Fans

Now that it's wired, power up the computer. You should still get the three beeps (because you haven't installed anything other than the memory and CPU yet), but all the fans should be running. You should now be able to control the speed of your heatsink fan, and the case and power supply fans.

Note   Before you turn your unit on, turn the knobs all the way to the lowest setting. You can then turn the power on and check that the respective fan responds to the knobs.

It works! Now, on to the next piece.

Install the Video Card

The video card is big. Huge. It is so big that when you place it inside the case it's going to take the space of two cards on the motherboard. When you try to fit it in, you're going to have to remove two protective expansion plates off the back of the computer. Not the biggest deal, but it just shows how large the card actually is.

It comes in one plastic unit complete with power connector cables, two VGA adaptors, and some sample software. To work on this installation, make sure your case lays flat.

Note
There are no VGA ports—this is only a DVI card. If you want to connect it to a VGA port, the box contains the correct adapters.

1. Do your best to move all the wires out of the way of the PCI Express slot. Don't pull any out when you move them around. (This slot is the longest black slot on the motherboard.)

2. On the rear of the computer, there are four screws that hold the purple and green PCI tool-free clip to the case. Remove the screws and thus remove the unit, as shown in Figure 12-51. This gives you full access to the metal brackets as well as uninhibited access of the motherboard.

Warning
We found it difficult to install the card by simply removing this bracket. As a result, we had to remove the entire tool-free bracket clip by unscrewing the unit from the back of the case. It's a convenient feature of the case because of the position of our motherboard, but it just gets in the way.

You're not going to put it back because anytime you want to make a change you'd have to remove it to make any change, adding to your steps.

3. Pop out two of the protective expansion covers — the third and fourth from the bottom — by inserting a straight-head screwdriver under the larger tab on the outside of the case. Gently twist the screwdriver in an upward motion, holding your hand inside the case to catch the covers as it pops off and into the case. You need to remove the two slots because the card takes up both.

Tip
You're supposed to be able to remove it without tools by sliding/pulling it straight up; however, if it doesn't work, insert a screwdriver under the metal tab on the back of the case, and twist up with one hand inside the case to catch the panel as it pops off.

4. Align the tabs on the bottom of the graphics card with the PCI Express graphic slot and slowly lower the card into the case, as shown in Figure 12-52.

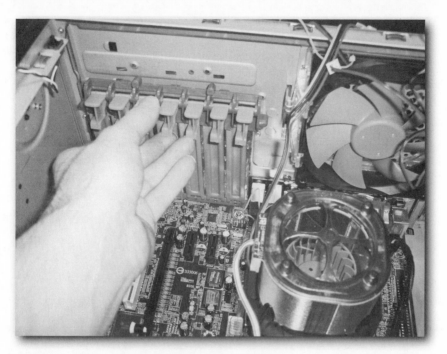

FIGURE 12-51: Remove the PCI tool-free clip from the case.

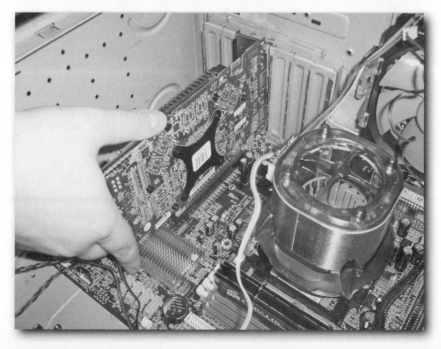

FIGURE 12-52: Lower the PCI Express card slowly into place.

5. Push firmly on the top of the card to seat it on the motherboard. It should fit snuggly into place with a dull click. Don't apply too much pressure. You don't want to crack the motherboard.

6. Insert one screw into the middle of the retaining bracket on the edge of the card to secure the card to the back of the case, as shown in Figure 12-53.

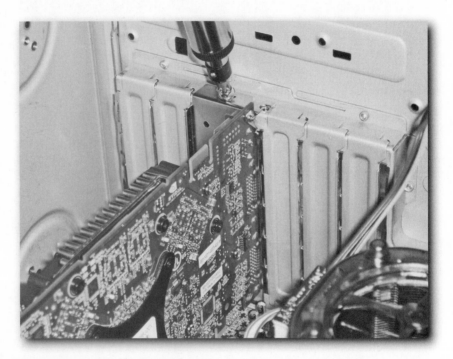

FIGURE 12-53: Secure the card with a screw.

 Note Sometimes the card and the case don't exactly line up. You may have to gently bend the case into position so that the screw can secure the card to the case.

7. Find the black and yellow cable that came with the power supply — it should have six pins, two rows of three on each end, and connect one end to the six-pin PCI Express connector on the power supply, as shown in Figure 12-54. Connect the other end to the six-pin power connector on the rear of the video card, as shown in Figure 12-55.

 Warning If you need to remove the PCI Express video card, there is a white retaining pin on the PCI Express slot on the motherboard. Pull this out to remove the video card. Do not attempt to remove the card without removing the pin; doing so damages the motherboard.

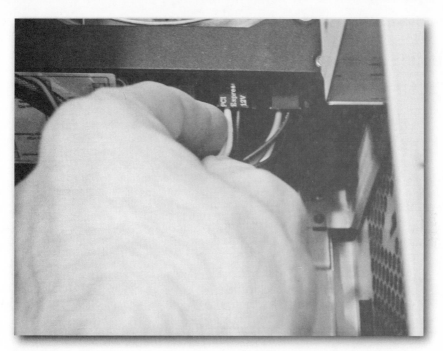

FIGURE 12-54: Connect the black and yellow cable to the power supply.

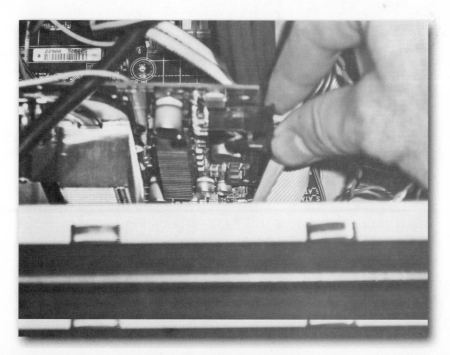

FIGURE 12-55: Connect the cable to the rear of the video card.

Your video card is now installed! Time to test....

Testing the Video Card

Plug in the computer to the outlet and turn your power supply on. Press the power button and watch the machine light up. You'll get one beep—success! Now on to the hard drives.

Install the Hard Drives

Besides the case itself, the hard drives are the heaviest components of your system. Unfortunately for you, heavy means speed. Now it's time to take your three SATA drives and install them in your system.

Find your two 74GB 10000-RPM Western Digital Raptor drives because those are the ones you use first.

1. Take the hard drive cage, which you removed when you wired up the power supply. Make sure that the clip on the top of the hard drive bay is facing you. If this is the case, the plugs on the hard drives are on the right as you insert them.

2. Slide one hard drive into the top of the cage, aligning the screw holes on the drive with those on the bay. We're putting the 74GB Raptor in the top bay of the hard drive cage.

3. Secure the drive with four screws, two on each side.

4. Slide the next 74 by 83 into the middle bay and repeat steps 1 through 3.

5. Slide the 250GB drive into the bottom bay and repeat steps 1 through 3. The full drive cage should look like Figure 12-56.

6. Locate the two four-pin peripheral and floppy power cables and connect them to the power supply. These cables have one end with a four-pin connector, two by two, and three female molex power connectors at the other end. Drape these over the side of the case for now, shown in Figure 12-57.

7. After all three hard drives are secure in the hard drive cage, clip the hard drive cage back into the case as shown in Figure 12-58 and secure the cage with the thumbscrew that you removed in the beginning.

FIGURE 12-56: The full hard drive cage.

FIGURE 12-57: The peripheral and floppy power cables.

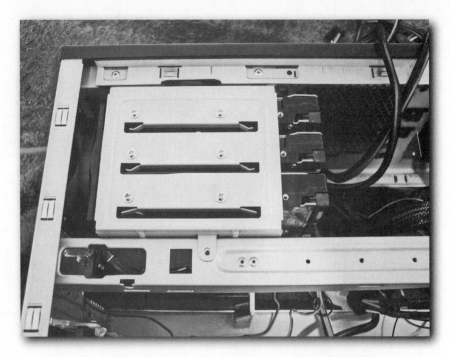

FIGURE 12-58: Clip the hard drive cage back into place over the power supply.

8. Connect your SATA data cables to the backs of your three hard drives. The cables, shown in Figure 12-59, are blue with black ends, and came with the hard drives.

Note   The SATA cables fit only one way on the back of the drives.

9. Secure the other end of the SATA cables to your motherboard's SATA slots (yellow orange), starting with the top SATA drive (Raptor drive) connecting to the socket labeled SATA0, the middle to socket labeled SATA1, and the bottom to the socket labeled SATA2, as shown in Figure 12-60.

Warning   The SATA sockets on the motherboard are not in order, so read the labels and the motherboard documentation carefully.

FIGURE 12-59: Connect the blue SATA data cables to the back of the hard drives.

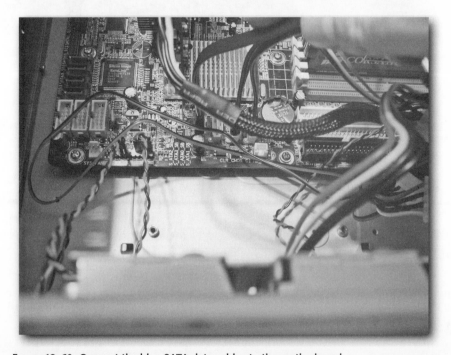

FIGURE 12-60: Connect the blue SATA data cables to the motherboard.

10. Take one of the power cables with the three four-pin molex connectors you draped over the case, and connect the three molex connectors to the back of each drive, as shown in Figure 12-61. They fit only one way; it doesn't matter which connector goes to which drive.

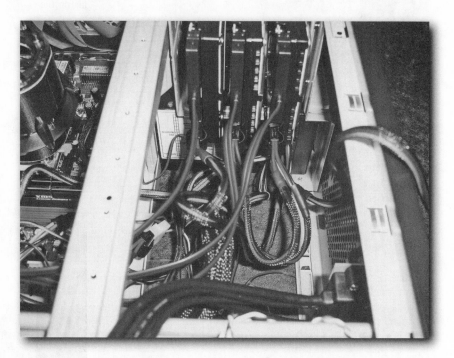

FIGURE 12-61: Connect the molex connectors to the back of each drive.

Tip You may find it easier to pull the hard drive cage back out to connect the power cables. It depends on how large the case is and how small your hands are.

No need to test. Why not? Because all drives need to be installed before you test again. On to the Memorex DVD drive.

Install the DVD Drives

In this section, you install the Memorex and Lite-On DVD drives. This should be another simple procedure; it's as easy as installing the hard drives. The main difference with these drives is that they're being installed in the front of the case, and not in the interior.

Installing the Memorex DVD Drive

For this, you need to stand the case upright.

1. You're going to pull out your third full bay from the top. This is the only bay without the clear clips on the sides. Reach in, push out the face place by raising the two tabs on the side, and pull the faceplate off, as shown in Figure 12-62.

FIGURE 12-62: Take the faceplate off the third full bay from the top.

2. Slide the DVD drive in through the front of the case, careful not to hit any wires that are inside the case. It may be a snug fit; slide it in, gently working it into place, as shown in Figure 12-63.

3. Secure the drive with four screws, two on each side, as shown in Figure 12-64, which slide in right underneath the support bar where the clear clip normally would be.

FIGURE **12-63**: DVD drive in place.

FIGURE **12-64**: Secure the drive in place.

4. Take the wide flat gray IDE cable (ribbon cable) that came with your DVD drive and connect it to the back of the DVD drive shown in Figure 12-65.

FIGURE 12-65: Connect the ribbon cable to the back of the DVD drive.

Warning

The ribbon cable is grooved, as if it were made up of many thin wires. One of these wires is colored red. This marks pin 1, which must align with a pin 1 marking on your DVD drive. In this case there is no marking, but there is a notch on the ribbon cable that indicates how it would be inserted.

5. Connect the other side of the ribbon cable to the IDE Channel 1 socket on your motherboard, shown in Figure 12-66. This socket is black with a notched groove, indicating the orientation of the ribbon cable.

6. Take the second power cable draped over the side of the case, and connect one of the molex power connectors to the DVD drive.

You're done with the installation of the DVD drive. If you did a power test now, with a monitor connected, you'd see a Note that says they recognize the drives. Now let's install the second DVD drive.

FIGURE 12-66: Connect the ribbon cable to the motherboard.

Installing the Lite-On DVD Drive

The Lite-On drive goes in the fourth slot down, just below the Memorex DVD drive. Simply follow steps 1 through 4 from the previous section and then proceed with the following:

1. Follow steps 1 through 4 from the Memorex DVD drive installation.

2. Connect the other side of the ribbon cable to the IDE Channel 2 socket on your motherboard, right next to the socket in which you plugged the Memorex DVD drive.

3. Power it up by connecting any free power cable with one of the molex connectors on the DVD drive.

4. Connect an analog CD cable (usually available separately but it came with our drive) from the back of the Lite-On DVD drive to the AUX port on the top of the SoundBlaster Card, third from the right.

Note With Windows XP, attaching this cable may no longer be necessary; however, you should attach it just in case you are running a different operating system.

The DVD drives are installed! That was easy. On to the floppy drive.

Install the Floppy Drive

We didn't purchase a floppy drive for this PC, but any floppy drive will do. They're relatively cheap — $8.00 to $15.00. They used to be cheaper, but as they become more obsolete, the prices are rising (as fewer manufacturers are making them). We are actually going to use one from an old computer we had laying around.

1. Pop the top bay out by undoing the clear clips on the side. The bay slides right out, as in Figure 12-67. Notice that, like the 3-1/2 inch bay holding the rocket cooler controller, it's designed to hold smaller drives such as the floppy.

FIGURE 12-67: Remove the top bay from the case.

Note You won't have much room to move the bay around because the wires are connected to the power button.

2. Push in the two black clips on the top and bottom of the bay and slide the faceplate right off, as show in Figure 12-68.

FIGURE 12-68: Remove the faceplate from the top bay.

3. As you did in the Gigabyte Rocket Cooler Controller installation, punch out the center of the faceplate. Put a little pressure on the front until it pops out of position. It may bend slightly, but chances are you won't use this piece again. If you do, it's easy to bend back into shape.

4. Slide the faceplate back on the front of the bay, as shown in Figure 12-69.

5. Gently work the floppy drive into the bay from the front, as shown in Figure 12-70, so that the holes on the side align with the holes on the bay.

FIGURE 12-69: Slide the faceplate back on the bay.

FIGURE 12-70: Gently work the floppy drive into the bay.

6. Secure the drive to the bay with screws, two on either side, as shown in Figure 12-71

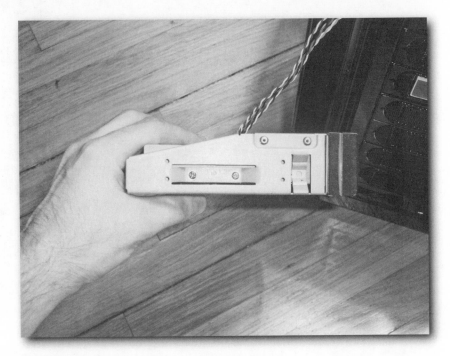

FIGURE 12-71: Secure the drive into the bay with screws, two on each side.

7. After the drive is secure, insert the bay back in the top slot. Be careful as you feed the wires back into the case so you don't accidentally pinch any of them.

8. After the drive is in place, lower the clear clips on the side and lock into place.

9. Along with the floppy drive, you should have gotten a thin IDE ribbon cable, not quite as wide as the ones you used for the DVD drives. Connect one end of this thin cable to the back of the floppy drive. Remember — the red pin should line up with pin 1.

10. Connect the other end of the ribbon cable to the FDD socket on the motherboard, located next to the IDE sockets that you plugged the DVD drives into.

Note Depending on how your wires worked out, the FDD slot may be hidden from view by the IDE cable coming from the DVD drive. Simply unplug the DVD drive, plug in the FDD, and replace the DVD IDE cable.

11. Off of one of the many power connectors, locate the wire that looks like Figure 12-72. This is your floppy drive power connector. Work it through the case until it can reach the back of the floppy drive.

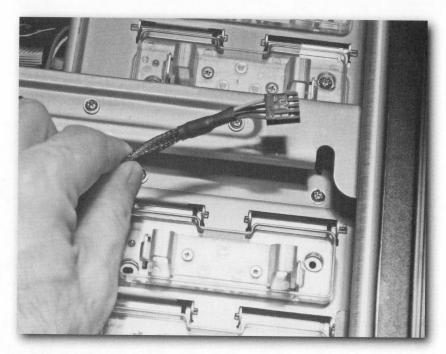

FIGURE 12-72: Floppy drive power connector.

> **12.** Normally, the power connector of the floppy is on the back-right corner. Just slide this connection onto the four pins of the power connector slot on the floppy drive.

The floppy drive is now installed. Next is the sound card.

Install the Sound Card

The SoundBlaster Audigy 2 ZS Platinum box is full of stuff. There are two primary components—PCI sound card that goes in the PCI slot on the motherboard and an external control panel that goes in one of the front bays of the case that houses all the input and outputs of the sound card in the front of the computer, including volume knobs, giving easier access and greater control. Also included are driver CDs, demo software, remote control, an extra molex power cable, an IDE cable, the audio cable that connects the card to the DVD drive, a stereo pin, additional faceplates for the drive—one white and one black so you can use the black or white one to match your case—a game port, and some weird type of adaptor you won't be using.

You're going to install the controller into the first full slot of the case first, and then install the card on the motherboard.

Installing the SoundBlaster Control Panel

The SoundBlaster Control panel goes in the first full bay of the case.

1. Remove the first full faceplate from the top of the case shown in Figure 12-73 by simply pushing the clips as you've done with every other drive installation.

FIGURE 12-73: Remove the faceplate from the front of the case.

 Note At this time, choose the faceplate that best matches the color of the case and, if necessary, replace the faceplate of the platinum drive. In our case, we're keeping the black face that came on it, since it matches our case. Simply undo the clips on both sides, snap off the plate, and snap on the one you prefer.

Before you proceed any further, attach all the cables to the platinum drive at this point. Usually, you'd attach these cables after the platinum drive is seated into the case, but you're doing this now because as you'd quickly find out, you're running out of room to work in the case and this makes it much easier!

2. With the knobs facing away from you, attach the gray ribbon cable to the rear of the platinum drive with the red-colored wire on the right side of the drive. (Fortunately, the cable only fits one way on the drive because of how the pins are oriented. It may be difficult to line up the pins. Be gentle so you don't bend the pins accidentally.)

3. Attach a four-pin female connector of the power splitter cable that came with the sound card (red, black, black, yellow cable) to the four-pin male connector to the right side of the platinum drive.

4. Take the internal FireWire cable, which is a black cable with a two-row, 10-pin female connector on both ends, and attach one end to the 10-pin, two-row male connector on the left side of the platinum drive. The connector is labeled SB1394.

Your platinum drive should look like Figure 12-74.

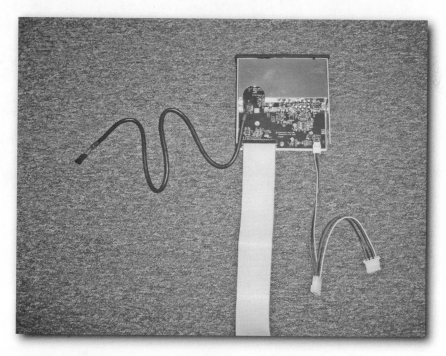

FIGURE 12-74: All three cables connected to the platinum drive.

Installing the Platinum Drive

To install the platinum drive in the front of the case, follow these steps:

1. Feed the wires now connected to the platinum drive through the front of the case, as shown in Figure 12-75

2. Slowly slide in the platinum drive until the empty 5-1/4 inch bays by lifting up the clear clip on the left side and slide the drive into the top bay.

FIGURE 12-75: Feed the cables through the case.

3. Gently work the platinum drive into place until the screw holes line up with the side of the case.

4. It takes four screws, one on the lower-left and upper-right on both sides. Lower the clear plastic clip in place to keep the platinum drive secure.

The live drive is now secure.

Installing the Card

Lay the case back on its side and we'll install the card.

1. Remove sound card from the static bag. Inside the static bag is a color sticker to apply to the rear of your sound card. Follow the diagram on the sticker to apply it to the card.

2. Put all wires that are not being used over the edge of the case so that they are out of the way.

3. Use a flathead screwdriver to pry open the last cover over the last PCI port (the bottom) as shown in Figure 12-76.

4. Locate the gray ribbon cable (AD Extension cable) from the back of the platinum drive and attach it to the right side of the sound card with the red wire (pin 1 designator) facing upward, as shown in Figure 12-77.

FIGURE 12-76: Use a flathead screwdriver to pry open the cover on the PCI port.

FIGURE 12-77: Attach the ribbon cable to your sound card.

Tip

Usually, you seat the card and then attach the ribbon cable; however, when we tried this, it was too difficult to maneuver inside the case. Attaching the ribbon cable before seating the card was a lot easier.

5. Take the SoundBlaster soundcard and line up the tabs on the bottom of the card with the last PCI slot on the motherboard, as shown in Figure 12-78.

FIGURE 12-78: Insert the card into the case, aligning the bottom of the card with the last PCI slot.

6. Press down firmly to seat the card into place.

7. Secure the card to the case with one screw at the top of the metal flange of the card (retaining clip) as shown in Figure 12-79.

8. Find the digital CD audio cable — the only cable that came with the case. It's a gray cable with two-pin female connectors, one on each end. Attach one end of cable to the right-most port on the top of the sound card, which is labeled "CD SPDIF." Attach the other end to the bottom-most port of the rear of the Memorex DVD drive.

FIGURE 12-79: Secure the sound card to the case with one screw.

Note With Windows XP, attaching this cable may no longer be necessary; however, attach it in case you are running a different operating system.

9. Attach the power extension cable to an empty molex connector attached to the cable attached to the DVD drive.

10. Finally, take the free end of the internal FireWire cable and attach it to the second port from the right on the top of the sound card, which is labeled SB1394. The sound card with all three cables connected is shown in Figure 12-80.

Note The cable should have *just enough* slack to connect it to the sound card. If you don't have enough slack, install the platinum drive into a lower bay.

The soundcard is now installed! The last thing you have to do now is install the USB ports and close up the case.

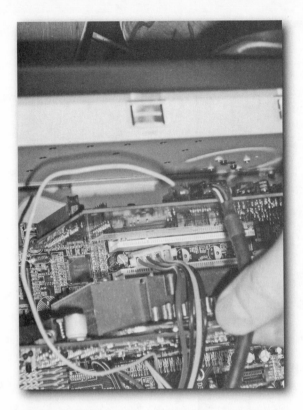

FIGURE 12-80: Ribbon cable, audio cable, and the FireWire cable all connected to the sound card.

Install the Extra USB Ports

You'll find you have four extra pieces — two USB ports and two USB ports with a mini-pin FireWire. We only install the one *without* the mini-pin FireWire, shown in Figure 12-81, because the FireWire expansion port on our motherboard has been covered by our PCI sound card. If your board is different, install this in the same way you install the two USB ports next.

1. Pop of the top-most bracket from the back of the case with a flathead screwdriver.

2. Insert the two USB ports by holding them flush with the case and sliding them down.

3. After they are in place, screw them in to secure.

4. Plug in the yellow, two-row, female, nine-pin end of the USB port into the yellow USB expansion slot, located near the LED connectors on the motherboard shown in Figure 12-82.

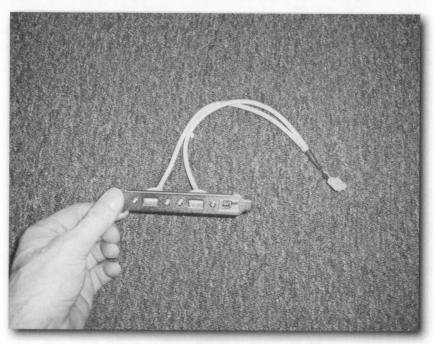

FIGURE 12-81: The last piece — the two USB ports.

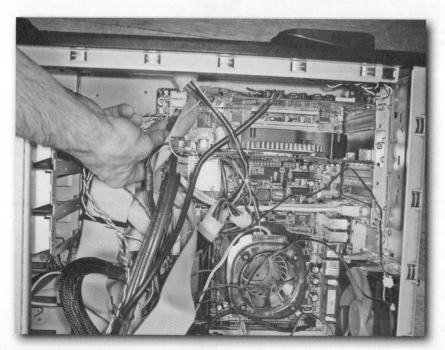

FIGURE 12-82: Connect the USB cables to the expansion slot.

We don't like to use these because, in our experience, this does not fit snuggly with the case; the lower end is loose, banging into the motherboard as you insert and unplug ports. It may be different with your case, but if you find yours is also loose, exercise care when using these ports, and only use them as your last ports (use the main ones first).

Complete the Installation

Congratulations! Everything is installed! The inside of your case should look like Figure 12-83.

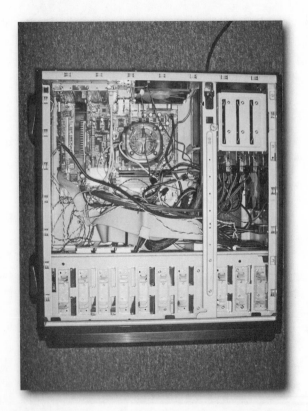

FIGURE 12-83: The inside of our case, with all devices installed.

Now, reapply the sides of the case, and stand the computer upright. Your computer should look like ours, shown in Figure 12-84.

FIGURE 12-84: Our computer, from the front and side.

Tip

Before closing the case, take the extra twist ties that came with all your equipment and bind the wires together so that they fit neatly into the case. This isn't necessary, but it does make for a neater inside.

It's time to connect the monitor and power on your computer for the first time. You should get one beep. The installation is a success! In the next chapter, you install the operating system and customize it to run games as effectively as possible. See you there!

Installing Your Software/OS

This chapter covers several details. It first looks at how to install your chosen operating system. Before you can install any games and get playing, you have to install Windows. You might have done a few of these installs before, and this one should only be slightly different from them. The big difference is how you configure all the hard drives with partitions and the creation of the RAID0.

If you haven't had a chance to do an install, don't worry too much; it is fairly straightforward and simple. The guide we have created walks you through setting up Microsoft Windows XP with Service Pack 2 from start to finish, including the drive setup, complete with detailed pictures. Following that lengthy section you can begin to optimize your system's software. You install your video drivers and adjust your screen resolution, along with moving your pagefile to the proper partition that you create for it. After that you move onto a nice collection of tweaks and modifications to Windows to make your gaming faster, sleeker, and more impressive. A good portion of this section is about freeing up resources that Windows is unnecessarily using on programs it runs in the background that you don't actually need.

This involves stopping certain programs that Windows automatically runs as well as turning off unneeded Windows Services. Again have no fear if any of this is new to you. This chapter walks you through everything in an easy step-by-step fashion.

After you are done tweaking your ultimate machine, we show you a few ways to maintain your high-performance machine. A computer is just like a car — if you don't take care of it, you will eventually run it into the ground. Take care of your computer and it won't be Game Over any time soon.

At the end of the chapter, when your computer is completely set up, you delve into benchmarking. Benchmarking is a way to gauge how well your system performs compared to other machines out in the world. Your focus, of course, is how well it can handle games. With this machine, expect great things!

Choosing Your Operating System

The first thing you must do is choose which operating system you want to use. There are a couple of current options — Microsoft XP Home and XP Professional, as well as the slightly older Windows 2000.

Although we have chosen to use Microsoft Windows XP with Service Pack 2, you can use whatever operating system you have. It is not recommended that the operating system you choose be older than Windows 2000. The hardware and the games you want to use just won't work nearly as well on Windows Me.

But what are the differences between the current versions of Windows? Well, let's talk about a few differences between the XP Home edition and the Professional edition that might matter to you as a gamer. Hopefully that will help you decide.

Let's start by explaining that Windows XP Home edition is the exact same as the Professional version minus a few features. Just think of the Professional version as the one on steroids. It can do everything the Home edition can, and then just a little more.

Another point to note is that XP Home is aimed at the average consumer; XP Professional is aimed more at the power users and corporate businesses. As a gamer with an incredible computer you can more than consider yourself as a power user if you like. If you have come this far along in building the ultimate gaming computer, the term *power* user was created to define people like you.

Beyond that, there are three main differences to consider when deciding which operating system to use. There is the price. Windows XP Home edition costs currently just over $100; the Professional version is just under $200. This means double the cost. That alone might help you decide to go with XP Home, which could be seen as a wise decision.

Tip   For the frugal shoppers who don't mind not getting their products in a pretty box there are also OEM versions of Windows XP Home that can be found for under $90 on the Internet. You can also get Windows XP Professional for around $140.

Let's see a couple of things you get for that extra $100, and then you can decide if it's worth it for you. There are a few operations Professional can do that Home can't, one being file encryption. Do you want to keep you data safe? All your notes and walkthroughs for all your game and save game files? File encryption is a good way to protect yourself because it simply helps prevent hackers from tampering with all the information on your machine. With file encryption you have a local security system that allows you to create permissions for all your files and folders. This is a feature that should not be overlooked.

Another point is that Windows XP Home edition is not a managed operating system. Professional is. This means that the Professional edition can look for and heed directions sent from a Windows server and log in to a domain. This is not something you need to worry about in gaming. We are creating one machine for gaming at home and not connecting to a corporate network. If you have a slightly different destination, you might want to go a different route, factoring in what matters to you.

There is a decent list of other differences between the two editions, such as Multi-Language Support, Dynamic Disk Support, Automated System Recovery, and Network Monitor features, but none of these have a huge impact on gaming. In the end if you can't afford to buy the Professional edition, the Home edition will suit your needs. If you decide to go with Professional, you just have a few more choices of features and operations you can do in the future.

Set Up RAID0

Now that you have picked your operating system, you need to get this machine in gaming order and create the RAID0 in the BIOS. In very simple terms the BIOS is software that lives on the motherboard to help it run. You have to tell the BIOS that you are planning to use a RAID0 so when the motherboard talks to the hard drives, it knows what to do.

This is not a long section in the book, but it's a very important section. Make sure before you continue that this step has been completed in full and that the RAID0 has been set up. If it is not set up properly, the RAID won't exist and you won't get the speed out of the drives that you desire.

Alright, let's get to it!

Creating the Floppy Driver Diskette

The only reason Windows XP ever needs a floppy these days is to allow it to load custom drivers for hard drive controllers it doesn't recognize. This is known as the "F6 floppy" because you have to press the F6 function key on your keyboard when Windows Setup is starting so you can load the driver. This includes drivers for RAID. Most motherboards come with either a floppy for this purpose, or have a utility on their driver CD that allows you to create one. In this case, you need to create a RAID.

To make Windows notice RAID0, you have to give it some new drivers. To make the floppy disk that holds these drivers, do the following on any extra computer you have access to that has both a floppy drive and CD-ROM drive.

1. Place a floppy in the floppy drive of any computer you have that can run Windows.
2. Place the CD-ROM that came with your motherboard into your CD-ROM drive. It may be labeled NVidianForce4 Series Utility CD, or at least be labeled motherboard driver CD.
3. Double-click My Computer.
4. Right-click the floppy drive and then choose Format from the context menu.
5. Select Quick Format.
6. Click OK.
7. Click to erase the floppy. In a moment the disk will be ready.
8. In My Computer, browse to the CD-ROM drive where you loaded your CD.

9. Go into the BootDrv folder. (Some motherboard CDs place the floppy creation utility under "Apps," the actual driver folder, or under a folder labeled "utilities.")

10. Double-click Menu.exe.

11. Press E for the NVidia XP drivers.

12. After a moment it will be done copying. Take the floppy disk out and put it aside.

That all it takes! Off you go back to your new computer.

Final Preparations for the Computer

Now that the computer is assembled you need some interfaces attached to it so you can communicate with the computer. Now is a good time to unpack your Saitek keyboard, Dell flat screen 2405FPW, and MX100 Logitech and get them connected. Basically, you need a working machine. If you don't have these particular parts, don't worry. Just attach any monitor, mouse, and keyboard you can find so that you can begin working on the computer. You can replace any of these later with the bigger, better, and more powerful parts.

After you have all of those connected and have set yourself up in a convenient and comfortable place, you are ready for that RAID setup.

Creating the RAID Volume

1. To make this RAID volume, we are going to use the Nvidia RAID BIOS program to help us. The good news is that this is already a part of your motherboard's BIOS software if you are using the GA-K8N Ultra-9 like we are. To use the Nvidia RAID BIOS to create your RAID, do the following.

2. Turn on your computer. A few seconds after starting up, as the BIOS information flows across your screen, it will stop for only a few short seconds with the following prompt: "Press F10 to enter RAID setup Utility." Press F10. If you missed it this first time, just restart your computer until you get it.

3. After the Nvidia RAID Utility -Define a New Array- window appears, you are ready for the next step. You first need to change the RAID Mode from Mirroring to Striping. Mirroring is a great option but we don't care about redundancy but more for speed, which striping gives us. If the text for Mirroring is not already highlighted in green, hit the Tab key until it is. Tab lets you select the window in which you are working. After Mirroring is highlighted, press the down arrow key once to change it to Striping.

4. Press Tab again until Free Disks is highlighted in green.

5. Using the up and down arrow keys, select the first WD740GD hard drive. When highlighted, press the right arrow key to move them over the box on the right designated the Array Disks.

6. Select the second WD740GD and move it to the right as well.

7. After both drives you want in the RAID are in the Array Disks box, press F7. A Clear Disk Data dialog box appears. Press Y to accept. You move to the Array List screen.

8. Press the B key to set this array as your boot device. Under the Boot designation on the far left, middle side, the No should change to Yes.

9. Press Ctrl + X to exit the Nvidia Raid Utility software. You should now be back at the BIOS screen.

That's it! RAID0 is now set up in the BIOS. Be sure to leave your computer on for the next step—installing the OS.

Installing Windows XP Professional SP2

You've got all the hardware out of the way, and now it's time for the software. This means that it's time to install the operating system.

If you chose to use Windows XP Professional that includes Service Pack 2, the following directions walk you through the OS installation. If you choose another version of Windows or Professional without Service Pack 2, you can still follow along but the steps may diverge slightly from what is written here. The most important and possibly most difficult part of the setup is going to be the hard drives. Fortunately, this should be similar if you use any of the XP operating systems.

Preparing for the Installation

So get yourself one step closer to gaming and start the operating system installation. You left your computer running because you have to put the Windows XP Professional SP2 CD-ROM into one of the DVD drives.

So our first step in this project is to insert the Windows XP Professional SP2 CD-ROM into our Memorex DVD drive.

Now turn your computer off and then on again.

As the computer boots up through the beginning DOS screens, watch the bottom of the screen for Boot from CD: When it shows up, quickly press any key. This launches the Windows OS installation.

If the hard drives are unformatted, the system should automatically boot from the CD.

If the Boot from CD: screen does not show up after about five minutes there is another change you should make. Do the following to make your DVD-ROM the first bootable drive in your computer:

1. Turn off your computer.

2. Turn on your computer, and as you do, on the bottom of the screen it will ask you to press Delete to enter the Bios Setup. Press Delete.

3. In a moment it will take you into the CMOS Setup Utility.

4. Press the down arrow key once so that on the left Advanced Bios Features becomes highlighted in red.

5. Press Enter to select this choice.

6. Press the down arrow key once so that the First Boot Device becomes highlighted in red.

7. Press Enter again to change this setting; it will likely be set to Floppy drive at the moment.

8. A First Boot Device menu appears. Press the down arrow key a couple of times until the square in the brackets is next to CDROM.

9. Press Enter to select this choice.

10. Press the Escape key to retreat one menu.

11. Press F10 to save and exit setup.

12. Press Y to save settings.

Now when you boot up you should be able to see the Boot from CD: prompt.

Setting Up Windows

A blue Windows Setup screen comes up. On the bottom of the screen it shows that it is loading files and prompts you to press F6. If you miss this prompt, restart you computer and try again until you press the key in time.

Eventually you come to a screen that says that setup could not find any mass storage devices. You know there are some drives; you just have to inform Windows of that, which is why you made the floppy disk with the drivers on it. Slide the floppy disk into the floppy drive and press S.

The following screen offers you two choices of what type of drivers you want to install. You need both! So highlight the top one and press Enter.

After that is done, it kicks you back to the first screen. Press S again so that you can load the other set of drivers.

This time select the second set of drivers and then press Enter again to load them.

Once again you are taken back to your original screen. At the top it notes the drivers you selected. If you do not see both of the drivers listed, press S again and load the one you missed. If both of these drivers are not there, Windows will not see the RAID properly. Press Enter after you are sure both drivers are loaded.

After Windows is done loading more files, a Welcome to Setup menu appears. You want to set up Windows, so press Enter.

The End-User License Agreement appears. Read through it if you desire and then press F8 to agree so that the installation continues.

Creating the Partitions

The following screen helps you create your partitions.

You actually want to create the partition that Windows will be held on first. To do this, you have to plan slightly ahead and know what other partitions you want on these drives as well so you can divide up the space as needed.

You can refer to Chapter 6, Choosing Your Ultimate Storage, in which we discuss partitions and make suggestions that might work for you.

With the two Western Digital Raptors in RAID0, we have 141GB of storage for our primary drives. We planned out dividing that space up in the following amounts:

- First Partition: Operating system and files 30GB or 30720MB

- Second Partition: Pagefile 4GB or 4096MB

- Third Partition: Games 116GB or 118784MB

You may notice now that the 250GB storage drive is not showing up. That is okay, because for that one we have to load the drivers inside of Windows. We will get to that a little later.

Partitions can be any size you want. You don't have to strictly follow our choices. If you have a different plan or goal, feel free to implement it.

The first partition is the OS partition and files partition.

1. Press C to create your first partition in the unpartitioned space. Enter the partition size in megabytes into the gray box. We are using 30GB, so that is 30720MB.

2. Press the down arrow to select Unpartitioned space, and press C again to create your next partition. The second partition you want to create is for your pagefile. Make your pagefile double the amount of space as RAM you have. For example, if you have 512MB of RAM, make your pagefile partition 1024MB. In our ultimate gaming PC, we have 2GB of RAM. We want our pagefile partition to be 4GB or 4096MB of space but we need a little buffer on the drive for Windows to work, so we will make it 5GB or 5120MB.

3. At the top, highlight the C: partition by using the up and down arrows and press Enter to set up Windows XP on the selected partition.

4. On the next screen use the down arrow to select Format the partition using the NTFS file system and then press Enter.

Note Formatting can take anywhere from a couple minutes to a half hour or more, depending on how large your partitions are.

5. After the formatting is completed, setup begins copying files from the CD-ROM to your OS partition. In a few moments of Windows doing its work, it may prompt you to insert a disk labeled Nvidia Raid Driver. If it does, place the floppy disk you have used to install the hard drive drivers back into the floppy drive and press Enter.

6. After the installation process is done copying files, the computer reboots. The hard part is over. The rest of the installation is automated with minimal needed input from you. After the computer starts back up on its own, it continues to load files.

7. Set up Regional and Language Options. Click Next on the first screen.

8. On the following screen, enter your name as requested. Organization can be left empty if you desire. We put in Ultimate Gaming PC.

9. Next you are asked to enter your product key that came with your Windows XP installation disc. Type in your product key and click Next.

10. Type in the name of your computer. Name it anything you want, but try to keep the name simple. We called ours Ultimate.

11. The lower half of the screen asks for an administrator password. You can leave this blank if you want, but in the world of the broadband and endless access to the Internet you would be safer putting in a password that is obscure, that uses numbers and letters, and nobody else knows. This helps prevent online hackers from accessing your computer and data. Press Enter.

12. Adjust the Date and Time settings as needed and then click Next.

13. The following screen asks you to choose your network settings. Typical Settings is highlighted by default and that is what you want. Click Next.

14. On the next screen leave it as the default settings again for Workgroup and click Next.

15. Setup continues for a few moments and eventually reboots your computer. When it comes back up, Windows notifies you that it is automatically adjusting your screen resolution. Click OK.

16. A box pops up asking if you can read it. This is nothing more than Windows verifying its automatic adjustments were accurate. Click OK if you can read it. If not, Windows will try again to adjust the screen or use a weaker resolution, which is fine until you install the video card drivers.

17. A Welcome to Microsoft Windows screen appears, thanking you for purchasing Windows. Click Next in the lower-right corner.

18. The following screen asks if you want Windows to help protect your computer. For now, take their recommendation and use their protection.

19. Create your user account. Type in your name, nickname, or handle in the Your name field and then click Next. We used GameMaster to keep the vibe going, but the choice is yours.

20. Microsoft again thanks you for choosing their product and tells you that you are done with your installation. Click Finish. Windows launches for the first time.

That's it! You are now at the Windows desktop! You are now so close to playing all the games you love. Before you can get to that point, though, you have just a few more quick stops to make, all of them involving getting Windows into shape. Off you go.

Installing Mouse Drivers from the CD-ROM

You now need to get your mouse up and running. The Logitech MX-1000 came with a CD-ROM with drivers on it. If you plan to use all the features of your mouse, you need to load the MX-1000 drivers onto the computer. Without these drivers you cannot get the full benefits of your new mouse such as being able to use all of the numerous buttons. To install the mouse drivers, do the following.

1. With your computer off, plug your mouse cradle into either a USB port or the mouse PS2 slot on the back of your computer.

2. Take the power adapter from the MX-1000 box and connect one end to the cradle and the other end to any free power socket that you have.

3. Turn the mouse over and turn it on from the bottom; then place it in the cradle.

4. Turn on your computer. Windows, after it starts, should recognize the mouse and start it running. Windows may also ask that you reboot so that the installation of the new device can complete

5. After the reboot, your mouse should begin working. Place the CD-ROM that came with your MX-1000 into your DVD drive. After a moment the CD begins to autorun.

6. Click the forward-facing arrow.

7. Click forward again on the next screen to choose English as the language, or change the language you desire; then click Next.

8. Logitech asks if you want to install the Logitech Desktop Manager, which can help with updates and support. Because we don't want extra programs running that we don't need on our computer, we choose not to install this; however, you can decide for yourself if this is something that you want. Make your decision and then click the forward arrow again.

9. Click the forward facing arrow to choose the default installation directory.

10. Check I Agree on the License Agreement page and then click forward.

11. To keep the install to a minimum, unless you want these programs on the following screen, uncheck Ebay Shortcut and Musicmatch from being installed; then go forward.

12. The installation should now begin. After it is done, it asks you to reboot.

13. After the computer comes back on, Logitech starts with a QuickTour. Feel free to take the tour so that you understand all the benefits of your new wireless mouse that allow you to customize it a little to your liking.

Now that the mouse is functional, it's time to get Windows looking a little bit prettier. To do that, you have to install your video card drivers. No sense waiting around. Let's get going.

Installing Video Card drivers

Logically the next thing you should do is install the drivers that make your video card work. It is kind of working now, but those are only the default drivers. You need the drivers that are cutting-edge and allow you to see brilliant graphics and vibrant colors. This also spiffies up the appearance of the computer, making it much easier and more pleasant to work with as you continue to begin to optimize it.

Your video card probably came with an installation disk. You can use this disk or go online to the manufacturer's Website to get the latest drivers.

 If you plan to go online to get the latest drivers, you have to connect your network cable to the back of your computer.

Installing Drivers from the CD-ROM

If you chose the BFG Geforce 6800 Ultra OC PCIe video card as we did, here are the instructions for installing the drivers.

1. Place the CD-ROM that came with your video card into your DVD drive. After a moment the CD begins to autorun.

2. When the menus come up from the CD, choose the appropriate language. We chose English.

3. Next click Install Drivers.

4. On the following screen, click Continue.

5. Click Next.

6. Click Continue Anyway.

7. After installed, reboot.

Note At the time of this writing the latest drivers available for the video card were included on the CD-ROM that came with the card. If you want to check to see if there are newer drivers, visit www.BFGTECH.com.

Adjusting the Screen Resolution

Now that you have your video card drivers installed, it is now time to put them to use. To do this you have to adjust your screen resolution settings. There can be a wide range of resolution settings for you to choose from, depending on which video card you purchased. Our chosen video card gives us the following choices: 800 Mlti 600, 1024 x 768, 1152 x 864, 1280 x 1024, 1600 x 900, 1600 x 1200, 1680 x 1050, and 1920 x 1200. The minimum range that you want for gaming is probably 1024 x 768 pixels. Some people like to go even higher to 1280 x 1024 pixels and beyond, which gives a tight, sharp look to your system. As for the Dell UltraSharp 2405FPW 24-Inch Wide Aspect Flat Panel LCD, the recommended resolution is a crazy 1920 x 1200. If this is the monitor you purchased, you probably saw this information on the clear protective sheet that protected the screen when you unpacked it.

There is no set resolution that you must have. The only factor that matters is what looks good to you. Keep in mind, though, while choosing your resolution, that the higher the resolution you choose, the more processing power, video card function, and system memory is required to make it happen.

To adjust your screen resolution, do the following:

1. Right-click your desktop.
2. Click Properties.
3. Click the Settings tab.
4. In the area for Screen Resolution, move the bar to the right to the setting you prefer or that is recommended by your monitor. For our monitor it is 1920 x 1200.
5. Make sure that Color Quality is set to at least 32 bit, as shown in Figure 13-1.
6. Click Apply.
7. At this point Windows tries to put the settings you have requested into effect. A box appears asking if you want to keep these settings. Click Yes.
8. Click OK.

That's it. The video settings have been adjusted. Now you can continue to load other drivers for the rest of the devices you have. Next are the Sound Blaster drivers so you can get optimum sound out of your machine.

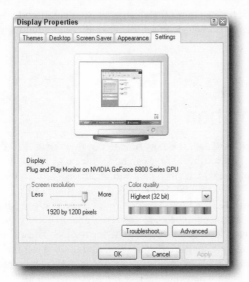

FIGURE 13-1: Video resolution settings for our computer.

Installing SoundBlaster Drivers from the CD-ROM

If you chose the SoundBlaster Audigy 2 ZS card as we did, here are the instructions for installing the drivers from the CD-ROM that came with the sound card.

1. Place the CD-ROM that came with your sound card into your DVD drive. After a moment, the CD begins to autorun.

2. When the menu comes up from the CD, choose the appropriate language. We chose English.

3. Click Install.

4. The following screen asks you to select your region. Do so by using the drop-down menu; then click OK.

5. Click Yes to accept the user agreement.

6. Click Next.

7. Click Next again.

8. Choose Full Installation and then click Next.

9. You now have to choose what type of speakers you have. Because we chose the Logitech Z-5500 Digital speakers, we chose the 5.1 option.

10. On the next screen choose No, that you don't want digital output as your default sound. Then click Next.

11. The following window lets you know that online documentation is available and wants you to let them know what product you bought. Select the SoundBlaster Audigy 2 ZS option; then click Next.

12. Click Next again. The files begin to copy to the hard drive.

13. Accept the user agreement again.

14. Click Next.

15. Click Full.

16. Click Next once more.

17. Click "Finish."

18. Click Exit to leave the SoundBlaster interface.

19. The SoundBlaster drivers require a reboot.

20. After the computer comes back on, you are asked to register your product. You can bypass this for now, if you choose.

Note Check the SoundBlaster Website for the latest drivers. You never know when some new ones might be out there.

You are now done with your SoundBlaster driver installation. But don't worry—you have more drivers to install. Next you install the rest of the motherboard drivers to make all your other onboard devices functional.

Installing Motherboard Drivers from the CD-ROM

The GA-K8N Ultra-9 motherboard came with a CD-ROM with drivers on it. This is the same one that we used for our SATA hard drive drivers. For our motherboard, we need that again to load more drivers onto the computer. Let's get to it.

1. Place the CD-ROM that came with your motherboard into your DVD drive. After a moment the CD begins to autorun. Notice in the right pane that you are missing drivers for a several devices—on our screen, six devices are shown in Figure 13-2.

2. With all of the drivers selected, click Go. The CD-ROM kick offs and tries to install the first driver. After it installs the first driver, it automatically reboots your computer.

3. After the computer restarts, the driver program tries to install the next device and then the next until it is completed. After it is done, click "OK" to reboot again.

This should install all the necessary drivers, putting all the driver fun behind you for now as you inch your way toward gaming heaven. Now let's get all the hard drives into shape.

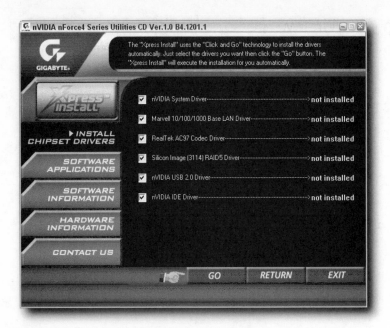

FIGURE 13-2: All the devices that need to be installed.

Setting Up the Hard Drive

You have shown Windows that you wanted a RAID, but you still have to format the other partitions you made as well as help Windows recognize your 250GB storage. After Windows sees the storage area, you need to break it up into a few more partitions.

Format the Other Partitions

No sense waiting around, so let's get to work.

1. Open My Computer from the desktop.

2. Double-click the E drive.

3. A prompt appears, asking if you want to format the drive. Click Yes.

4. Another box immediately appears. Click Start.

5. A warning box appears stating that all data will be lost on the drive. Click OK to start the formatting process.

6. Repeat this process for the F drive. After both the E and F drives are formatted, continue with the steps in the following section.

Making Sure Windows Sees the Partition

Now you have to make Windows take notice of your 250GB drive. Unfortunately to do so you have to go back into the BIOS and make two changes. Not a big deal but it means you have to reboot. To make Windows see your storage drive, follow these steps.

1. Reboot your computer.

2. When it starts to boot up, press the Delete key to enter the BIOS.

3. Press the down arrow twice and choose Integrated Peripherals. Press Enter to select this choice.

4. Scroll down to SATA 2 Primary and then press Enter to accept the change.

5. Press the up arrow key until the box is next to disable.

6. Scroll down to SATA 2 Secondary and then press Enter to accept the change.

7. Press the up arrow key until the box is next to Disable.

8. Press F10 to save your changes and quit.

9. Press Y to save and exit.

The computer reboots. After you are in Windows again, you can finish up with this drive. You need to partition and format it. For our 250GB Western Digital drive we planned to divide the space in the following amounts:

- First Partition: Backup space for files from the RAIDed drives 40GB or 40960MB

- Second Partition: Storage space 83GB or 84992MB

- Third Partition: Storage space 127GB or 130048MB

   To create this, perform the steps in the following section.

Partitioning the Western Digital Drive

1. Click Start and then choose Programs.

2. Right-click the My Computer Icon and choose Manage to open the Computer Management dialog box.

3. In the left pane, click Disk Management.

4. A box titled Initialize and Convert Disk Wizard should appear. This box indicates that Windows now sees your other drive. Click Next.

5. Click Next again.

6. On the next screen check the box next to the Disk 0 and then click Next again.

7. Click Finish.

Still with us? Great! Then let's continue.

Breaking up the Drive

You now need to break up this large 250GB drive into different partitions. Use the same Disk Management software, so keep the Disk Management window of the Computer Management dialog box open. Let's begin.

1. With the Disk Management window open, look for the new drive bordered black and noted as 232GB in size. Click where it says Disk 0 near the icon.

Warning

Important! Don't click the area to the right where it says unallocated! That won't get you to where you need. Click the far left side where it says Dynamic so the menus change to what we need. Much time has been wasted at this point by many people over the years.

2. Right-click and Convert to Basic Disk. In a moment it will be complete and you will have a large basic disk.

3. Right-click the Unallocated space and click New Partition.

4. Click Next.

5. Click Next to select this first partition as primary.

6. Enter the size of this first partition. You want to create this first partition on the drive to use as backup space for all your files from the RAIDed drives, so this partition should be about 40GB or 40960MB.

7. Click Next.

8. Click Next again.

9. Click Finish.

Creating the Next Partition

With that done, you have to create your next partition. There are only two more to go! Don't worry; the bright light at the end of the tunnel really is getting closer. No, really it is. Anyway, here are the next steps.

1. Right-click again on the unallocated space, which should now be 192GB. Click New Partition again.

2. Click Next.

3. Click Next to select this first partition as primary.

4. This partition will be for storage space and should be 83GB or 84992MB in size. On this screen that comes up, fill in that size.

5. Click Next.

6. Click Next again.

7. Click Finish.

Creating the Last Partition

Here's at the last one. Let's get it out of the way so you can move on to the next part of the setup.

1. The last partition is for more storage as needed. Right-click the remaining unallocated space and for the last time click New Partition.

2. Click Next.

3. Click Next to select this first partition as primary.

4. This partition uses the remainder of the drive. Leave the default at 112522MB.

5. Click Next.

6. Click Next again.

7. Click Finish.

Now all the drives are formatting.

OS Tweaking and Management

Buying some of the best hardware on the market and installing your operating system were just the first couple steps in building the ultimate gaming PC. Now that you have it altogether, it is time to fine-tune Windows a little to make it more suitable and powerful as a gaming rig.

Optimizing your system settings in the most efficient way allows for a better gaming experience. The following section gives you a simple overview of what you can do to help make Windows run faster.

There are programs that can help you do all this — some for free and some that cost money. We will go over those at the end of the section, but we also show you how you can do it yourself with relative ease and at no extra cost.

 Just a friendly reminder that the following was written in regards to Microsoft Windows XP SP2, the most current and versatile operating system currently available for the PC gaming market. Not all of the following optimizations work, or are found in the same place on other versions of the Windows operating system.

Optimizing Your Ultimate PC

You are ready to begin the process of optimizing the PC.

Optimization Step #1: Naming Your Drives

Naming your drives helps you stay organized. Luckily it is also a very simple thing to do. With each drive labeled, you can quickly tell what information is on which drive, especially with as many partitions as we have created. It's a simple yet very effective way to help maintain your data. When naming your drives try to use simple, short names that clearly define the drive's purpose. As an example the partition you created for your pagefile could simply be called Pagefile.

To name your hard drives do the following:

1. Double-click My Computer.

2. Right-click the first drive listed.

3. Click Rename to highlight the drive's name.

4. Clear the current name by pressing the Delete key.

5. In the empty Name box type the name you want that drive to have. For instance our firstdrive is C and we want an OS drive. So we typed in OS.

6. Repeat steps 1 through 5 for each of your other drives, naming them appropriately.

If you followed our exact setup, your drives should be labeled as the following : the C drive is OS, the E drive is Pagefile, the F drive is Games, the G drive is Backup, the H drive is Storage 1, and the last drive, the I drive, is Storage 2.

Optimization Step #2: Adjusting the Location of Your Pagefile

We have talked about the pagefile before in the storage chapter as well as in this chapter, and about why we want it on a separate drive. A simple refresher here couldn't hurt. A pagefile is space Windows uses to temporarily store information while it is running. A pagefile, because it writes and deletes so much information in a very short amount of time, causes fragmentation of a drive, and that hurts the drive's performance significantly. By putting the pagefile in its own little area, you restrain the area on the drive that it can fragment. By doing this you help maintain and increase the drive performance.

You have already made your partition for the pagefile, and have named the drive in the previous step. Now all you have to do is tell Windows where you want the pagefile to reside.

To adjust the location of your pagefile, do the following:

1. Right-click My Computer.

2. Click Properties.

3. Click the Advanced tab.

4. Under Performance click Settings.

5. Click the Advanced tab.

6. Under the Virtual Settings section, click Change.

7. Select the partition that you chose for you pagefile. (Ours was the 5GB drive.) You can tell which drive is which by looking at how much space is on the partitions, as noted in the area Space Available. It might be just slightly less than 5094 by a few megabytes because the actual creation of the partition takes up a little space.

8. Select Custom Size.

9. Click Set. You should see your sizes appear next to your chosen drive.

10. Now you have to remove the default paging file from the OS partition. Highlight your OS partition.

11. Select No Paging File.

12. Click Set.

13. Before you click OK, make sure your window looks like the one shown in Figure 13-3; then click OK.

FIGURE 13-3: New pagefile settings.

14. Reboot for the settings to take effect.

Optimization Step #3: Disabling Automatic Updates

You can save resources and bandwidth by turning off the Windows Automatic Updates. Updates is a process that contacts Microsoft across the Internet to check if all the OS software on your computer is up to date. The problem with this, as a gamer, is that the auto update process might try to connect on its own and download the latest updates while you are in the middle of an online match of Half Life 2. When Windows Automatic Updates does this, it hurts your performance for several reasons. It takes up CPU power and time. If it finds needed updates, it instantly begins downloading them, which can potentially begin strangling your Internet connection and causing a lag.

The solution to this is to stop Windows from automatically trying to update your computer.

Warning Only disable the Automatic Updates service if you are confident that you can remember to check the Microsoft site regularly for the latest updates and patches. Disabling this feature may save you bandwidth and processing power, but you should have all the latest patches from Microsoft. Disabling the automatic updates means you have to go and check for updates yourself because Windows no longer does this for you automatically. The updates often are security fixes that help protect your computer from any vulnerabilities found within the software, making them a good thing to have as a responsible gamer.

To turn off your Automatic Updates, do the following:

1. Right-click My Computer.

2. Click Properties.

3. Click the Automatic Updates tab.

4. Select Turn off Automatic Updating, as shown in Figure 13-4.

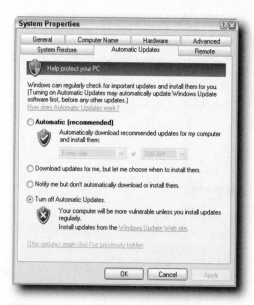

FIGURE 13-4: Turning off Automatic Updates.

5. Click Apply.

6. Click OK.

Optimization Step #4: Reducing the Overheard of the Windows Interface

A nice feature with Windows is that it does its best to look visually appealing. This is great, but aesthetics come with a price. The price, of course, is that it takes up resources, both in CPU processing and in memory to create all those clean-cut, crisp, and bright graphics you have on your interface. Not many people do it, but there is a way to reduce this wasted processing power so it can be steadily diverted into rendering the next cyber-babe-avatar you come across.

The reason most people don't divert the processing power away from their beautiful interface is because it makes Windows look much less attractive. This is something you have to judge for yourself. If you don't mind the toned-down, blotchy-looking, less-colorful interface, this is a great way to save on overhead processing power.

This only reduces the graphic quality of the Windows interface and does not affect any games in the same way

With a computer as powerful as the one you are making, you won't really see a huge savings by doing this. Still, however, it is a viable way to save resources if you find you ever need that little extra power or extra frame rate.

To reduce the overhead of the Windows interface, do the following:

1. Right-click My Computer.

2. Click Properties.

3. Click on the Advanced tab.

4. Under Performance, click Settings to open the Performance Option dialog box.

5. On the Visual Effects tab, select Adjust for Best Performance, as shown in Figure 13-5.

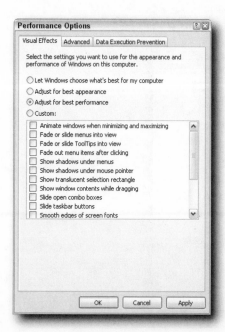

FIGURE 13-5: Adjusting Windows visual performance.

6. Click Apply.

7. Click OK.

Optimization Step #5: Turn off Remote Assistance and Remote Desktop Sharing

Remote Assistance and Remote Desktop Sharing is a useful feature that allows another computer to connect to your computer and have access to your files. It can be helpful if you are in need of some tech support, but it does add to your boot time and takes up overhead after Windows is running. It is also a potential security risk that could allow unethical people to do bad things to your computer after they take control of it. A good idea is to turn off Remote Assistance and Remote Desktop Sharing for now. This has a double benefit of safety and performance, and you can easily turn it on again later if you ever decide you need it.

To turn off Remote Assistance and Remote Desktop Sharing, do the following:

1. Right-click My Computer.

2. Click Properties.

3. Click the Remote tab.

4. Uncheck the boxes next to Remote Assistance and Remote Desktop, as shown in Figure 13-6.

5. Click Apply.

6. Click OK.

FIGURE 13-6: Turning off Remote Assistance.

Optimization Step #6: Turning off Windows Messenger

Windows Messenger and Outlook Express 6 are linked together like most Microsoft programs. If you have Outlook Express 6, your Windows Messenger program is designed to start every time you boot. This is just another program that takes up resources you would rather have free to run your games. The solution to this is to stop Windows Messenger from starting up on its own. Our plans won't stop you from using the chat client if you desire, but rather allow you to control when it is active and when it is not.

To stop Windows Messenger from starting, do the following:

1. Click Start/All Programs/Outlook Express.

2. Click Cancel on any box that pops up asking you to create an account.

3. Click Tools/Windows Messenger/Options.

4. Click the Preferences tab.

5. Uncheck the box next to Allow Windows Messenger to run in background.

6. Uncheck the box next to Run Windows Messenger when Windows starts.

7. When your Options page looks like Figure 13-7, click OK.

8. Close Outlook Express.

FIGURE 13-7: Stopping Windows Messenger from automatically starting.

Optimization Step #7: Stopping Windows Services That Are Not Needed

This is one of the longer, more involved optimization steps, but can be worth the effort. Windows Services are small programs that Windows uses to do different jobs. Like all programs, though, these services take up system resources. Each program uses only a little, but add a few of them together and you can start noticeably losing a fair amount of your total power. There are a few services that are running on your ultimate gaming rig that as a dedicated and avid gamer you never need or use. This means that you can turn them off for now, and then later, if the need ever arises, you can go back and turn them on. With gaming, our goal for this computer is the least amount of programs running on our computer as possible is best.

The following gives a list of the least or possibly not ever used services you might want to stop from automatically starting when Windows boots up. You have to make the final decision whether to stop it or not, based on your personal needs. If it sounds like something you might need, err on the side of caution and leave it on.

Warning

It is important to point out that these are standard Windows Services that Windows uses to run and that turning them off could have some strange result on your particular computer. We have never witnessed any problems, but you should be aware that there is a risk of undesired effects.

To begin turning off Windows Services, do the following:

1. Right-click My Computer.
2. Click Manage.
3. Double-click Services and Applications in the right pane.
4. Double-click Services in the right pane.
5. Double-click the service you want to change.
6. In Startup Type, change the setting to Manual.
7. Click Apply.
8. Click OK.
9. Repeat steps 5 through 8 for each service you want to change. Figure 13-8 shows a good selection of services that can be set to Manual.

The following processes are most likely running at the moment and can be set to Manual, which means they only start up if you go in and start them. After these processes are set to Manual, they continue to run until you reboot.

- Computer Browser
- Distributed Link Tracking Client
- Error Reporting Service
- Help and Support
- Network Location Awareness (NLA)
- Portable Media Serial Number

- Protected Storage

- Remote Registry

- Routing and Remote Access

- Secondary Logon Server

- SSDP Discovery Service

- System Restore Service

- Task Scheduler

- TCP/IP NetBIOS Helper

- Themes

- Windows Time

- Wireless Zero Configuration

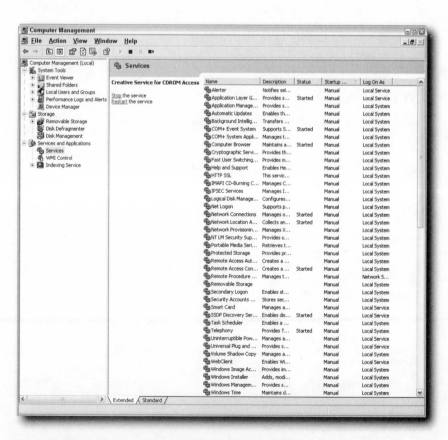

FIGURE 13-8: Services set to Manual will no longer start unless you want them to.

The following should already be set to Manual. If they are not, you can make them so:

- Alerter
    - Application Management
    - Background Intelligent Transfer Service
    - ClipBook
- COM+ System Application
- Distributed Transaction Coordinator
- Indexing Service
    - IPSEC Services
    - Logical Disk Manager Administrative Service
    - MS Software Shadow Copy Provider
    - Net Logon
    - NetMeeting Remote Desktop Sharing
    - Network DDE
    - Network DDE DSDM
- NT LM Security Support Provider
    - Performance Logs and Alerts
- QoS RSVP
    - Remote Desktop Help Session Manager
    - Remote Procedure Call (RPC) Locator
- Removable Storage
    - Smart Card
    - Smart Card Helper
- Telnet
- Uninterruptible Power Supply
    - Universal Plug and Play Device Host
    - Volume Shadow Copy
    - Windows Image Acquisition (WIA)
    - Windows Installer
- Windows Management Instrumentation Driver Extensions
- WMI Performance Adapter

Software to Help You Optimize Your PC

At the beginning of the section we briefly mentioned that there is also software available that can help you tweak your computer for better gaming. A lot of the steps we did can be done by these programs. The reason we gave you detailed instructions on how to do them is so that you can personally control what is being changed on your computer. If you would rather take a shorter road, you can download any of these programs and let them work their magic on your computer.

There are many programs floating around the Internet and the majority of them are free. One of the free ones that we like is GameXP, which is made by Theorica Software. It does a lot of the tasks we just did and a whole bunch more. What sets GameXP in the lead for us is that it is designed to optimize your computer for gaming. There are many programs available that tweak Windows for a better performance, but not many of them are purely aimed at gaming. GameXP is fast, quick, and simple to use. A great feature that Theorica put in GameXP is to make it ask you to back up your system state, or how Windows is currently running, before it makes any changes. You can undo everything if you happen not to like the results. It's a nice safeguard because whenever you start tweaking your computer, there is a chance of something unexpected happening.

All you have to do is click the Warp Speed button on the interface and wait a few minutes until the process is complete. The GameXP Website gives a nice rundown of all the major tasks that it performs so you won't waste space here listing them all, but you might find it a worthy addition to your software collection.

GameXP can be found at www.theorica.net/GameXPHelp.htm.

There are countless tweaking and optimization software packages out there so to help narrow it down for you here are a few others that are along the same lines as GameXP and are also free.

- Xteq X-Setup can be found at www.xteq.com
- Fresh UI can be found at www.freshdevices.com
- Windows Configuration can be found at www.freeware.prv.pl

If you don't mind spending money, another good one is Tweak-XP Pro 4 from Totalidea Software. You can try it for 30 days before you have to buy it. Tweak-XP Pro 4 can be found at www.totalidea.com/frameset-tweakxp.htm.

Optimization Step #8: Turning off Windows Firewall

Windows XP SP2 automatically turns on a software firewall for you. We go over what firewalls do and how they can help you in the next chapter, so you might not want to be hasty to turn off the Windows firewall until you read that. The Windows firewall is a program on the computer that Microsoft put there to help protect your computer. It does its best to stop unwanted and potentially dangerous attacks on your computer from the Internet or any network that you are on.

The problem is it could potentially stop some games from allowing you to connect when playing over the Internet. If you feel safe and have a hardware firewall, you can turn off the Windows firewall with the following steps.

1. Click Start/Control Panel.

2. Double-click Windows Firewall.

3. Click (Off) Not Recommended.

4. Click OK.

That's it. The Windows firewall is now off. Again, make sure you have some other form of protection on your computer after doing this.

Maintaining Your Ultimate PC

So far all the optimization steps have been things you should do before you start gaming to help increase your gaming PC's performance out of the gate. The next section is a list of tasks you can do regularly to maintain your PC so it continually makes those laps around the track at spectacular speeds. Take care of your computer and it will take care of you, at least in terms of playing the latest games!

Maintenance Step #1: Disk Defragmenter

To help maintain your hard drives' lightning performances you want to keep them in top form. One of the best ways to do this is to run the Disk Defragmenter. When information is written to any hard drive, the drive places the data wherever it finds empty space. This space can be anywhere on the drive because as files are deleted and removed, empty space appears. The hard drive fills in the information in the given space until it runs out of room. If there is still more of the file to be written, the hard drive finds another empty space on the drive to write the next piece of data. It continues this process until the file is completely written. When the file is called upon again, the hard drive has to search around for all the pieces that are spread out across the drive, causing the length of time it takes to access the file to increase. This is called fragmentation.

As a simple example, imagine that your name is the data being written to your hard drive, but currently there is only enough space in each empty space to write one letter. The hard drive then has no choice but to place the G on the first part of the hard drive. The A on the next. And the R and Y in two other far-off locations. When you want that information again, the hard drive has to move all around the drive, wasting time in an effort to collect all the spaced-out letters.

The cure for this is Disk Defragmenter. It goes through the entire drive, pieces together all the separated files, and puts them neatly back together in one place where they can easily and quickly can be found. The bottom line is that a defragmented drive accesses information much faster than a fragmented one.

Note You should defragment your hard drives at least once a month. Another good suggestion is to do it overnight. The process can take quite some time, up to several hours to complete, depending on your drive size. So just before you go to bed, start defragging and by morning you will be ready once more for fast, endless gaming.

To defragment your hard drives do the following:

1. Click Start/All Programs/Accessories/System Tools/Disk Defragmenter.

2. Click Analyze.

3. After Analyze is done, click Defragment as shown in Figure 13-9.

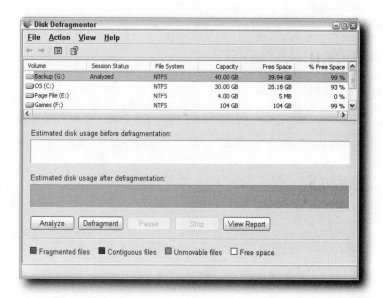

FIGURE 13-9: The Disk Defragmenter Utility.

Maintenance Step #2: Disk Clean Up

Over the course of your computer's life, it is good to make sure that the OS partition or any partition that holds your programs never gets close to being full. You should always have a little empty space on every drive for the programs to work. This space may be used for a variety of tasks, but most important to us is the location where our saved games are going to be.

Always make sure you have plenty of free hard drive space for Windows to work. When your drives start getting full, it is time for a little disk clean up to make some free space. This free space can come from removing programs you no longer use, cleaning up your temporary Internet files, or cleaning out your Temp folder.

Freeing Up Space

The first step to clean up some space on your drives is to remove any temporary Internet files. You would be surprised as to how much space these can take up over time. To do this, follow these instructions:

1. Click Start/Programs/Internet Explorer.

2. Click Tools/Internet Options.

3. Under the Temporary Internet Files section, click Delete Files.

4. When a box pops up check the box next to Delete all offline content.

5. Click OK.

6. After Internet Explorer is done cleaning up all the extra files, close out of the program.

Cleaning Out Your Temp Folder

The second step you want to take is to clear out any files in your Temp folder. This folder is the second place the Internet Explorer can place files it downloads. Also when programs are installing they often extract themselves from their packaged form and temporarily store files in this folder as well. All these files can add up eventually so it's good to every now and again come in and clean them out. To clean out your Temp folder, do the following:

1. Double-click My Computer.

2. Double-click the C drive.

3. Double-click the Temp folder.

4. Press Control+A.

5. Press Delete.

6. Click Yes to send all the files to the Recycle Bin.

7. Go to the Desktop.

8. Right-click the Recycle Bin.

9. Click Empty Recycle Bin.

Removing Unnecessary Programs

The last thing you can do to free up space is to remove old or unused programs. There is no sense in wasting hard drive space for software that you are not using. This can be a big way to clear up some space.

To remove unused programs, do the following:

1. Click Start/Control Panel.

2. Double-click Add/Remove Programs.

3. After the list is populated with all the programs you have installed, scroll through them and find ones you would like to remove. Highlight the first program you would like to remove.

4. Click Remove on the right side. This begins the uninstallation process for that program. Each program is installed and removed differently from all other programs, so the following prompts will be different. If you want to remove the program, accept all requests but make sure you keep your Save Game files if it asks you! You don't want to lose those in case you ever want to play that game again.

Maintenance Step #3: Spyware Removal

Not everybody in the world is nice. If they were, there would be no spyware and you wouldn't need to spend loads of time cleaning up the pesky, invasive, annoying stuff. Unfortunately the reality is that spyware is here and we have to deal with it on a regular basis.

One of the worst things about spyware is that it hurts your computer's performance. Each piece of spyware takes up a small bit of resources from your computer to allow itself to run. Now multiply that little bit by several hundred pieces of spyware and suddenly you have a significant decrease in the quality of your PC.

The solution to this is to remove spyware on regular intervals so it doesn't build up. It is hard to say how often somebody should clean their computer of spyware, but the more you are on the Internet, the more spyware you accumulate — that is just a fact. If you are frequently on for several hours a days hitting tons of gaming sights you need to clean your computer more often than somebody who only browses the Pricewatch.com specials once a week. At the absolute minimum you should clean your computer of spyware at least once a month.

Fortunately to aid us in controlling spyware infestation, there are many free spyware removal tools available. And because they are free, you can grab several and run them all. The reason you want to do this is that more often than not one program will miss a few pieces of spyware and you can run the other programs in hopes of catching what was missed.

The following is a list of places from where you can download free spyware removal tools.

- For Adaware visit www.Lavasoft.com
- For Spybot-S&D visit http://www.safer-networking.org/en/download/
- For SpywareBlaster visit http://www.javacoolsoftware.com/spywareblaster.html

Maintenance Step #4: Antivirus Software

In addition to the evils of spyware, we also have the long-standing virus nemesis to deal with. Just as you need to protect your ultimate gaming PC from spyware, so must you protect yourself from malicious viruses that can set back your gaming for days as you reinstall Windows and all your games.

The only thing different about using anti-virus software on a gaming PC and your regular home PC is that on the gaming PC you don't want it to be always running, if possible. Why? Well, as you probably guessed, if it is running continually it takes up resources.

This gives you two choices, the first is having whatever anti-virus software you choose running on your computer that you can turn off whenever you start playing games. This solves the problem of keeping the computer protected while not draining resources during gameplay.

Your second option is to not have anti-virus software on your computer; instead, you can use any of the Internet-based software that doesn't require you to install it and therefore is not regularly running on the local computer and taking up valuable resources.

If you decide to use one of these Internet-based anti-virus software programs, a couple can be found by visiting either of the following Websites.

- For Trendmicro's HouseCall go to http://housecall.trendmicro.com/
- For Panda Software's ActiveScan go to http://www.pandasoftware.com/products/activescan/com/activescan_principal.htm

Maintenance Step #5: Updating Drivers

It is always good to keep your drivers up to date. Go to the manufacturer's Website for the device you want to upgrade. The big one you want to watch for, of course, is your video card drivers. Keep those up to date and you are likely to continually see slightly faster and better responses from your video card. You should check for new drivers every month or so if you have the free time between games.

There are also impressive alternate third-party drivers for Nvidia and ATI devices, such as those made at Omegacorner. These are geared toward gaming and improve visual quality instead of raw speed, which corporate drivers tend to do and sacrifices visual quality. The theory is that a ton of frames per second don't amount to much if they don't look very nice.

A couple of good third-party driver sites are www.Driverheaven.net and www.Guru3d.com.

Maintenance Step #6: Clean out System Tray and Extra Startup Programs

One of the best maintenance steps you can continually do over time is keep the number of programs you have running on your computer minimized. What we mean by this is that as you use your computer you continually install new software and programs. Some of these programs start up every time you boot. You often see these types of programs filling up your System Tray on the lower-right of your screen.

These programs increase your boot time as well as taking system resources to allow those executables to run. An example of a file like this is AOL's Instant Messenger (AIM). After installed, AIM starts up every time you turn on your computer. One program won't really make a huge difference, but programs can add up because even the smallest program takes up memory.

The following instructions show you how to clean out those files from auto starting, allowing you to decide when they run.

Disabling Auto Starting Programs

To stop unwanted programs from starting up, make sure the following folders are empty. Note that %username% means the name of your account that you log under.

- C:\Documents and Settings\%username%\Start Menu\Programs\Startup
- C:\Documents and Settings\All Users\Start Menu\Programs\Startup

Updating the Registry

The next step involves the registry. The registry is the brains of Windows. One wrong step while working with it could render your computer useless until you reinstall Windows.

Working with the registry should only be done if you are confident in your computer abilities. If not, we recommend for your own sanity and time that you move past this step. With that said there are two main locations in the registry that might hold information that instructs programs to launch.

To get to the first location in the registry do the following:

1. Click Start.
2. Click Run.
3. Type in Regedit.
4. Double-click HKEY_LOCAL_MACHINE.
5. Double-click Software.
6. Double-click Microsoft.
7. Double-click Windows.
8. Double-click CurrentVersion.
9. Double-click Run.

Look in the right pane for the names of any files you recognize as something you installed and have noticed starting up. If, and only if, you are absolutely sure that you know what the registry entry is and you don't want it to run, highlight it and press the Delete key. The registry key is permanently removed and the only way to replace it is to reinstall the software to which it was related.

Figure 13-10 shows a bunch of registry settings that should be left alone. They are part of the system and if you remove them, some devices such as SoundBlaster won't work properly.

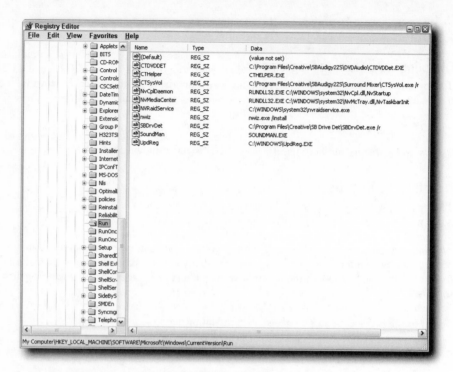

FIGURE 13-10: Registry settings that should be left alone.

The get to the second location in the registry, do the following.

1. Click Start.

2. Click Run.

3. Type in Regedit.

4. Double-click HK_Current_User.

5. Double-click Software.

6. Double-click Microsoft.

7. Double-click Windows.

8. Double-click CurrentVersion.

9. Double-click Run.

Again, look in the right pane for the names of any files you recognize as something you installed and have noticed starting up. If you are a 100 percent sure that you know what the registry entry is and you don't want it to run, highlight it and press the Delete key. The registry key is permanently removed and you have to reinstall the software associated with it to replace the entry.

Benchmarking

What is benchmarking? Benchmarking enables you to see how well your monster gaming rig can handle everything that the top-of-the-line games can throw at it. There are several different types of benchmarking. You can test just the gaming aspect of the machine, which is mostly hardware, or test just the memory. You can also do an overall benchmark to see how the system as a whole performs in a variety of tasks.

Some games like Final Fantasy 11 have benchmarking programs available that will allow you to see how your computer rates while running that game. It measures exactly how the game performs on your particular system. Where this is great, it is also very specific because even if you benchmark one game and the results are good there is no guarantee that your computer runs all games equally as well. So if you only ever plan to play FFXI, this is the only real benchmarking test you would probably need or want. If you plan to play more than a few games, however, it's best to have a program that tests the system in a more general way and not just the way one specific game utilizes the hardware.

Also some games that have built-in benchmarking use time demos. Time demos are a long sequence game play used to test the computer's capabilities. The problem with these is that they may not be actual gameplay footage and may just be following along a smoothly written script with no user interaction. These likely produce different results from real-time gameplay where reactions and inputs are more sporadic. You want your benchmark to be taken from actual game play, if possible, where the game is being played in its truest, most resource-demanding mode.

Another fallback of in-game benchmarking is that you most likely never have exactly the same game experience each time you play. This means that you may move your character differently, shoot a different weapon at a different time, and jump more frantically as the Drones of Malik 5 pour over the ridge after you with Vibro Blades +5. So it is necessary to run the benchmarking program a few times and take the median of those as your overall result.

Pure benchmarking programs that are not specific to any other application are the best way to go. There are a slew of programs available for this and some are listed in the following section. The reasons these are better is because they test the system, and not just under the specific set of standards that an in-game program would do. This saves time in the end because it tests the exact same things in the exact same order every time, and therefore you only have to run it once instead of multiple times.

You may ask why you want to benchmark at all. Simply — because it's really cool to see all the big numbers flicker up onscreen and know your computer can handle everything there is on the market. Bring on Doom 4!

Types of Benchmarking

This section goes into more detail on the various types of benchmarking so you can decide which, if any, you would like to run. You spent a lot of time planning, ordering, building, sweating, and dreaming about your ultimate computer, and this is a great way to gauge and judge the results of your endeavor. Imagine it as a report card for your computer.

Trust us — if you made the computer anything close to what is presented in this book, you will be getting all A's.

Gaming

Gaming benchmarking tends to measure 3D graphics and CPU utilization on Direct X, Windows-based computers. This involves high-end graphics tests such as Masked Environment Mapping, Particle Count, Large Scale Vegetable Rendering, Volumetric Fog, Vertex and Pixel Lighting, Fill Rate, along with a slew of others. They may also test image quality, sound quality, and CPU speed.

There are many programs out there from which to choose to help you in your testing. The Futuremark Corporation makes a variety of benchmarking software. Their 3dMark05 is the first benchmarking software designed specifically for testing Direct X 9.0 hardware that is capable of Pixel Shaders 2.0. It's not even worth trying to run 3dMark05 unless you have Pixel Shaders 2.0 on your video card because it won't halt at startup and recommends that you use 3dMark05's older, and still popular, brother 3dMark03, which does pretty much the same things just for the non-Pixel Shaders 2.0+ generations. It is also one of the standards in benchmarking.

To visit Futuremark Corporation's Website, go to http://www.futuremark.com/download/.

They offer free versions of their 3dmark software that has very limited capabilities with relatively cheap, full-blown editions.

Aquamark is another maker of benchmarking software that is very easy to use and also has a free trial edition with the option to upgrade to the complete retail edition. Like all brands, the retail edition has many more features. They have one version of their software, Aquamark3, that is kept updated and can test all Direct X 9.0 systems. It can even go as low as running Direct X 7. We will be using Aquamark3 to test our system.

To visit and download the Aquamark Website, go to www.aquamark3.com.

FRAPS is also worth mentioning — not because it's a robust benchmarking software, because it isn't. It can measure only FPS, in any game, at any time you desire. The reason it is worth mentioning is that in-game movies are becoming more and more available on the Web, such as videos of people showing tricks they learned, showing strategies to get past the final battle without firing a bullet, or movies of matches they have won versus top opponents to prove their victory. FRAPS can help you make those in-game movies as well as having the ability to take an instant in-game screen capture and have it labeled and dated in a folder instantly without you doing any extra work. It already can take advantage of PCI Express during its video capturing to make full use of the newly acquired bandwidth. It's not the best tool for benchmarking, but it has other worthwhile uses.

To visit FRAP's Website, go to http://www.fraps.com/.

Memory

Memory tests, as you would guess, test memory. There are different approaches to testing memory. Your best bet, though, is either Memtest86 or Memtest86+, two pieces of software that are free for everybody. Memtest86 doesn't test memory performance, but rather tests memory reliability.

These two pieces of software use algorithms to test the individual cells on each stick of memory. The common failures in memory are a cell's interaction with the other cells around them. The algorithms test whether each cell can hold the appropriately assigned 0 or 1 while the surrounding cells are assigned the opposite number to see if the first cell can retain its proper assignment.

Whichever you choose you likely have to make a bootable disk unless you have knowledge in bootable binary. The type of disk, whether CD or floppy, is dependent on which version of the software you chose to use.

This software does not require any OS to run, so you also might want to visit their Website prior to using either Memtest86 or Memtest86 + and copy down the list of commands and further instructions. You won't be able to surf the Internet after you have the program running.

To visit Memtest86's Website, go to http://www.memtest86.com/.

To visit Memtest86+'s Website, go to http://www.memtest.org/.

Overall

PCMark 04, is also made by Futuremark Corporation, is just like all the others we mentioned except that it measures overall computer capabilities by doing large application testing. It tries to use real applications to test your computer rather than a set program it contains, which for accuracy can be a real advantage.

Good and Poor Results of Benchmarking

Scores and results are shown differently from program to program. Aquamark3 can give you a score in the ten of thousands while 3dmark03 can get you a score in the hundreds. So there can be no correlation of results between programs. You have to find the meaning and merit of your score for the program you are using.

The benchmarking software score sometimes appears as a simple chart that tells you how your computer responded. Aquamark3 has this feature. A few programs, such as 3dmark03, have no charts to compare to on the results screen and only have online databases that you can add your results to, to see where you fit in among other scores of those people who used 3dmark03.

With your ultimate gaming PC, though, have no doubt. There are many people far below your massive score!

The Current Game to Benchmark Against

A popular game to benchmark while running is Halo PC. The reason many people use this game is because of the drastic dark and light areas on many of the maps that, when moving from one to the other, cause the computer to do a lot of work.

Doom 3 is another good game to test against simply because of the enormous system requirements that the game demands. With an Nvidia TI4600, a 2GB Intel processor, and 512MB memory on the board our old system could barely handle medium textures without frame stuttering rising to annoying levels.

If you can play Doom 3 on max resolutions and settings, you truly have the ultimate gaming PC.

Our Benchmarking Results

We ran some of the benchmarks we mentioned to see just how ultimate our ultimate PC is. We tested ourselves with Doom 3, a rigorous and highly intensive hardware game that pushes what a current computer can do. After that, we ran Aquamark 3 and compared our results online.

We are very proud of our Doom 3 results, mostly because we have played it on lower-end machines and could see just how much power the game required to play it. So the good news is that we were able to play Doom 3 with not only high detail, but with Ultra resolutions! (Ultra is Doom 3's highest system setting.) This is an impressive feat in the world of PC games. When you see Doom 3 at that resolution, the clarity and detail of it all is stunning and makes it all that much more immersive, especially with a wide screen format monitor.

It wasn't perfect at first, to be honest, when we first launched Doom 3 with Ultra settings. We got a "ripple" effect in the graphics whenever we turned very fast, also causing the environment to "tear" slightly. So we thought we would throw just a little more power at the game. We quit Doom 3, went to our desktop settings, and turned our video resolution for just Windows down to 800 x 600. It had been set at 1920 x 1200, which is what we want, but it takes a bit of CPU power to manage. Because we were playing Doom 3, we weren't really browsing around Windows and we didn't care what it looked like at that point.

When we re-launched Doom 3 the slight rippling was gone and all was good and grand in the gaming world.

With that under our belt we thought we would check out where we ranked in the world of benchmarking versus other computers. We ran Aquamark 3 on our ultimate gaming PC. We quickly downloaded the sample software and spent a few minutes running it; the software itself is entertaining to watch. When the test was done, a large number flashed onscreen — 75,212.

At first that number didn't mean a whole lot to us, but at the bottom of the results screen it gives examples of what our numbers might mean. It said to play the game AquaNox 2: Revelation at high resolution and textures, we would need a score of 30,000. Well, we surely surpassed that by more than double! That gave us a slight idea of how powerful our gaming PC is.

Next we compared our results online versus everybody else who has benchmarked their computer. And people who bother with benchmarking tend to be people who care about their results and the power of their computers. Chances are we were going to have some tough competition.

In the end, out of 80,752 other benchmarking results, we came in at 4,282. This puts us in the top 5 percent of all computers tested to date! We would have liked even higher — and who wouldn't — but the only machines that beat us were machines that cost much more money, possibly thousands more, than ours did.

Regardless, at the end of the day we proved that for gaming, this truly is an ultimate gaming PC that can handle anything currently on the market. After a lot of planning, searching, price checking, waiting, and assembling, this machine is all we could ever want.

What's Next?

Oh! What? You're still here? Really? We thought you would be off gaming by now. Because you are still sticking around, let us tell you what is next in this book. Even though you are itching to game, there are still a few more tasks we can do to make it all even better.

In the last chapter, Multiplayer Gaming, we show you how to get connected to the online world and begin gaming not just with yourself but with an infinite number of other people. Whether you have played online games before or not, you will likely find a few useful tidbits in the next chapter.

Advanced Gaming

part

IV

Multiplayer Gaming

There is something about the frantic, adrenaline-charged pace of a multiplayer game that you are trying to win in unison with your closet gaming friends. There can be a greater sense of accomplishment and camaraderie in winning such a game, especially in most cooperative games where the levels of the game dramatically increase in difficulty to balance out having extra players.

In this chapter we show you what you need to know to get your machine ready for multiplayer gaming. This includes connecting your computer to the Internet while trying to get the lowest ping possible.

We also briefly explain how firewalls, both physical and software, can factor into your multiplayer gaming. Although being a much-needed security device, firewalls can also hamper your playing. We explain how to find a happy, safe median. And, we talk about how the location of a host server affects game performance. Don't want to use the Internet? No problem — the last section of this chapter talks about LAN parties.

in this chapter

- ☑ Online gaming
- ☑ Defense for your computer
- ☑ Networking choices

Key Terms

Before you dive into connecting your gaming PC up for multiplayer gaming, here are some key terms with which you should be familiar.

- LAN (Local Area Network): The connection between computers located close to each other that allows for communication between the computers.

- RJ45 or Cat5: Networking cables that are certified at 10/100 Mbps speeds.

- Hub/Switch: A local device that allows for the transferring of data between machines. Hubs broadcast all requests to all attached clients, blindly forwarding every packet. Switches read the data packets that travel through it to identify to whom it should direct the data and only sends it to the designated client.

- ISP (Internet service Provider): A company that provides a connection to the Internet, usually for a monthly fee.

- DSL (Digital Subscriber Line): An ISP service that provides a connection to the Internet through the copper wires of a phone line.

- Cable: Another ISP service that provides a connection to the Internet. It is faster than DSL because it runs over the same, much larger bandwidth, cable line that delivers cable television to homes.

- Router: A piece of hardware that allows interconnection between multiple networks.

In Case You Need Convincing...

You've played the games against the computer before, maybe because you didn't have the best machine for gaming, or maybe because you're not convinced that multiplayer gaming is for you. Whatever the reason, you haven't delved into the multiplayer gaming world yet. There's no better time than the present. Fire up that monster PC and prepare for the challenges of multiplayer gaming.

If you're a hardcore gamer, you're familiar with playing Warcraft III against computer-controlled armies. This is fun and can be challenging, but the computer-controlled avatars are predictable. They have limited movement and reactions, and after you figure out their pattern, the game gets easier to play. Pretty soon, you've beaten the computer on each level setting, and you're bored. Game over.

Hooking up Warcraft III into the multiplayer world changes everything. Playing with other gamers against the computer changes the feel of most every game. Playing against human-controlled avatars is unlike playing against the computer. Avatars with limited movements and tactics now think and react, and respond appropriately to your attacks. They learn and counter each of your movements. Your strategy has to change to beat these guys, no matter what the playing level.

It's not limited to Warcraft III. We can't even begin to count how many hours Halo PC has stolen from our lives, and even so long after it's been released we still load it up regularly. Multiplayer gaming, if you enjoy it, can greatly extend the value of your games, thus increasing the value of the money you spent. The multiplayer aspect adds replay ability to your game. Add the human factor, and the game is never over.

Your ultimate gaming PC system was built to game and handle all the games on the market. This is your chance to finally play all those games that you never had the system specifications for in their full glory. What are you waiting for?

Getting Started with Online Gaming

You don't have to pack up your computer and lug it to someone's home to play a multiplayer game. It's a lot easier on your muscles to connect to other gamers over the Internet. But there are a few things you'll need to decide before you can play the first game.

Note If you already have an Internet connection, you can skip this section and pick up at the section "How Do I Protect My Gaming Computer Online?" later in this chapter.

Pick a Connection Type

Playing on the Internet requires some of the same choices as accessing your favorite Website or email. Your first step is to select an Internet Service Provider (ISP) to connect you to the Internet. There are so many ISPs from which to choose — in the United States alone there are somewhere around 2,000 different providers and about 200 different ones in the United Kingdom. With so many vendors, it can be difficult to choose which one to use.

To navigate through this world of ISPs, start by deciding if you want a dial-up connection or broadband. Dial-up connects your computer to the Internet through a standard phone line. Broadband connects either through a Digital Subscriber Line (DSL) that runs over the phone line, or via the cables (cable modems) that are provided by the cable TV companies.

Dial-up is becoming increasingly less useful and probably is near being obsolete in playing high-profile computer games, mainly due to the meager amount of bandwidth it offers. Times have changed and technology has moved forward. No longer does a simple phone line pack enough power to play many of the latest games online without some ill effect, like lagging. Additionally, dial-up connections are well known for dropping the connection, much more so than say a cable broadband connection. On the bright side one of the good things about dial-up is that it is much cheaper than all broadband services. This is because it is currently the low man on the totem pole in regards to Internet connections.

It is cheaper than DSL or cable, most of the time by nearly half or more, and that is definitely something you want to consider.

Note Blizzard's Battlenet, which allows you to play all their games like Diablo 2 and Warcraft III, is still accessible via a dial-up connection; we're doubtful that Doom III would run as smoothly over dial-up as it would over broadband. Battlefield 1942 or Battlefield 2 requires broadband for smooth play.

Broadband is more expensive than dial-up, but your connection becomes much faster. A 56.6K modem is sending and receiving information at a capped 53.3 Kbps, but the current cable service we have while writing this book is giving us a connection of 3841.8 Kbps. That is 72 times faster than a dial-up connection.

Broadband cable with its thick wiring currently offers a range of speeds between 1.5 Mbsp and 6 Mbps; 6 Mbps is the fastest of any standard broadband that you can find and is equal to a T3 connection. On average, a cable connection is the fastest type of broadband connection you can buy. The only drawback is that it does not guarantee uplink speed, unlike DSL.

Broadband DSL, which runs over slower telephone wires, offers a much lower range of speed, between 144K to 1.5 Mpbs Kbps. Because it is considerably slower than cable, you might wonder why anybody would want DSL over cable. The most common reason is that it offers a guaranteed uplink speed. This means that you cannot only download files quickly, but you can upload them quickly as well, which is very useful if you are hosting a server. Just like DSLs download speed, you can have an upper limit of upload speed of 768 Kbps.

There are a few areas that support even higher DSL connections. Check with your local phone company to see if they're one of them. Note that DSL is also limited by the distance to the local telephone company switch. The farther you are from the switch, the lower the maximum possible speed. If you're too far away, you can't get DSL at all.

A fast connection has many advantages that can affect you, such as being able to quickly download the latest patch to your favorite game. What might take 20 minutes on dial-up could take only a minute or two from your DSL connection. Getting the patch sooner means getting to play sooner as well, and what is better than that?

Finding a Provider

After you have decided what type of connection you are going for, you need to narrow down the total number of providers in the world by finding out what providers are in your local area. There are many good tools on the Web to help you do this. We found a really good one at CNET (http://reviews.cnet.com/Internet_services/2001-6536_7-0.html?tag=glnav). Their Website allows you to choose your choice of dial-up, cable, or DSL, whichever you prefer, fill in your location, and press Enter. The site then tells you what providers are available in your area.

Another great resource is Broadband Reports (http://www.broadbandreports.com). In addition to helping you research local ISPs, it also offers a variety of tools to help you test your downstream and upstream speeds.

Another similar Website is found at EZISP (http://www.ezisp.info). The main difference between this Website and CNET's is that here you choose your local provider by state, then area code. They also give direct links to the provider's Websites and price comparison between the listed providers, along with a detailed list of features you get with your package. Some of the more common ISP's are Verizon DSL, Cox, Earthlink, SBC/Yahoo, Comcast, Roadrunner, Speakeasy, and MSN. After you find a few providers in your area that interest you, you can find reviews on the Internet to see how good their services are. You ideally want an ISP that has

- Friendly, round-the-clock support, preferably both by email and phone
- The fastest connection for the lowest price you can afford
- Free installation and setup
- A price discount for the first few months

Warning

Bear in mind that DSL often takes longer to get installed than a cable connection. Your DSL provider has to work with your local telephone company to set up your connection because a DSL line runs through the extra wires you have in your phone line. This cooperation can take a few weeks to a month at times.

While looking for an ISP, keep in mind that you may come across a variety of Internet access packages. Remember, it is not necessary to purchase any service faster than cable or DSL for casual Internet gaming. Internet games are designed to be bandwidth conscious of the 10 Mbsp mark, so getting an Internet connection faster than that would just be a waste of money.

After you have decided on which provider to go with, they will help you with everything else you have to set up, including any special software or networking settings you may need.

Tip

We mentioned CNET and their resources for helping to find an ISP. They also have a useful bandwidth tester that gives you a good view of how your connection rates in comparison to other types of connections, such as dial-up or a T3. You can find the bandwidth tester at http://reviews.cnet.com/Bandwidth_meter/7004-7254_7-0.html?tag=tool.

How Do I Protect My Gaming Computer Online?

Now that you have an ISP, the next step you need for safe multiplayer Internet gaming is a firewall. A firewall protects your network or computer from unwanted Internet traffic by enforcing an access control policy between the two. The purpose of a firewall is to prevent unwanted and malicious traffic from entering your network. A firewall allows you to do what you want on the Internet while preventing incoming requests from the Internet to directly access your private network resources, such as your computer, printer, or even your attached digital camera.

There are three types of firewalls — Physical, Software, and firewalls built into the operating system (which are a kind of software firewall). We'll go into more detail about each of these in the next section. For now, know that your physical firewall should live between your computer and your connection to the Internet. It is a filter for all traffic from your home network to the world. Software firewalls and the one built into Windows XP do the same thing, but are located on the computer itself. Their job is to monitor all information coming through the network card to the rest of the computer.

Regardless of its location, a firewall checks and verifies all the information that is sent through it to make sure it is desired traffic. If it is not, the firewall blocks the transmission, saving your computer from receiving potentially dangerous data or preventing hackers from browsing your machine.

The challenge with gaming and firewalls is that it takes time for the firewall to scan data and then send your gaming packet on. The firewall is trying to stop remote logins, SMTP session hijacking, denial of service attacks, email bombs, spam, and more, but it can slow down the receipt of the information that you actually want. When information about your game is sent through the firewalls, it can slow down the response of the games as they are waiting for information to arrive.

A lot of games indicate that certain ports must be opened in your firewall if you want to play that game over the Internet. For example, according to the Blizzard Website, makers of Warcraft III, Diablo, and Starcraft, the ports you need open to play Diablo II are

- Port 6112 TCP, both out and in traffic
- Port 4000 TCP out, if you want to play realm games
- Port 4000 TCP, both out and in if you want to host open games

A port is nothing more than a doorway in the firewall; by opening a port you are telling the firewall that all information that is sent to this door is okay and should be allowed to pass freely without inspection. These ports vary from game to game, but having them open allows the information for your game to travel freely through the firewall. All the firewall has to do is to route the packet through the open port directly to its destination.

Exact directions are hard to give on how to open ports on a firewall since there are so many different firewalls on the market. All of them have their own Web interface that you can access to make the changes. The problem is each Web interface is different from all the others. You just have to click around a little bit until you find what you are looking for, and it is recommended that you read the user manual that came with your firewall for more help.

The delay that the firewall can cause is called latency or lag. The good thing about latency is that if everybody is using a firewall, any lag experienced from information traveling through a firewall is mutually experienced and is less likely to be unbalancing, not really giving any person a speed advantage.

Physical Firewall

A physical firewall, also called a hardware firewall, is a piece of hardware that you can actually touch. It is a box-like item that you have to go to the store and buy. It normally comes as part of a router or gateway. Some of the more popular firewall/routers are made by D-Link, Linksys, and Netgear. All brands have their following and all get the job done; choosing between them all comes down to personal choice, like how easy to use you find the Web interface menus.

Routers isolate your internal network from the outside world. So even if you have only a single PC, an inexpensive router is probably a good idea. It helps keep your PC "invisible" to other systems on the Internet that may try to compromise your system. If you want to have an internal network of several PCs, a router is even more strongly recommended. Managing multiple PCs is much easier when the internal network isn't exposed to the Internet.

One of the big pros to having a physical firewall is that they tend to come as part of router. Because you need a firewall anyway, having a router can be just an added bonus. It protects your computer and allows you to create a small LAN inside your house that can split your ISP connection among several computers. This can be great for gaming (see the section on LAN Parties later in this chapter). You can do the same thing with a switch, which is just a device that allows PCs to connect to the network. And you can certainly connect your broadband modem to the switch directly, but then your entire network would be visible to anyone on the Internet. Plus, you have to deal with having multiple dedicated IP addresses. It's much better to use a router, which can automatically manage internal IP addresses for the PCs on your LAN. Routers direct information in a much better fashion. They read the data packets that travel through it to learn who to direct the data to and sends it only to the designated client.

Another advantage that physical firewalls have over software firewalls is that because it is a physical object, they tend to be much more difficult to hack and manipulate than a software one. This makes them incredibly secure.

The last beneficial factor is that they are not very expensive. A firewall you buy is also a router and can act like a hub. It can be found on sale almost every week for under $100 — sometimes even a lot less after rebates, approximately the price of a computer game or two. It is not that much when you think about what it does and the protection it offers.

There are not very many cons with a physical firewall. They are easily the better and safer bet. But one factor that might seem like a hindrance is the difficulty in setting up the device. It can be fairly straightforward, but to those without any experience it can be a task that keeps you busy for a few hours or longer.

Another con is, as we mentioned, the interface with which you must use to manage your firewall and router. Whether you are trying to set up a Virtual Private Network (VPN), logging activity, filtering URLs, or opening ports, the Web interface to do so may not be the most friendly and useable for you. Because each router seems to have its own terminology, it can be very confusing and difficult to figure out what each menu really means and does.

The last con is that it's a stationary defense. You are only protected by the physical firewall while you are on your home network. It's not likely that you will be taking your computer out much, so this may not be a concern. But if you also have a laptop and you spent your money on a physical firewall, remember that when you go roaming outside the house, the firewall can't go with you.

Software Firewall

Software firewalls do the exact same things as physical firewalls, but instead of being another piece of hardware you have to connect, it is a piece of software you have to install on your computer. Software firewalls are programs that work between your computer, the operating system, and the drivers of your network card. They monitor all traffic into the computer and do their best to stop anything deemed hostile or intrusive.

A big benefit to choosing a software firewall is that some come with built-in spyware removal tools and pop-up blockers. With the amazing increase in spyware on the Internet, free, quality spyware blocking tools should never be casually overlooked. Spyware, in large amounts, can drain system resources, and this is not something you want to happen on a machine designed for gaming. Pop-up blockers, on the other hand, aren't as usefully correlated to gaming. They can help your Web browsing go more smoothly and with less unwanted interruptions, which can make shopping for the next big game or reading its reviews more pleasurable. This feature of a software firewall is just gravy.

The next benefit is that it is a portable defense. A physical firewall isn't designed to be moved around. After it's set up, it is pretty much left alone and is stationary. If you went to a local café with a laptop, your hardware firewall can't protect you; if you had a software firewall, it goes wherever your machine goes, whether a laptop or a desktop.

Probably the biggest benefit of using a software firewall is that you can find a few of them for free on the Internet. Not having to put out any money after spending a ton of cash on your gaming computer might be a nice relief. Most free firewalls are for personal use only, but are also licensed for commercial use. A listing of several free firewalls can be found at http://www.homenethelp.com/web/howto/free-firewall.asp.

Because software firewalls are running on the local machine they take up local resources, which is the opposite goal of what we are aiming for in an ultimate gaming PC. You want optimum resources for gaming. You want your computer to be completely free of all extra work so that it can deliver the best game experience possible. The software firewall takes up resources; so does the spyware removal tools as well as the pop-up blocker. Anything that does not apply to gaming is just taking up valuable resources and can make all the work you did in tweaking Windows to run faster a waste.

Another of the drawbacks of software firewalls is that by the time any hacker starts to attack your machine, they are already on it because that is where the software firewall lives. With physical firewalls, they must first get through the hardware and then on to your machine. Because software firewalls are installed into the OS and any OS has its flaws, we find that software firewalls are weaker in defense than a physical one.

 Warning Before you use a personal software firewall on a Windows XP machine, you have to turn off the firewall built into the operating system. This is not a major con, but it is something you have to do. You never want to run two software firewalls together because they can conflict with one another.

Windows Firewall (XP SP 2)

Since Service Pack 2 came out for the Windows XP, any fresh installation of the operating system with the service pack included has had the Windows firewall turned on by default. This is

Microsoft's way of helping to protect all users, especially those that wouldn't be able to turn it on themselves.

Every time a program tries to access the Internet for the very first time a Windows Firewall dialogue box pops up asking you if you wish this program to be allowed to connect to the Internet or whether it should be blocked. This can be annoying when you launch all your programs for the first time on a freshly built machine, but after you get through all the prompts, this firewall can be a very useful tool for protecting your computer. Windows stores your answers to the prompts and will not ask you to allow the same program to connect again.

The Windows firewall is also adjustable in terms of protection. You can mark off exceptions that you want to the firewalls protection. By exceptions, we mean you can populate of list of all the programs you want to run freeing through the Windows firewall by scanning through all the programs installed on your computer and selecting them.

The biggest pro to running the Windows XP firewall is that it is free if you are running Windows XP. You don't have to use their firewall, but it is already a part of your computer. If you don't have SP2 on your machine all you need to do is download it from the Microsoft Website. To get SP2 go to the following link: http://www.microsoft.com/athome/security/protect/windowsxp/choose.mspx

Another bonus is that it is part of the operating system and designed by Microsoft. This means that it is as compatible as it can get with Windows and not likely to cause any conflicts that a third-party piece of software might.

Much like a software firewall, the Windows firewall offers the same portable protection, meaning that wherever you go, you at least have some form of defense against unsolicited requests and Internet attacks.

Similar to the software firewalls, because the Windows firewall is software it is running on the local computer, it is taking up resources. This is something that you may want to avoid to get more power out of your system for gaming. In addition, because it is part of the operating system and not something physical, there is a chance it can be hacked or manipulated.

Other Forms of Protection

In addition to a firewall, it is also a good idea to have other forms of protection. Having anti-virus software running on your computer is always a good idea if you spend a lot of time online or even receive email on your gaming machine. Viruses come in all forms — Trojans, worms, mass-mailing viruses — and the best protection is anti-virus software that is updated and run regularly. It's true that you could go without it and may be lucky enough to never get a virus, but it is really not worth the risk of losing any data you have stored on your hard drive, or the time it would take to reinstall your operating system if you are infected.

Note Trend Micro Incorporated sells Internet security and anti-virus software at their Website.

Other popular anti-virus programs are Symantec's Norton Anti-Virus Software and McAfee VirusScan. You can purchase their products from their Websites at

- http://www.mcafee.com

- http://www.symantec.com/index.htm

Tip If you can't afford anti-virus software, Trend Micro also offers a free virus scan over the Internet. Their Website is http://housecall.trendmicro.com/. Also, AVG offers a version of their anti-virus software that's free for personal use, http://www.grisoft.com/doc/40/lng/us/tpl/tpl01.

Running a spyware removal tool on a regular basis helps maintain your computer's performance. The more spyware you have collected on your computer, the more resources you lose for gaming because those resources are spent running the spyware. If you don't browse the Internet on your gaming PC, this is not a major concern; however, if you do, you will no doubt end up with spyware. Find an anti-spyware program and, just like the anti-virus software, run it regularly.

As mentioned in an earlier chapter, having more than one spyware removal tool is also not a bad idea. What one tool can't find, the other might. It's good to run at least two of them back to back to make sure everything that can be removed is removed.

Tip Run each tool after a fresh reboot before you launch any programs, especially any Internet ones. Sometimes a piece of spyware that is in use, which can be caused by launching an Internet browser, may not be removed.

Lavasoft makes an exceptional spyware removal tool called Ad-Aware. They also offer a free non-commercial version for the average user. Their Website is http://www.lavasoft.com/. Another popular spyware removal tool is SpyBot Search & Destroy, located at: http://www.safer-networking.org.

What Kind of Networking Hardware Do I Need?

In addition to an Internet connection, you need networking hardware. You have two choices in networking—free roaming wireless or hard-wired Ethernet. The following is an overview of each to help you decide what suits your needs most.

Wireless Connections

Why do you want wireless? That depends on your needs, but often people decide to go with wireless network connectivity because there is one computer somewhere in the house that is too far away from the router to run a cable to. Besides, not many want an ugly blue wire running across the house. In this case its might be time to create a Wireless LAN (WLAN) by buying an access point and a wireless interface card that can be installed on the remote computer. Other people choose wireless just because they don't like dealing with the tangles of networking wires, or they have a laptop and like to roam free about the house. Others simply choose wireless because it is the newest technology available in networking.

Access points bridge the wireless network with the wired network so that communication can occur. Access points receive the wireless traffic and packets from the wireless clients and send them to the router or switch that the access point is hard-wired to. It basically transfers wireless information to wired. You can also find combination devices that bundle a router, network switch, and access point into a single device.

Tip If you are building a home network from scratch, this is a good way to go because there is only one device to set up. If you already have a router that doesn't have an access point built in, it may be cheaper to buy an access point than a new router with this feature.

Some routers have wireless technology built into them, so you can have both wired and wireless clients connected to it. This removes the need to buy an access point because it is already apart of the router. The only drawback with using your router as your access point is that only a small number of clients can connect to a router at any given time, usually between 4 and 10. Access points can have many more. How many is usually defined by what you buy, but generally speaking a home unit can handle 150 concurrent connections although a few currently available can handle 255. You can have hundreds of friends and family logged into your wireless network! But remember — the more active users you have, the slower the entire network becomes because it is saturated with connections. Staying below 30 users ensures you don't experience any huge decrease in your wireless networking performance.

One of the big factors in the quality of your wireless is operating range. The range at which your device can work inside and outside of the house varies greatly. The farther away you are from the wireless access point, the slower your connection becomes as the signal gets weaker. When you are outside, perhaps in the backyard and the access point is in a window on the rear of your house, you could go much farther away and still have a connection, albeit a much slower one. If you are indoors with the wireless access point on the third floor of your house, you might not get any signal at all when you are in the basement.

Just remember — the closer you, are the better the connection. (But if you are too close, why bother with wireless in the first place?)

Types of Wireless Standards

The Institute of Electrical and Electronics Engineers organization (IEEE) helped to create the wireless standards we use for computers and communication devices. Before you can decide what type of wireless network you might like to set up, it is good to know what is available.

There are three main wireless standards currently available. IEEE 802.11g is the newest standard, preceded by IEEE 802.11a and IEEE 802.11b. Each standard is defined by their speed and frequency on which they send their information. Their speed is measured in how many millions of bits per second (Mbps) they can transfer wirelessly. The more Mbps, the better and faster the connection. Table 14-1 compares these three standards.

IEEE 802.11b, which runs on a frequency of 2.4 GHz, transfers data at speeds of 11 Mbps at distances up to 300 feet. IEEE 802.11g, which is also on the 2.4 GHz radio band, can get speeds of nearly five times that with 54 Mbps.

Tip

It is good to know these standards so that when you shop for a device you buy something that is adequate to your needs. But because speed is your main requirement, we recommend IEEE 802.11g.

Table 14-1   Wireless Standards Compared

Wireless Standard	Connection Speed	Wireless Band or Frequency
802.11a	Up to 54 Mbps	5 GHz
802.11b	5.5 and 11 Mbps	2.4 GHz
802.11g	Up to 54 Mbps	2.4 GHz

Fortunately because IEEE 802.11b and IEEE 802.11g share the same band, IEEE 802.11b devices can be used on a Wireless Grouter (G) network. IEEE 802.11g routers are cleverly backwards compatible with IEEE 802.11b. What this means is that if you have some old IEEE 802.11b network cards lying around, they can communicate with IEEE 802.11g router. The connection, of course, will only be at the IEEE 802.11b speed, but for secondary or non-gaming computers, this might be fine for you and a cheaper solution than buying new hardware.

There are companies such as Belkin that have sought to link the two wireless bands, the 2.4GHz and 5GHz frequencies, together in one device. They call it the Dual-Band Wireless A+G Suite. If you have already ventured into creating a wireless network back in the days of IEEE 802.11a and want to upgrade your ultimate gaming computer to at least IEEE 802.11g, you can do so without upgrading all the other computer network cards in your house. It is another way you can save money in the short term.

There is even boosted Wireless G that grants speed of 108 GHz. Boosted Wireless Grouter uses a compression algorithm on the router and the wireless card to achieve even greater local speeds.

Finally, there's an emerging standard known as 802.11n. It's basically the same as 802.11g, but adds "quality of service" capability. This is really aimed at using the wireless network to watch video or listen to audio without dropping data packets, so it's not a must-have for gaming.

How Do I Get the Best Results from My Wireless Router?

You want fast gaming, and depending where you place your wireless router or access point you may experience a different quality in your wireless connection. The following is a list of points to keep in mind when choosing placement for your device to make sure it does not hamper any Internet activity, especially gaming. Following these instructions ensures you get the best and most continually reliable service the majority of the time.

- After you set up your device and you are receiving a weak signal, move it to a new location and try again. Hopefully after time you can find someplace suitable and your gaming can commence.

- Try not to place your wireless router near any large object made of metal. The metal structures hamper the signal and therefore can dampen it when you are trying to send information. Basically don't place it right next to your ultimate gaming computer or your refrigerator.

- Try to choose a location that gives you an unobstructed connection from your wireless networked ultimate gaming computer to the router. There is a loss of speed in transferring data when the signal has to pass through physical objects. The less objects, such as cement walls, tables, couches, and bookcases that are in the way, the stronger the signal will be because it does not have to pass through objects and can get directly to its destination.

- Do not place your wireless device near any other object that also uses the same frequencies as your router. As we mentioned earlier, this is the 2.4 GHz and 5 GHz ranges. The signals conflict, leaving you with a weaker connection and speed. A few of these types of objects are microwaves, radios, and televisions. You can go into your router and tune it to different channels if this does become a problem. The standard 802.11b is particularly susceptible to interference from phones or microwaves; 802.11g is more robust.

- Place your device as high up as you can. This becomes helpful in multistory houses where you are sharing the signal with more than your gaming PC. Even going through the upper floor it is still closer to those upstairs who need it. This also helps with the other point we made of keeping it unobstructed, the higher it is, the fewer objects that would be in the way of its signal.

- Finally, you can buy aftermarket antennas that can boost transmission distance, which may be helpful in difficult situations. Also, companies that sell wireless access points and routers also offer range extenders, which are essentially small relay boxes for wireless networks.

Figure 14-1 shows a good example of how to set up your wireless network in a room. Note that the wireless router is at the highest point in the room for the best connection.

Wireless routers come with an option to restrict who has access to the router. This is called Wired Equivalent Privacy (WEP). You should set up WEP security so that any nearby neighbors can't steal your signal and bandwidth, leaving you with a slower connection.

You can also turn on data encryption in your router, using a technology known as WPA, so that any of your information traveling through the airways is less likely to be stolen. The problem with encryption is that it takes time for the router of a wired interface card to encrypt the data and then time for the other to decrypt the data. The time this takes can noticeably slow down your connection. The higher the encryption, the more time it takes. If you decide to turn on encryption, keep it as low as possible so as not to hurt your gaming. A 40-bit data encryption is the minimum; most systems are 128bit and above. The lower the encryption, the easier it is to break. But to put that in perspective, 40-bit encryption would take about a week of work for somebody to crack. It also protects from packet sniffers that allow people to see your data on your actual machine after they have the header information they can send that packet back to you. The clever hackers can use this as a way into your machine and force whatever information they want, such as your passwords.

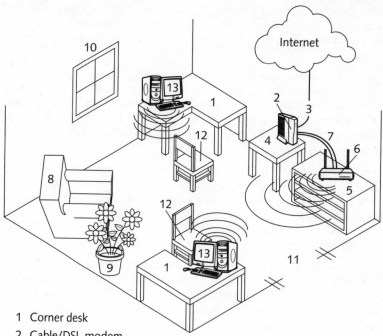

1 Corner desk
2 Cable/DSL modem
3 Cable/DSL line
4 Table to hold cable/DSL line
5 Bookcase to hold wireless router up high
6 Wireless router: Emanating wireless rings
7 Ethernet cable connecting modem to router
8 Plush chair
9 Flower in pot
10 Window
11 Doorway
12 Chair
13 Computer: Emanating wireless rings

FIGURE 14-1: Wireless network setup.

Ethernet Connections

After going into details on wireless, explaining Ethernet is much simpler because there aren't so many choices. Ethernet connections are also known as Cat5, Cat5e, or Rj45 and perform networking with the IEEE standard of 802.3 specification. Ethernet transfer rates range from 1 Mbps to 1Gbps. Some large enterprises are even moving to 10 Gbps Ethernet. Many high-end motherboards suitable for gaming PCs now have gigabit Ethernet built in, but the network switches and routers are still expensive.

Note that the different wiring names relate to different maximum speeds. Standard CAT5 cabling is rated to 100 Mbps. If you plan to run a gigabit LAN, you'll want CAT6 wiring. For gaming on a local area network, 100 Mbps is more than enough.

So why would you want an Ethernet network? Well, Ethernet is a stable, solid connection. It doesn't suddenly go weaker like a wireless connection can at times. You don't have the same problems with it as you do with wireless, like worrying if your phone is interfering with the connection.

You might ask yourself if Ethernet is 100 Mbps and wireless has a maximum of 54 Mbps, why did we say before that they are comparable in speed? What you need to know is that the common bottleneck that limits your Internet speed is not your private network setup, but rather your ISP speed. We mentioned already the maximum speed you would get from a broadband connection is 6 Mbps, so it doesn't matter how fast your system can talk if the Internet connection that you are talking over is forcing you to talk much slower.

Additionally unless you are buying a high-end specialty router for several thousands of dollars the outgoing port on your router, wireless or otherwise, is only 10 Mbps, not the 100 Mbps that most people assume it is. Internally your router is a 100 Mbps, which is great for your local LAN but if your maximum connection to the Internet is limited by your outgoing port, and it is, you are capped at 10 Mbps. (This is really not much of a concern because half the people running networks are still running at 10 Mbps, not 100 Mbps.)

Even with the full cable broadband speed of 6 Mbsp you still are not reaching your maximum capabilities built into your hardware. This is another reason why the outgoing port is only 10 Mbps — the router manufacturers know that you are being limited by your ISP, so there is no need to add a more expensive piece of hardware where a cheaper one will do.

Note To further explain and put all that in perspective, back up toward the beginning of the chapter where we ran a bandwidth test. The most speed we were receiving from our cable Internet connection was 3841.8 Kbps. That equals 3.8 Mbps, which is only 30.8% of your maximum throughput.

Gigabit Ethernet

Where Ethernet transfers data at 100 Mbps, gigabit Ethernet transfers at a staggering 1000 Mbps. This is a huge increase but sadly for current Internet gaming you will never reach that cap because your total speed is limited by your ISP — and games are only designed to take advantage of 10 Mbps anyway.

Where gigabit Ethernet currently can be of use to you is through in-house multiplayer gaming. If you have a gigabit switch, which is available for around $150–$200, you can create your own super LAN for multiplayer madness. You of course need to have gigabit Ethernet cards in all the machines connected to your new switch, but if you did you could have lightning fast games without the remote chance of the network slowing you down. Note, however, that 100 Mbps is more than enough for most gaming. Gigabit comes in handy when moving around large files, or installing large games over a network.

One warning, though, is that if you have a gigabit Ethernet LAN and one machine does not have a gigabit card, your total communication with that machine will still be limited to the type of NIC (network interface card) you have installed in it.

If you decide this is the path you want to take, you need to be careful when you go shopping for a gigabit router because some companies are selling "gigabit routers" that only have a single GB port. These are ultimately useless; if only one machine can connect at 1000 Mbps and every other port is only 100 Mbps, then your 1000 Mbps machine will only be able to talk at everybody else's cap because that is the fastest they can receive data. If there is nobody to talk to at 1000 Mbps, why bother?

Having just one machine with a gigabit NIC, unless you have a gigabit switch and have other networked computers with gigabyte NICs, won't produce any speed difference.

In the end a gigabit network might be a little over the top and the improved results you might see may not be enough to justify the cost. It would be fun to have for your personal LAN gaming, but a gigabit network currently gets most use out of transferring very, very, large files or on business networks.

 Warning Even though a gigabit Ethernet is 1000 Mbps that speed is only for the inter-network because the outgoing ports on these routers are also just 10 Mbps like all 100 Mbps models.

How Do I Choose Between Wireless and Hardwired?

As we have said again and again in our book, speed and power are the driving factors in all your decisions. Based on this criteria, the decision is really up to you. Both the wireless and Ethernet networks are equal in power. The deciding factors might be the roaming conveniences of wireless or the constant solid connection of Ethernet.

Ethernet connection is continuous, solid, and reliable. With a wireless device you have to worry about signal strength and your neighbors trying to siphon your bandwidth. As much as you try, there can still be interference in the air, even from your cordless phone that could hamper your wireless signal. Wireless is a wonderful technology, but a wired Ethernet is more consistent.

On the other hand, IEEE 802.11g wireless connection speed is comparable to Ethernet. Although you are only connecting your ultimate gaming PC to the Internet for gaming, you may have other computers to want to connect around the house. Wireless might be a good and simple solution for this without having to deal with a tangle of RJ45 wires running around your house. Wireless is also easier and cheaper to set up when compared to a hardwired network.

A drawback of wireless is that the more people on wireless the more that 54 Mbps is divided up. Two people connected to a 54 Mbps wireless router makes each connection only 27 Mbps. With three people it is shared even more. The wireless router can only receive so much information at once and that total is divided up among all who are connected. The good news is that newer routers have more antennas and an additional NIC to handle more users to help more concurrent connections achieve 54 Mbps speed.

Other options? You can also buy Ethernet routers that have wireless access built in. This can solve your problem of serving both your gaming needs and that of any other remote computers you may have.

Figure 14-2 shows the same room we set up with our wireless setup, but now we have migrated to plain Ethernet. It serves as a good example of what the wiring would look like for the computer to be connected.

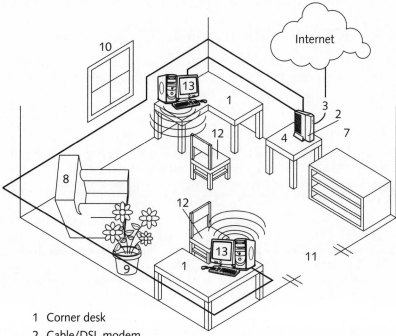

 1 Corner desk
 2 Cable/DSL modem
 3 Cable/DSL line
 4 Table to hold cable/DSL line
 5 Tall bookcase
 6 Ethernet cable connecting the computers
 7 Ethernet cable connecting modem to router
 8 Plush chair
 9 Flower in pot
10 Window
11 Doorway
12 Chair
13 Computer: Emanating wireless rings

FIGURE 14-2: Ethernet network setup.

You could also go with the gigabyte LAN, but as we said that is a lot of power, most of which you will probably never get to use. This is a technology that only in the coming years will become more useful in household rather than just at the corporate office.

In the end, the choice is yours. The information offered here should give you enough insight to decide what is best for your house, plans, and networking setup. If your ultimate gaming PC is the only computer you are connecting to the Internet, hardwiring it might be the way to go, or if you have many computers in your house and you don't want to share the bandwidth.

What Can Affect My Online Gaming?

Now that you have your PC connected to the Internet, it's important to know what can affect your online gaming experience. Perhaps the topic that most significantly affects your gaming experience is ping.

Ping

Ping is the exact time it takes a packet of information to travel from your computer to another computer and back to you. These other computers tend to be the ones with which you are trying to play a game. The lower the ping rate, the better, as it represents the total time it takes the packet to make the entire trip.

Ping rate is more important to some games than others. It is less important in a build strategy game like Warcraft III because the timing of a single click really can't spell complete doom for you unlike in a First Person Shooter (FPS) like Halo PC. Strategy games are much more forgiving in this regard. If you don't play a lot of FPS, your ping is not nearly as important. But if you play a lot of FPS and are thinking of playing competitively, your ping rate is extremely important. Let's see why.

Halo PC is a FPS game. You can select your weapon of choice. If both you and your opponent, using the same uber weapon of destruction, target each other and click the fire button at the same time, who wins?

Sounds like a math equation, doesn't it? If all other things are equal, the person with the best ping to the host computer will win. That player clicks the fire button and that data travels from their mouse, across their motherboard, through the CPU, through their network card, and out across the Internet to the host first. Your click of the fire button does the same thing, but because your opponent's ping is faster, their message to the hosting server arrives first, and thus you are slain by a one-bullet frag. You don't even want to know what the advantage of actually being the host can be at times. It can be a beautiful, but unfair to the other players, kind of thing.

What can give you a good ping? Your firewalls can be very important in this as well as your level of encryption because a firewall, by inspecting the packet, adds to the total travel time of a packet. Your Internet Service Provider is also another factor. If you don't have a very good connection to the Internet, your ping will be unfavorably high. Your location in regards to your

ISP's hub is another factor. This is part of having a good connection to the Internet; just know that the closer you are to your ISP's network hardware, the faster your connection will be.

As long as you open the proper ports, your Internet gaming should be smooth as long as all those people you play against are not several continents away. For example, after the release of Asherson's Call 2, an online persistent role playing game, there was a big push by the players of the UK to get a localized server because of the latency involved with them playing on the U.S. servers. When they did actually get their own server, the problem was alleviated and their gaming was smoother. Proximity to your host is another important factor in lag free gaming.

Warning

A ping to the hosting server or other players of 20–30 milliseconds is an excellent connection speed and what is most desired if you are lucky enough to get it. A ping in the range of 60–80 milliseconds—standard for cross-country traffic in the business world—is good and is what you are most likely to have. Any ping that is above 100+ milliseconds is too slow; people will often quit out of games if you are the host, especially if it reaches over 200+ milliseconds, because there is a likely chance it will be laggy.

Location

Another thing that can affect your online gaming experience is your proximity or physical distance between you and the other players. The farther away you are, the more distance your game information has to travel. When eight people are playing on a remote server, the response time of the game is often gated by the performance of the most distant, highest ping player, relative to that server. Longer distances can cause latency or lag.

Tip

Lag can be such a big issue in gaming, so much so that Battlenet is broken into regions to help with this to make sure you play with people somewhat close to you.

For the optimum gaming experience, find a host server that is close. The closer the server is to you, the less distance any packet has to travel and therefore ensures a smoother game experience. The latency between Australia and the United States is quite significant. If the host is in the U.S., the U.S. player will have an advantage over the Australian player because the host is closer to the U.S. player, giving the host a noticeable advantage over the other player. Find hosts that are as local as possible and choose servers that have the lowest ping rating.

The Ping Rate of Your Friends

The connection speed of your friends can slow you down as well if somebody's connection isn't as good as yours. If one person's connection is lagging out, all players will likely suffer hampered game play since the data from that client is being waited for. Equal connection speeds are important for fair and fun game play.

When a connection is made over the Internet between your computer and another to play games or even browse the Internet, the link you make is not direct. You have to bounce or be redirected by other servers to get to your destination. Each of these stops is called a hop. The number of hops between your computer and the computer you're playing with can also affect your game play because the more hops it takes, the more time it takes. Hops are one of the factors that determine ping speed.

You always want the person with the fastest connection to be host of your online game. To achieve better game play for all involved, it is important that the host send and receive information faster than everybody else. A fast host can help to ensure your computer gets all the data that you need by the time you need it.

Tip If you choose to connect to the Internet via dial-up, don't try to be the host of any games that you play with other people. If someone else playing has a faster connection, allow them to host for a smoother game. The reason for this is to achieve better game play for all involved because a faster host can send and receive information faster than everybody else. A fast host can help ensure you're getting all the data that you need by the time you need it.

Number of Players

The amount of players on the server can also affect your gaming experience. In general, the more players, the slower the play. If the server is hosting 12 players, its total upload bandwidth is split between all 12 players. The fewer players on the servers, the fewer people it has to divide up its bandwidth among, thus making its server capabilities faster. The actual type of hardware that is in the server can also be a factor into how many players it can host. The better the server, the more it can host without diminished play. What the numbers are is hard to say because it varies from game to game.

The Game

Some games have higher bandwidth requirements than others. Battlefield 1942, for example, requires 32KB per second (that's kilobytes, not kilobits) of bandwidth *per player* on the server. That can saturate a home DSL connection if you try to run a server with more than a few players.

Internet Traffic

General Internet traffic can also affect your gaming experience. Sometimes the Internet, as a whole, is just slower because more and more people are on. Other times, perhaps late at night when less people are on, your connection can be faster than normal. There is no way to judge or control this, but sometimes the speed just won't be there.

Hosting a Small LAN Party

Now that you have just built your ultimate gaming PC and have connected your computer to the Internet, it's time to celebrate and show off your spectacular PC. What better way to do this than to throw a small lag-free gaming fest in which your machine of monstrous power can help you lay a smack down on all your friends in a mass of multiplayer madness! LAN parties can be huge, and at times, hard to run and organize. But because you want to be able to play and take part in your event so that you can use your new computer, here is a simple guide to throwing a small LAN party at your house for true multiplayer fun.

A LAN party usually consists of a bunch of people getting together in the same location with their computers, which are then networked together so that multiplayer games can be played by those in attendance. The fun of a LAN party, rather than just playing over the Internet, is seeing and hearing your friends' reactions to your great skills, techniques, or just plain smitings. There is something about seeing the look of defeat, and even victory, on a friend's face after a hard-fought game that you just never get over the distance of the Internet.

In cooperative games it makes communication much faster and clearer than if you where playing over the Internet using headsets. Some games don't even have voice communication, which can make things even harder as you try to type warning messages to your friends while you are also defending yourself against an attack. When your companions are in the same room with you, it's amazing how much faster you can react to a situation and how much easier it is to win.

Whether it ends up being a deathmatch against your friends or a full on war against the computer, LANs bring a completely new and refreshing aspect to games. They can enliven an old forgotten game, and they can bring you closer to your friends. Most of all, they are fun.

Note We're only going to cover LAN parties very briefly here. For a more in-depth guide for planning and hosting your own LAN party, check out *Extreme Tech's LAN Party: Hosting the Ultimate Frag Fest* by William "the Ferret" Steinmetz (Wiley 2004).

The Invitation List

How many people you should invite is really up to you — some huge gaming fests have 50 or more people. But for your pint-sized LAN party, that really shouldn't be your goal. For a small and fun LAN party you only need a couple people to play, so we recommend inviting at least four friends. At a maximum, 20 people. Beyond that number you can run into challenges with spacing, power, too much noise for the neighbors, and of course, confusion.

Try to keep the number small and manageable. If all your friends are mature, quiet, and willing to help, you can easily increase the number. They might be willing to help with whatever needs to be done and they won't be running amuck around your house. If the majority of your friends are boisterous, lazy, and loud, maybe try to stay at the lower end of the spectrum so you don't make too much work for yourself. The idea is to enjoy your event, not spend your time worrying or cleaning.

When inviting people it may also be good to keep in mind the general rule about attendance at weddings. Normally only 80% of those that are invited are able to attend any given wedding with advanced notice. Just because you invite 10 friends does not mean they will all be able to make it. Using that rule of thumb, only 8 of them will. It's risky because you never know who will be able to make it but it might be a good idea to invite a few extra people to make sure you have enough to suit your LAN party needs. Don't invite too many, though, just in case you break the law of averages and everybody is miraculously able to attend.

The number you invite in the end really depends on how much work you want to do and how big your house is. Remember — the more people you have, the harder it is to coordinate, and you do want to participate. We have found that 10 to 12 people are good numbers for this. It can get slightly crazy, but not so much that it is out of control.

Invite everybody you want to show off your ultimate gaming PC to, of course! Truthfully though, invite anybody you want that has his or her own computer and that you like spending time with. If you are going for a bigger party and not sure that enough of your friends can attend, to fill up all your slots you can pass along extra invites to your friends and ask them to hand them out to people they might know that would be interested in playing.

When inviting your friends it is also a good idea to let them know if the invitation is strictly for them or if they are allowed to bring a friend or two. Quite often an extra person or two shows up that you may not have even ever met, and this can overload your house if you are not prepared. If they know of somebody else who would like to come, it's best if they run it by you first so that you can determine if there is room for them after you get a better gauge of how many people are coming.

Also try to give each person a couple weeks' notice of when the party is going to be so that they can make arrangements and plan to be there. Last-minute invites are normally much harder to accept, especially if they have to lug their computer around.

How Long Should the LAN Party Be?

If you're hosting the party at your home, schedule a full day. It's short and sweet and keeps your workload to a minimum without having to deal with overnight guests. You could start at 10 in the morning and play as long as you like into the night. Another good thing to remember is that at a LAN party you will be amazed at how fast the time flies by as the games blend seamlessly into one another, whether they be a victorious battle or one of defeat. Before you know it, your guests will be breaking down all their computers, packing them up, and disappearing into the night. You will go to bed that night tired and hopefully with great memories of a really fun and exciting day.

If you can have some of your friends help you organize, you can easily run a weekend event. If you go for a party that spans days, you need to arrange for sleeping accommodations for your guests (again, the smaller number of people you have the less worrisome this becomes). This can make for an exhausting weekend, most likely with minimal sleep, but most of the time it is worth it.

Whether you can have a full weekend event probably depends on who you live with, if anybody. If you live by yourself, well, no worries; there is nobody else in the house to bother. If you live with your parents, getting their permission for such an event might be difficult, just as it might be from a significant other. In any regard it is good to be considerate of those you live with as well as your neighbors, if they are close by, when planning the length of your event.

What Do I Need Besides a Location to Run a LAN Party?

Having the party at your house saves on a lot of headaches that you might get from hosting a huge LAN fest where you have to rent a venue, mail invites, make promotional paraphernalia, obtain insurance, rent tables and chairs, and so forth. The list goes on and on but fortunately that is not going to be us. We want simple and fun. Even so, having the right supplies on hand and ready before the party starts is important to getting the event kicked off without a hitch or wasting time frantically driving to BestBuy to purchase a much-needed extra networking cable.

To help make sure you don't forget anything, the following is a checklist of common items you need to run a successful and fun LAN party. Having all this prepared and ready to go when the guests start arriving reduces the amount of hiccups in getting the party off the ground. It also might not be a bad idea to ask one of your more responsible friends if they could show up a little early to help you get everything prepared. Here's what you need:

- A desk or table for each person to put their monitor on; their computer can go on the floor beneath it to save space
- A chair or something for each person to sit on
- Electrical outlets, or power supplies for each guest's computer and monitor
- A couple of extension cords to get power to where there might not be any
- Network cable for each person (you can make your guests responsible for this)
- Hubs, routers, or access points enough to connect all your friends
- Food and drinks
- Prizes (optional for match and/or game winners)

How Much Does It Cost to Run a LAN Party?

Cost really depends on how you because the main cost will be food. You can ask your guests to bring their own nourishment, you can buy it yourself, or you can split the cost of the day's food among all those in attendance.

If you ask them to bring their own food, that can make it a very simple and a negligible responsibility for you. If you decide to split the cost, the total depends on how many people you invited and how long your LAN party will be. If only three of your friends are coming over to your house, there may be no need to ask for an admission fee to cover costs. But if 12 friends show up, the cost of hosting greatly increases, and this may become financially unreasonable. You then have to decide if you will be asking for an "entrance fee" to participate. This can reduce the cost of the party by splitting the cost among all the participants.

It's not rude to ask for a few dollars to pitch in if you are hosting it at your house and you bought tons of chips and soda to feed everybody. If they each pitched in $8 to $10, this could cover you for snacks and also may allow you to buy a bunch of plain pizzas. You can go with toppings if you want but the price per slice can go up considerably. You have to know how much food in your area costs, how much a whole pizza is going for. You then have to do a little math, divide it fairly among all those you invited, and let them know when you invite them that you are asking everybody to pitch in to cover food and other costs.

A good way to cut down the cost a little is that if you know your party is in a few weeks, read the supermarket flyers and look for good deals on soda and chips so you can stock up at a good price for the food that you want. Some of your invitees might even bring stuff on their own without you asking.

If you plan to have some fun prizes, whatever you think is appropriate among your friends, for the winners of the matches or of your own little tourney the money you collect can go toward that as well.

Like we already said it is also important to be upfront with your guests and let them know if there is a cost to attend and how much it will be as soon as you can so they know well in advance and can plan on paying you.

What Games Should Be Played?

Nobody knows the answer to that question better than you and your friends. You know better than us what type of games you like to play, be it Warcraft III, Doom 3, Far Cry, or Half Life 1 and 2. So decide which you think the entire group would enjoy the most and schedule those. You can even ask for your guests to vote and use that as a measure of what should be played. Don't be afraid to mix it up by changing the game after each match is complete. This type of rotation can give anybody a chance to be happy because their favorite game will eventually come up once or twice.

It's important to let everybody know what the gaming roster is, and that they have the games already installed, including all patches, and ready to go before they show up. It's no fun having everybody wait around to start a game because a few people don't have it currently installed or forgot the disks at home. This can really slow things down, so make it a firm requirement that their computers must be ready to go when they arrive or maybe they have to sit out the first round while everybody else who is ready begins. They can then use that time to get their computer up to date.

How Do We Get Wired?

The next thing you must do before your LAN party is to come up with a plan to wire or network everybody together. Do you want a mass of RJ45s linking you all up to multiple routers, or to a single switch, or do you want to go all wireless? This is just one more thing everybody needs to know when they are invited so they can be prepared.

Wireless is, of course, the easiest and the neatest, but not everybody has a wireless card. You can set those that do to a wireless access point and just run networking cables to those that need to be hardwired. Either way, make sure you have enough hubs or access points for everybody. You can ask your friends to bring extra hubs as needed. Most likely somebody has one you can use.

If you have a choice between a hub and a router, go with the router because it is much smarter at communicating than a hub. A hub sends all packets it receives across all the connections it has linked up to it. This wastes a lot of bandwidth and creates useless traffic because only one client actually needed those sent packets. Routers are smart enough to know who to send the packet to when it receives it, and so it does not forward it across all ports but only to the actual person it was meant to go to. This makes for faster responses across the network as there is much less traffic.

It might also be good to designate one person to fix any computers that do not have the proper networking settings. This person, of course, should be the most knowledgeable about the subject because inevitably one person's computer is always tweaked differently than everybody else's and will need to be adjusted to make it work. Hopefully you have a good networking IT friend that can fill in this regard.

If you don't have such a person, the best thing you can do to minimize network problems is to make sure everybody is on the same page. The easiest thing to do is try to get all your invitees to match the following settings:

Ask all your guests to make sure their computers are part of the generic workgroup called "Workgroup." In Windows XP this can be done by following these steps:

1. Right-click My Computer.

2. Click Properties.

3. Click the Computer Name tab.

4. Click Change as shown in Figure 14-3.

5. Make sure in the Workgroup field it says Workgroup as shown in Figure 14-4.

FIGURE 14-3: Computer name dialog box. Click Change on this screen.

FIGURE 14-4: Make sure the Workgroup Field says
Workgroup.

6. Click OK.

7. Click OK again when the box pops up to say the workgroup has been changed.

8. Reboot to make the changes take effect.

Make sure their TCP-IP settings are set to DHCP, meaning they automatically receive an IP Address without anybody having to manually assign one.

In Windows XP this can be done through the following steps:

1. Click Start.

2. Right-click My Network Places.

3. Click Properties.

4. Right-click Local Area Connection (or the connection that you will be using).

5. Click Properties.

6. Highlight Internet Protocols (TCP/IP) as shown in Figure 14-5.

7. Click the Properties button.

8. Make sure you select Obtain an IP Address Automatically twice, as shown in Figure 14-6.

9. Click OK.

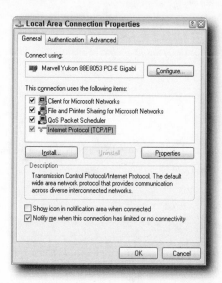

FIGURE 14-5: Select Internet Protocols (TCP/IP) and then click the Properties button.

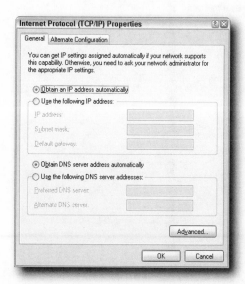

FIGURE 14-6: Make sure Obtain an IP Address Automatically is checked in both sections of the dialog box.

Have the Windows firewall (only on XP) turned off as well as any other firewall software that might be running.

Follow these steps to turn off the Windows firewall in Windows XP with SP2:

1. Click Start.

2. Right-click My Network Places.

3. Click Properties.

4. Right-click your Local Area Connection, or whatever main network card you will be using.

5. Click Properties.

6. Click the Advanced tab.

7. Click Settings.

8. Next make sure the bullet next to "Off (not recommended)"is selected as shown in Figure 14-7.

FIGURE 14-7: Make sure that the firewall is turned off.

9. If a warning box pops up asking if you are sure you want to disable the firewall protection, click Yes.

Tip

After the LAN party is over, remind your guests to turn on all their protective software so that after they get back home and on the Internet their computer is once again safe. You don't want to be responsible for anything ill happening to their computer after a fun and exciting day.

What Should Each Attending Person Bring?

When inviting your guests it's good to let them know what they need to bring so they can plan ahead and be prepared and the whole event runs smoother. Here is a list of things they might need to bring:

- Their complete computer, including mouse pad, and keyboard
- Their monitor
- All games from the play roster installed with all current patches
- A networking cable (if you are making them responsible for this)
- For every four to eight people, one four-or eight-person hub as needed
- A power strip
- If they want to be helpful, they can brings snacks and food as well
- Headsets, as too many sets of speakers can get very loud very quickly
- CD-ROMS of all the games that will be played

Should I Have a Game Server?

If you have time and parts to set one up, a game server can be very useful in raising the enjoyment level of everybody at the LAN party. If you don't know what a game server is, it is nothing more than a computer that acts as a host for the game. It keeps track of, and calculates, all the players' actions, locations, deaths, troops, victories, and so on between all the computers playing the game it is hosting.

If you have an extra computer laying around, perhaps the computer that you just upgraded from, it can be a good idea to use it as a server for your LAN gaming. This can save a lot of resources on the machines in the LAN party that somebody is using to play on and thus make gaming more pleasurable.

Having the extra computer reduces the workload off the other computers and this can reduce any sluggish play caused by slower machines. How well your server works depends on the game you are playing, the specifications of the server itself, and the amount of players you plan to host. Depending what games you are playing, the game server doesn't have to be very powerful because it won't be running all the fancy hard-to-render graphics. Some games can require a pretty powerful machine to act as a server, but other games like Battlefield 1942, Vietnam, or Warcraft III do not.

We have seen a dedicated Neverwinter Nights server hosting two to eight people with only the following, easy to achieve, system specifications and hardware:

- **OS:** Windows XP
- **CPU:** Intel PIII 800
- **RAM:** 128MB SD Ram
- **HDD:** 40GB Western Digital with 8MB Buffer

And we have seen servers running even less.

Running a Half-Life 2 server for up to 10 people has been done on the following computer specifications:

- **OS:** Windows XP
- **CPU:** Celeron 1.06 GHz
- **RAM:** 512MB SD Ram
- **HDD:** 40GB Western Digital with 8MB Buffer

Again we have seen servers running even less, for fewer people, as low as the following for eight people:

- **OS:** Windows XP
- **CPU:** Intel PIII 800
- **RAM:** 256MB DDR RAM
- **HDD:** 20GB Western Digital

The reason we didn't list the video cards requirements is, as we said previously, because they are almost negligible in the performance of the hosting server. The computer running the Neverwinter Nights server, for example, only had a very outdated 16 mg video card within it. If your video card can run whatever version of Windows you plan to use, it is most likely sufficient to run your gaming server.

Later on if this works out well for you and you like the aspect of having a gaming server, you could toy with the idea of having a dedicated gaming server. By dedicated we mean the server is available at all times, mostly over the Internet, and the server does nothing but run games. This can greatly increase your flexibility to play games with your friends without having them come to your house all the time for LAN parties. One of the best things is that it is your server, so it's your rules for all your games and matches.

There is another Extreme Tech book called *LAN Party: Hosting the Ultimate Frag Fest* by William "the Ferret" Steinmetz, which goes into a lot more detail on how to set up such a server and host LAN parties on a much bigger scale. So if you are looking for more information that is a good place to start.

What Should I Do to Guarantee Fair Play?

Depending who your friends are or who they end up inviting, it can be hard to guarantee fair play because cheaters abound as any person who played Halo 2 on Xbox Live in the first few months of its launch, before it was patched, can easily attest to. The thing about Xbox Live and Internet gaming in general is that there is complete anonymity when playing out there. A person can cheat without any real physical threat of retaliation coming back at them except for perhaps maybe a few angry words from their victims, which the cheaters seem to thrive off of anyway.

This is your LAN party though, and because it is not being played over the Internet it does not offer the complete anonymity that goes on there. We could hope that this would mean there would be less cheaters when playing face to face and that is probably true, but that does not mean there aren't any.

A good rule to put in effect from the beginning is that any form of cheating or hacking will not be tolerated at your LAN party. You have gathered these people to your home, at the cost of your time, energy, and money, for a fun and stress-free day or weekend, and cheating can easily and utterly destroy all your efforts.

Cheating can be any form of game manipulation that gives one person an advantage over another. Inform your guests that they should not use any trainers, unauthorized mods, or cracks, or third-party patches they have come across.

You are here for honest, fair entertainment and you expect everybody to respect that and each other. This may seem frivolous at first, but cheating can strip the fun out of the event very quickly as tempers rise. You would not be out of line, for the sake of everybody's fun, to warn your guests that anybody caught cheating or tampering with a game in progress will instantly be asked to leave and will not be invited back to any future events that you may have.

What Do I Need to Do Before and After the Event?

Just before the LAN fest it's good to have everything set up before the guests arrive. This means that the tables are cleared off to hold monitors, that fold-up tables have been unfolded, that extension cords are run to all the locations where they're needed, and that beverages are in the refrigerator. Do everything that you can think of so that after your guests arrive, there is a minimal amount of extra work to be done other than setting up computers.

As the event is under way, make sure to take pictures to remember your party and how much work you put into setting it up. Pictures of laughing friends having a good time can be a very rewarding keepsake for all the effort you put in. You can also use the pictures from this LAN party to promote your next one on a Website or on a color invitation.

Also ask the guests as the session commences not to swap or take files from any computer that is in a game because it can slow down the machine and reduce the owner's fun.

Make sure everybody is comfortable, that you have reasonable air conditioning or heat as needed or requested. Every now and then check to see that everybody is having a good time, and remember to take it easy on them when the games begin. Chances are their computer just won't be able to compete with yours.

That's it! It's all done! You have built your computer, tweaked and installed the OS, got it connected to the Internet with the fastest connection you could find, and thrown a small party to show it off and truly appreciate its power. Now it's time to get to all those games you could never play before. Go! Have fun! You deserve it, and get a few frags for us!

Index

Index

C

cable connection to Internet, 296, 297, 298
cable management system, 144
cables
 Cat5, 296, 308
 installing
  binding with twist ties, 251
  black cables, 205
  overview of, 181–182
  power button, case speaker, and case
   lighting, connecting, 204–207
  power supply, connecting to motherboard
   and heatsink, 197–204
  ribbon, 234–235, 240, 244, 245–246
  for sound card, 247
 RJ45, 296, 308
 secondary power connector, 198
 24-pin main connector, 197, 200
cache
 hard drive and, 88, 89
 Intel Extreme Edition and, 28
 memory and, 24, 26–27
Call 2 (Asherson), 313
capacitor, 141
case
 airflow and, 127–128, 129, 130, 136
 cooling system and, 127, 131–132
 ease of use of, 132–134
 features of, 129–134
 heat transfer and, 127–128
 inserting motherboard into, 186–188
 manufacturers of, 134
 material of, 128, 131
 modding, 135
 motherboard and, 131
 orientation to, 180
 as providing structure for components,
  125–126
 removing from box, 179
 removing panels from, 181
 safety and, 126
 saving money on, 137
 scratches to, 181
 selecting, 135–136
 shopping for online, 137

 size of, 129–131
 terminology, 126
 view of, after installation, 250, 251
 wiring power supply and, 199
Caslis, Russ, *Going Mod,* 135
Cat5 cable, 296, 308
cathode-ray tube (CRT)
 description of, 150
 monitor
  description of, 152–155
  features of, 158–160
CD drive
 overview of, 98–100
 selecting, 103–104
CD-ROM
 booting from, 257
 drivers, installing from
  motherboard, 265–266
  for mouse, 261–262
  SoundBlaster, 264–265
  video card, 262–263
ceiling fan, installing, 221–222
center channel of surround sound, 108
chassis alarm, 207
cheating, 325
chipset, 38, 40
choosing
 case, 135–136
 DVD or CD drive, 103–104
 hard drive, 97–98, 100–103
 Internet connection type, 297–298
 memory, 67
 monitor, 160–162
 motherboard, 50–51
 network type, 310–312
 operating system, 254–255
 power supply, 145–146
 processor, 33–34
 sound card, 119–120
 speakers, 121–122
 video card, 82–84
clock speed, 24, 25–26
CNET Website, 298, 299
communications between components, 38,
  40–41

compression of soundtrack, 107
Computer Management dialog box, opening,
267
Computer Name Changes dialog box, 320
connection speed, 312–313
connections on sound card, 116
connectors on power supply, 144
controller card, 92
controllers
Logitech Rumblepad 2 Vibration Feedback
Gamepad, 168–169
Nostromo N52 Speedpad, 169–171
overview of, 168
Saitek R440 Force Feedback Wheel, 171–173
cooling system
case and, 127, 131–132
installing
case fan controller, 212
ceiling fan, 221–222
front fan, connecting, 222
Gigabyte Rocker Cooler fan controller,
217–219
hard drive fan, connecting, 223
new case fan, 210–211
overview of, 210
testing after, 223
power supply and, 141
3D Rocket Cooler Pro (Gigabyte)
connecting power supply to, 197–204
description of, 173–174
fan controller, installing, 217–221
installing, 192–195
cordless mouse, Logitech MX 1000 Laser,
164–167
core frequency, 30
core logic, 40
Corsair (manufacturer), 67–68
cost. See also budget; saving money when
building PC
of building PC, 6–8
of buying PC from gaming PC Website, 5
of case, 137
of floppy drive, 237
Internet shopping and, 12
Internet shopping portal and, 13
of LAN party, 317–318

memory and, 61
of monitor, 157
price match policy and, 15
rebates and, 14, 95
of shipping
monitor, 157, 159
PC, 4–5, 12
CPU
AMD
core frequency and, 30
Front Side Bus and, 31
FX series, 35
FX-55 2.6 GHz Socket 939, 188
FX-57 chip, 42
integrated memory controller, 30
Intel processors compared to, 31–32
64-bit capabilities of, 29
cache and, 26–27
description of, 23, 25
future of, 32–33
in generic gaming PC, 4
grounding self before touching, 189
heatsink, installing, 192–195
installing onto motherboard, 188–192
Intel
AMD processors compared to, 31–32
core frequency and, 30
Extreme Edition, 28–29, 35
Front Side Bus and, 31
hyperthreading and, 27
saving money on, 34–35
selecting, 33–34
speed of, 25–26
terminology related to, 24
Creative Labs (manufacturer)
Audigy 2 ZS Platinum, 119–120
EAX technology, 107, 112, 115
Crossfire (ATI), 79, 80
CRT (cathode-ray tube)
description of, 150
monitor
description of, 152–155
features of, 158–160
Crucial (manufacturer), 64, 66, 67
current, 140

D

DC (direct current), 139, 140–141
DDR (Double Data Rate), 54, 57–58, 59
DDR Memory Controller (AMD), 56
DDR2, 54
dead pixel, 159
decoding capability, 115
decoding surround sound, 107–108
decompression of soundtrack, 107
default pagefile, 94
Dell UltraSharp 2405FPW Flat Panel
    description of, 160–161
    resolution for, 263–264
design of speakers, 118
desktop case, 126, 129, 130
Diablo II (game), 300
dial-up connection, 297, 314
digital signal processor (DSP), 113
Digital Subscriber Line (DSL), 296, 297,
    298, 299
Digital Theater Systems (DTS), 107
Digital Visual Interface (DVI), 150, 152, 158
direct, buying, 64
direct current (DC), 139, 140–141
DirectX, 75, 82, 111
disabling
    auto starting programs, 285
    Automatic Updates, 271–272
    Remote Assistance and Remote Desktop
        Sharing, 274
    Windows Firewall, 279–280, 322
    Windows Messenger, 275
    Windows Services, 276–278
Disk Clean Up, 281–283
Disk Defragmenter, 280–281
Disk Management, 268–269
Disk Striping, 96
Display Properties dialog box, 263, 264
D-Link firewall/router, 300
Dolby Digital, 107
Dolby Digital Surround EX, 110
Doom 3 (game), 289, 290
Double Data Rate (DDR), 54, 57–58, 59
downloading SP2, 303
DPI (dots per inch), 151

drive. *See also* hard drive
    CD, 98–100, 103–104
    DVD
        installing
            Lite-On, 236–237
            Memorex, 232–236
        making first bootable drive, 257–258
        overview of, 98–100
        selecting, 103–104
    floppy, 99, 237–241
    multiple, and pagefile, 94, 95
drive installation, tool-free, 132
driver
    loading custom, 255
    motherboard, installing, 265–266
    mouse, installing, 261–262
    optimization and, 77
    SoundBlaster, installing, 264–265
    updating, 284
    video card, installing, 262–263
DSL (Digital Subscriber Line), 296, 297,
    298, 299
DSP (digital signal processor), 113
DTS (Digital Theater Systems), 107
DTS Extended Surround, 110
dual core, 24, 32–33
Dual-Band Wireless A+G Suite (Belkin), 306
duration of LAN party, 316
DVD drive
    installing
        Lite-On, 236–237
        Memorex, 232–236
    making first bootable drive, 257–258
    overview of, 98–100
    selecting, 103–104
DVI (Digital Visual Interface), 150, 152, 158

E

EAX technology, 107, 112, 115
eBay, buying monitor on, 157
ECC technology, 54, 60
efficiency of processor, 26
electricity, 139, 140–141
encryption of files, 254, 307
Enermax (manufacturer), 144

Continued

Intel Extreme Edition and, 28
risks of, 57
video card and, 78, 83
overhead of Windows interface, reducing,
    272–274

P

pagefile
    adjusting location of, 270–271
    multiple drives and, 94, 95
paging data to hard drive, 55, 62
Parallel ATA, 90
partitions
    creating, 259–261
    formatting, 266
parts. *See also specific parts*
    bargain versus brand, 10, 64, 98
    harvesting from old PC, 9
    intertwining of, 68
    making sure all are ready for assembly, 177
    OEM (original equipment manufacture), 11
    priorities, setting, 9
    removing from boxes, 178
    researching and selecting, 15–16
    retail, 10–11
PC Power & Cooling (manufacturer), 144,
    145–146
PCI Express lanes, 38
PCI Express (PCIe)
    connection, 44–45, 81
    expansion slot, 38
    video slot, 38
PCI slot, 38, 44–47
PCI sound card, 46, 49
Pentium 4 (Intel)
    AMD Athlon 64 compared to, 26, 33–34
    specs, 33
performance
    cache and, 26–27
    efficiency and, 26
    frames per second and, 76–77
    of hard drive, 89, 96
    hyperthreading and, 27–28

maintaining
    antivirus software, 283–284
    Disk Clean Up, 281–283
    Disk Defragmenter, 280–281
    spyware removal, 283
    System Tray and extra Startup programs,
        cleaning out, 284–286
    updating drivers, 284
    memory and, 55
    monitor and, 157–158
    multiple hard drives and, 95
    north bridge/south bridge chipset and, 40–41
    of power supply, 143–144
    sound card and, 115
    speed of processor and, 25–26
    video card and, 75
    of wireless router, 306–308
Performance Options dialog box, 273
perspective in 3D game, 72
phone support from manufacturer, 83
physical firewall, 300–301
ping
    of friends, 313–314
    online gaming experience and, 312–313
pixel
    dead or stuck, 159
    description of, 150
pixel assembly line, 71–72
pixel density, 151
pixel response time, 154
placement of wireless router, 306–308
platter density, 89
playback of in-game audio, 110–111
point-to-point connection, 39
pop-up blocker, 302
port
    description of, 38
    Diablo II and, 300
    FireWire, 38, 49
    IEEE1394, 49
    USB
        description of, 38, 47–48
        installing, 248–250
positional audio, 106, 111–112
power button, connecting, 204–207

Continued

How to take it to the Extreme.

If you enjoyed this book, there are many others like it for you. From *Podcasting* to *Hacking Firefox*, ExtremeTech books can fulfill your urge to hack, tweak and modify, providing the tech tips and tricks readers need to get the most out of their hi-tech lives.

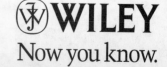